I0405581

ABOUT THIS PUBLICATION

FOR SERVICE ASSISTANCE

Customer Service
1.704.898.0770

www.visionbooks.org

Copyright © 2015 by MMGGC
All rights reserved!

TID: 5107799
ISBN (10) digit: 1503243613
ISBN (13) digit: 978-1503243613

123-4-56789-01239-Paperback
123-4-56789-01239-Hardback

First Edition

090520140547

Printed in the United States of America

1

2015 EDITION

North Carolina Criminal Law And Procedure-Pamphlet # 76

Printed In conjunction with the Administration of the Courts

North Carolina Criminal Law and Procedure
Pamphlet Reference Guide

5

9

11

12

13

14

Article 12.

Junkyard Control Act.

§ 136-141. Title of Article.

This Article may be cited as the Junkyard Control Act. (1967, c. 1198, s. 1.)

§ 136-142. Declaration of policy.

The General Assembly hereby finds and declares that although junkyards are a legitimate business, the establishment and use and maintenance of junkyards in the vicinity of the interstate and primary highways or within the vicinity of North Carolina routes in counties that have no interstate or federal aid primary highways within the State should be regulated and controlled in order to promote the safety, health, welfare and convenience and enjoyment of travel on and the protection of the public investment in highways within the State, to prevent unreasonable distraction of operators of motor vehicles and to prevent interference with the effectiveness of traffic regulations, to attract tourists and promote the prosperity, economic well-being and general welfare of the State, and to preserve and enhance the natural scenic beauty of the highways and areas in the vicinity. It is the intention of the General Assembly to provide and declare herein a public policy and statutory basis for regulation and control of junkyards. (1967, c. 1198, s. 2; 1993, c. 493, s. 1.)

§ 136-143. Definitions.

As used in this Article:

(1)   The term "automobile graveyard" shall mean any establishment or place of business which is maintained, used, or operated for storing, keeping, buying or selling wrecked, scrapped, ruined, or dismantled motor vehicles or motor vehicle parts. Any establishment or place of business upon which six or more unlicensed, used motor vehicles which cannot be operated under their own power are kept or stored for a period of 15 days or more shall be deemed to be an "automobile graveyard" within the meaning of this Article.

15

(2)   "Interstate system" means that portion of the National System of Interstate and Defense Highways located within the State, as now officially designated, or as may hereafter be so designated as interstate system by the Department of Transportation, or other appropriate authorities. As to highways under construction so designated as interstate highways pursuant to the above procedures, the highway shall be a part of the interstate system for the purpose of this Article on the date the location of the highway has been approved finally by the appropriate federal authorities.

(3)   The term "junk" shall mean old or scrap copper, brass, rope, rags, batteries, paper, trash, rubber, debris, waste, or junked, dismantled or wrecked automobiles, or parts thereof, iron, steel, and other old or scrap ferrous or nonferrous material.

(4)   The term "junkyard" shall mean an establishment or place of business which is maintained, operated, or used for storing, keeping, buying, or selling junk, or for maintenance or operation of an automobile graveyard, and the term shall include garbage dumps and sanitary fills. An establishment or place of business which stores or keeps for a period of 15 days or more materials within the meaning of "junk" as defined by subdivision (3) of G.S. 136-143 which had been derived or created as a result of industrial activity shall be deemed to be a junkyard within the meaning of this Article.

(5)   "Primary system" means that portion of connected main highways, as now officially designated, or as may hereafter be so designated as primary system by the Department of Transportation or other appropriate authorities. As to highways under construction so designated as federal-aid primary highways pursuant to the above procedures, the highway shall be part of the federal-aid primary system for purposes of this Article on the date the location of the highway has been approved finally by the appropriate federal or State authorities.

(6)   "Unzoned area" shall mean an area where there is no zoning in effect.

(7)   "Visible" means capable of being seen without visual aid by a person of normal visual acuity. (1967, c. 1198, s. 3; 1973, c. 507, s. 5; c. 1439, ss. 1-5; 1977, c. 464, s. 7.1.)

§ 136-144. Restrictions as to location of junkyards.

16

No junkyard shall be established, operated or maintained, any portion of which is within 1,000 feet of the nearest edge of the right-of-way of any interstate or primary highway, or a North Carolina route in a county that has no interstate or federal aid primary highways, except the following:

(1)   Those which are screened by natural objects, plantings, fences or other appropriate means so as not to be visible from the main-traveled way of the highway at any season of the year or otherwise removed from sight or screened in accordance with the rules and regulations promulgated by the Department of Transportation.

(2)   Those located within areas which are zoned for industrial use under authority of law.

(3)   Those located within unzoned industrial areas, which areas shall be determined from actual land uses and defined by regulations to be promulgated by the Department of Transportation.

(4)   Those which are not visible from the main-traveled way of an interstate or primary highway or a North Carolina route in a county that does not have an interstate or federal aid primary highway at any season of the year. (1967, c. 1198, s. 4; 1973, c. 507, s. 5; 1977, c. 464, s. 7.1; 1993, c. 493, s. 2.)

§ 136-145. Enforcement provisions.

Any person, firm, corporation or association that establishes, operates or maintains a junkyard within 1,000 feet of the nearest edge of the right-of-way of any interstate or primary highway, after the effective date of this Article as determined by G.S. 136-155, that does not come within one or more of the exceptions contained in G.S. 136-144 hereof, shall be guilty of a Class 1 misdemeanor, and each day that the junkyard remains within the prohibited distance shall constitute a separate offense. In addition thereto, said junkyard is declared to be a public nuisance and the Department of Transportation may seek injunctive relief in the superior court of the county in which the offense is committed to abate the said nuisance and to require the removal of all junk from the prohibited area. (1967, c. 1198, s. 5; 1973, c. 507, s. 5, c. 1439, s. 6; 1977, c. 464, s. 7.1; 1993, c. 539, s. 999; 1994, Ex. Sess., c. 24, s. 14(c).)

§ 136-146. Removal of junk from illegal junkyards.

Any junkyard established after the effective date of this Article as determined by G.S. 136-155, in violation of the provisions of this Article or rules and regulations issued by the Department of Transportation pursuant to this Article, shall be illegal and shall constitute a public nuisance. The Department of Transportation or its agents shall give 30 days' notice to the owner of said junkyard to remove the junk or to make the junkyard to conform to the provisions of this Article or rules and regulations promulgated by the Department of Transportation hereunder. The Department of Transportation or its agents may remove the junk from the illegal junkyard at the expense of the owner if the said owner fails to act within 30 days after receipt of such notice. The Department of Transportation or its agents may enter upon private property for the purpose of removing junk from the junkyards prohibited by this Article without civil or criminal liability. Any person aggrieved by the decision declaring the junkyard illegal shall be granted the right to appeal the decision in accordance with the terms of the rules and regulations enacted by the Department of Transportation pursuant to this Article to the Secretary of Transportation who shall make the final decision on the agency appeal. (1967, c. 1198, s. 6; 1973, c. 507, s. 5; c. 1439, s. 7; 1977, c. 464, s. 7.1.)

§ 136-147. Screening of junkyards lawfully in existence.

Any junkyard lawfully in existence on the effective date of this Article as determined by G.S. 136-155 which does not conform to the requirements for exceptions in G.S. 136-144 hereof, and any other junkyard lawfully in existence along any highway which may be hereafter designated as an interstate or primary highway or a North Carolina route in a county without an interstate or federal aid primary highway and which does not conform to the requirements for exception under G.S. 136-144 hereof, shall be screened, if feasible, by the Department of Transportation at locations on the highway right-of-way or in areas acquired for such purposes outside the right-of-way in such manner that said junkyard shall not be visible from the main-traveled way of such highways. The Department of Transportation is authorized to acquire fee simple title or any lesser interest in real property for the purpose required by this section, by gift, purchase or condemnation. (1967, c. 1198, s. 7; 1973, c. 507, s. 5; c. 1439, s. 8; 1977, c. 464, s. 7.1; 1993, c. 493, s. 3.)

§ 136-148. Acquisition of existing junkyards where screening impractical.

(a)   In the event that the Department of Transportation shall determine that screening of any existing junkyard designated in G.S. 136-147 hereof would be inadequate to accomplish the purposes of this Article, the said Department of Transportation is authorized to secure the relocation, removal or disposal of such junkyard by acquiring the fee simple title, or such lesser interest in land as may be necessary, to the land upon which said junkyard is located, through purchase, gift, exchange or condemnation.

(b)   The Department of Transportation is authorized to move and relocate junk located on lands within the provisions of this section, and is authorized to pay the costs of such moving or relocation.

(c)   The Department of Transportation is authorized to acquire by purchase, gift, exchange or condemnation, fee simple title or any lesser interest in real property for the purpose of placing and relocating the junk required to be moved under this section or permitted by G.S. 136-146 hereof to be removed. The Department of Transportation is authorized to convey in the manner provided by law for the conveyance of state-owned property, the lands on which junk is to be relocated, to the owner of the junk with or without consideration, under such conditions and reservations as it deems to be in the public interest.

(d)   The Department of Transportation is authorized to convey in the manner provided by law for the conveyance of state-owned property any property acquired under the provisions of this section, under such conditions and reservations as it deems to be in the public interest.

(e)   The Department of Transportation upon a determination that the same is necessary for the removal of any junkyard which is prohibited by G.S. 136-144 may acquire by gift, exchange, purchase or condemnation, the junk located on any junkyard which is acquired under this section and may acquire by gift, exchange, purchase or condemnation the fee simple title or lesser interest in land for the purpose of storing said junk by the Department of Transportation and may dispose of said junk in any manner which is not inconsistent with this Article. (1967, c. 1198, s. 8; 1973, c. 507, s. 5; 1977, c. 464, s. 7.1.)

§ 136-149. Permit required for junkyards.

19

No person shall establish, operate or maintain a junkyard any portion of which is within 1,000 feet of the nearest edge of the right-of-way of the interstate or primary system or a North Carolina route in a county that does not have an interstate or federal aid primary highway without obtaining a permit from the Department of Transportation or its agents pursuant to the procedures set out by the rules and regulations promulgated by the Department of Transportation. No permit shall be issued under the provisions of this section for the establishment, operation or maintenance of a junkyard within 1,000 feet to the nearest edge of the right-of-way of interstate or primary system except those junkyards which conform to one or more of the exceptions of G.S. 136-144. The permit shall be valid until revoked for the nonconformance of this Article or rules and regulations promulgated by the Department of Transportation thereunder. Any person aggrieved by the decision of the Department of Transportation or its agents in refusing to grant or revoking a permit may appeal the decision in accordance with the rules and regulations enacted by the Department of Transportation pursuant to this Article to the Secretary of Transportation who shall make the final decision upon the agency appeal. The Department of Transportation shall have the authority to charge fees to defray the costs of administering the permit procedures under this Article. The fees for junkyard permits to be issued under this Article shall not exceed a twenty dollar ($20.00) initial fee and a fifteen dollar ($15.00) annual renewal fee. (1967, c. 1198, s. 9; 1973, c. 507, s. 5; c. 1439, s. 9; 1977, c. 464, s. 7.1; 1983, c. 604, s. 3; 1993, c. 493, s. 4.)

§ 136-149.1. Judicial review.

Any person who is aggrieved by a final decision of the Secretary of Transportation after exhausting all administrative remedies made available to him by rules and regulations enacted pursuant to this Article is entitled to judicial review of such decision under this Article. In order to obtain judicial review of the Secretary of Transportation's decision under this Article, the person seeking review must file a petition in the superior court of the county in which the junkyard is located within 30 days after written copy of the decision of the Secretary of Transportation is served upon the person seeking review. Failure to file such a petition within the time stated shall operate as a waiver of the right of such person to review under this Chapter.

The petition shall state explicitly what exceptions are taken to the decisions of the Secretary of Transportation and what relief petitioner seeks. Within 10 days after the petition is filed with the court, the person seeking the review shall serve copies of the petition by registered mail, return receipt requested, upon the Department of Transportation. Within 30 days after receipt of the copy of the petition for review, or within such additional time as the court may allow, the Department of Transportation shall transmit to the reviewing court a certified copy of the written decision.

At any time before or during the review proceeding, the aggrieved party may apply to the reviewing court for an order staying the operation of the decision of the Secretary of Transportation pending the outcome of the review. The court may grant or deny the stay in its discretion upon such terms as it deems proper. The review of the decision of the Secretary of Transportation under this Article shall be conducted by the court without a jury and shall hear the matter de novo pursuant to the rules of evidence as applied in the general court of justice. The court, after hearing the matter may affirm, reverse or modify the decision if the decision is:

(1)   In violation of constitutional provisions; or

(2)   Not made in accordance with this Article or rules or regulations promulgated by the Department of Transportation;

(3)   Affected by other error or law.

The party aggrieved shall have the burden of showing that the decision was violative of one of the above.

A party to the review proceedings, including the agency, may appeal to the appellate division from the final judgment of the superior court under the rules of procedure applicable in other civil cases. The appealing party may apply to the superior court for a stay for its final determination or a stay of the administrative decision, whichever shall be appropriate, pending the outcome of the appeal to the appellate division. (1973, c. 1439, s. 10; 1977, c. 464, ss. 7.1, 32, 33.)

§ 136-150. Condemnation procedure.

The Department of Transportation shall use the condemnation procedure as provided by Article 9 of Chapter 136 of the General Statutes for the purposes of this Article. (1967, c. 1198, s. 10; 1973, c. 507, s. 5; 1977, c. 464, s. 7.1.)

§ 136-151. Rules and regulations by Department of Transportation; delegation of authority to Secretary of Transportation.

The Department of Transportation is authorized to promulgate rules and regulations in the form of ordinances governing:

(1)   The establishment, operation and maintenance of junkyards permitted in G.S. 136-144 which shall include, but not be limited to, rules and regulations for determining unzoned industrial areas for the purpose of this Article.

(2)   The specific requirements and procedures for obtaining a permit for junkyards as required in G.S. 136-149 and for the administrative procedures for appealing a decision at the agency level to refuse to grant or in revoking a permit previously issued.

(3)   The administrative procedures for appealing a decision at the agency level to declare any junkyard illegal and a nuisance as pursuant to G.S. 136-146.

(4)   The specific requirements governing the location, planting, construction and maintenance of material used in the screening or fencing required by this Article, all as may be necessary to carry out the policy of the State as declared in this Article.

The Department of Transportation, in its discretion, may delegate to the Secretary of Transportation the authority to promulgate such rules and regulations on its behalf. (1967, c. 1198, s. 11; 1973, c. 507, s. 5; c. 1439, s. 11; 1977, c. 464, s. 7.1.)

§ 136-152. Agreements with United States.

The Department of Transportation is authorized to enter into agreements with other governmental authorities relating to the control of junkyards and areas in the vicinity of interstate and primary systems, and to take action in the name of the State to comply with the terms of such agreement. (1967, c. 1198, s. 12; 1973, c. 507, s. 5; 1977, c. 464, s. 7.1.)

§ 136-153. Zoning changes.

All zoning authorities shall give written notice to the Department of Transportation of the establishment or revision of any industrial zone within 660 feet of the right-of-way of interstate or primary highways. Notice shall be by registered mail sent to the offices of the Department of Transportation in Raleigh, North Carolina, within 15 days after the effective date of the zoning change or establishment. (1967, c. 1198, s. 13; 1973, c. 507, s. 5; 1977, c. 464, s. 7.1.)

§ 136-154. Alternate control.

In addition to any other provisions of this Article, the Department of Transportation shall have the authority to acquire by purchase, gift, exchange, or condemnation, such interests in real property as may be necessary to control the establishment and maintenance of junkyards in accordance with the policy, standards and regulations set out herein. (1967, c. 1198, s. 14; 1973, c. 507, s. 5; 1977, c. 464, s. 7.1.)

§ 136-155. Availability of federal aid funds.

The Department of Transportation shall not be required to expend any funds for the regulation of junkyards under this Article, nor shall the provisions of this Article, with the exception of G.S. 136-152 hereof, have any force and effect until federal funds are made available to the State for the purpose of carrying out the provisions of this Article, and the Department of Transportation has entered into an agreement with the United States Secretary of Transportation as authorized by G.S. 136-152 hereof and as provided by the Highway Beautification Act of 1965 or subsequent amendment thereto. (1967, c. 1198, s. 15; 1973, c. 507, s. 5; c. 1439, s. 12; 1977, c. 464, s. 7.1.)

Article 13.

Highway Relocation Assistance Act.

§§ 136-156 through 136-174: Repealed by Session Laws 1971, c. 1107, s. 2.

Article 14.

North Carolina Highway Trust Fund.

§ 136-175. Definitions.

The following definitions apply in this Article:

(1)   Repealed by Session Laws 2013-183, s. 4.7, effective July 1, 2013.

(2)   Transportation Improvement Program. The schedule of major transportation improvement projects required by G.S. 143B-350(f)(4).

(3)   Trust Fund. The North Carolina Highway Trust Fund. (1989, c. 692, s. 1.1; 2004-124, s. 30.21(a); 2013-183, s. 4.7.)

§ 136-176. Creation, revenue sources, and purpose of North Carolina Highway Trust Fund.

(a)   A special account, designated the North Carolina Highway Trust Fund, is created within the State treasury. The Trust Fund consists of the following revenue:

(1)   Motor fuel, alternative fuel, and road tax revenue deposited in the Fund under G.S. 105-449.125, 105-449.134, and 105-449.43, respectively.

(2)   Motor vehicle use tax deposited in the Fund under G.S. 105-187.9.

(3)   Revenue from the certificate of title fee and other fees payable under G.S. 20-85.

(4)   Repealed by Session Laws 2001-424, s. 27.1.

(5)   Interest and income earned by the Fund.

(a1)   Repealed by Session Laws 2013-183, s. 4.8(b), effective July 1, 2013.

24

(a2)   Repealed by Session Laws 2002-126, s. 26.4(b), effective July 1, 2002.

(a3)   through (a5) Repealed by Session Laws 2013-183, s. 4.8(b), effective July 1, 2013.

(b)   Funds in the Trust Fund are annually appropriated to the Department of Transportation to be allocated and used as provided in this subsection. A sum, in the amount appropriated by law, may be used each fiscal year by the Department for expenses to administer the Trust Fund. Operation and project development costs of the North Carolina Turnpike Authority are eligible administrative expenses under this subsection. Any funds allocated to the Authority pursuant to this subsection shall be repaid by the Authority from its toll revenue as soon as possible, subject to any restrictions included in the agreements entered into by the Authority in connection with the issuance of the Authority's revenue bonds. Beginning one year after the Authority begins collecting tolls on a completed Turnpike Project, interest shall accrue on any unpaid balance owed to the Highway Trust Fund at a rate equal to the State Treasurer's average annual yield on its investment of Highway Trust Fund funds pursuant to G.S. 147-6.1. Interest earned on the unpaid balance shall be deposited in the Highway Trust Fund upon repayment. The sum up to the amount anticipated to be necessary to meet the State matching funds requirements to receive federal-aid highway trust funds for the next fiscal year may be set aside for that purpose. The rest of the funds in the Trust Fund shall be allocated and used as specified in G.S. 136-189.11.

The Department must administer funds allocated under this section in a manner that ensures that sufficient funds are available to make the debt service payments on bonds issued under the State Highway Bond Act of 1996 as they become due.

(b1)   Repealed by Session Laws 2013-183, s. 4.8(b), effective July 1, 2013.

(b2)   There is annually appropriated to the North Carolina Turnpike Authority from the Highway Trust Fund the sum of forty-nine million dollars ($49,000,000). Of the amount allocated by this subsection, twenty-five million dollars ($25,000,000) shall be used to pay debt service or related financing costs and expenses on revenue bonds or notes issued for the construction of the Triangle Expressway, and twenty-four million dollars ($24,000,000) shall be used to pay debt service or related financing expenses on revenue bonds or notes issued for the construction of the Monroe Connector/Bypass. The amounts appropriated to the Authority pursuant to this subsection shall be used by the Authority to pay

25

debt service or related financing costs and expenses on revenue bonds or notes issued by the Authority to finance the costs of one or more Turnpike Projects, to refund such bonds or notes, or to fund debt service reserves, operating reserves, and similar reserves in connection therewith. The appropriations established by this subsection constitute an agreement by the State to pay the funds appropriated hereby to the Authority within the meaning of G.S. 159-81(4). Notwithstanding the foregoing, it is the intention of the General Assembly that the enactment of this provision and the issuance of bonds or notes by the Authority in reliance thereon shall not in any manner constitute a pledge of the faith and credit and taxing power of the State, and nothing contained herein shall prohibit the General Assembly from amending the appropriations made in this subsection at any time to decrease or eliminate the amount annually appropriated to the Authority. Funds transferred from the Highway Trust Fund to the Authority pursuant to this subsection are not subject to the formula in G.S. 136-189.11.

(c)   Repealed by Session Laws 2013-183, s. 4.8(b), effective July 1, 2013.

(d)   A contract may be let for projects funded from the Trust Fund in anticipation of revenues pursuant to the cash-flow provisions of G.S. 143C-6-11 only for the two bienniums following the year in which the contract is let.

(e)   Subject to G.S. 136-189.11, funds may be used for fixed guideway projects, including providing matching funds for federal grants for fixed guideway projects. (1989, c. 692, s. 1.1; c. 770, ss. 68.2, 74.6; 1989 (Reg. Sess., 1990), c. 1024, s. 46(a), (b); 1991, c. 193, s. 9; c. 280, s. 1; c. 689, s. 62; 1995, c. 390, s. 27; 1995 (Reg. Sess., 1996), c. 590, s. 6; 1996, 2nd Ex. Sess., c. 18, s. 19.4(a); 1998-212, s. 27.2; 1999-237, s. 27.1; 2000-140, s. 31; 2001-424, ss. 27.1, 27.23(d), 27.23(e), 27.23(f); 2002-126, ss. 26.4(a), 26.4(b), 26.9(b); 2002-133, s. 3; 2002-159, s. 41.5; 2003-284, ss. 29.4, 29.22; 2003-383, ss. 1, 2, 3; 2004-124, ss. 30.3(a), (b), 30.21(b); 2006-203, s. 78; 2007-323, s. 27.17; 2008-107, ss. 25.1, 25.5(b), (d), (f), 25.15; 2009-56, s. 1; 2010-31, s. 28.7(c), (g), (k); 2011-145, s. 28.32(c), (d); 2011-391, s. 55; 2012-142, s. 24.19(b); 2013-183, s. 4.8.)

§§ 136-177 through 136-180: Repealed by Session Laws 2013-183, s. 4.9, effective July 1, 2013.

§ 136-180.1: Repealed by Session Laws 2002-126, s. 26.10(b), effective July 1, 2002.

§ 136-181: Repealed by Session Laws 2013-183, s. 3.2, effective July 1, 2013.

§ 136-182: Repealed by Session Laws 2013-183, s. 2.9, effective July 1, 2013.

§ 136-183: Repealed by Session Laws 2001-424, s. 27.1.

§§ 136-184, 136-185: Repealed by Session Laws 2013-183, s. 4.9, effective July 1, 2013.

§ 136-186. Reserved for future codification purposes.

Article 14A.

North Carolina Mobility Fund.

§§ 136-187 through 136-189: Repealed by Session Laws 2013-183, s. 4.9, effective July 1, 2013.

§ 136-189.1: Reserved for future codification purposes.

§ 136-189.2: Reserved for future codification purposes.

§ 136-189.3: Reserved for future codification purposes.

§ 136-189.4: Reserved for future codification purposes.

§ 136-189.5: Reserved for future codification purposes.

§ 136-189.6: Reserved for future codification purposes.

§ 136-189.7: Reserved for future codification purposes.

§ 136-189.8: Reserved for future codification purposes.

§ 136-189.9: Reserved for future codification purposes.

Article 14B.

Strategic Prioritization Funding Plan for Transportation Investments.

§ 136-189.10. Definitions.

The following definitions apply in this Article:

(1)   Distribution Regions. - The following Distribution Regions apply to this Article:

a.   Distribution Region A consists of the following counties: Bertie, Camden, Chowan, Currituck, Dare, Edgecombe, Gates, Halifax, Hertford, Hyde, Johnston, Martin, Nash, Northampton, Pasquotank, Perquimans, Tyrrell, Washington, Wayne, and Wilson.

b.   Distribution Region B consists of the following counties: Beaufort, Brunswick, Carteret, Craven, Duplin, Greene, Jones, Lenoir, New Hanover, Onslow, Pamlico, Pender, Pitt, and Sampson.

c.   Distribution Region C consists of the following counties: Bladen, Columbus, Cumberland, Durham, Franklin, Granville, Harnett, Person, Robeson, Vance, Wake, and Warren.

d.   Distribution Region D consists of the following counties: Alamance, Caswell, Davidson, Davie, Forsyth, Guilford, Orange, Rockingham, Rowan, and Stokes.

e.   Distribution Region E consists of the following counties: Anson, Cabarrus, Chatham, Hoke, Lee, Mecklenburg, Montgomery, Moore, Randolph, Richmond, Scotland, Stanly, and Union.

f.   Distribution Region F consists of the following counties: Alexander, Alleghany, Ashe, Avery, Caldwell, Catawba, Cleveland, Gaston, Iredell, Lincoln, Surry, Watauga, Wilkes, and Yadkin.

g.   Distribution Region G consists of the following counties: Buncombe, Burke, Cherokee, Clay, Graham, Haywood, Henderson, Jackson, Macon, Madison, McDowell, Mitchell, Polk, Rutherford, Swain, Transylvania, and Yancey.

(2)   Division needs projects. - Includes only the following:

a.   Projects listed in subdivision (3) or (4) of this section, subject to the limitations noted in those subsections.

b.   State highway routes not included in subdivision (3) or (4) of this section.

c.   Airports included in the NPIAS that are not included in subdivision (3) or (4) of this section, provided that the State's total annual financial participation under this sub-subdivision shall not exceed eighteen million five hundred thousand dollars ($18,500,000).

d.   Rail lines not included in subdivision (3) or (4) of this section. This sub-subdivision does not include short-line railroads.

e.   Public transportation service not included in subdivision (3) or (4) of this section. This sub-subdivision includes commuter rail, intercity rail, and light rail.

f.   Multimodal terminals and stations serving passenger transit systems.

g.   Federally funded independent bicycle and pedestrian improvements.

h.   Replacement of State-maintained ferry vessels.

i.   Federally funded municipal road projects.

(3)   Regional impact projects. - Includes only the following:

a.   Projects listed in subdivision (4) of this section, subject to the limitations noted in that subdivision.

b.   U.S. highway routes not included in subdivision (4) of this section.

c.   N.C. highway routes not included in subdivision (4) of this section.

d.   Commercial service airports included in the NPIAS that are not included in subdivision (4) of this section, provided that the State's annual financial participation in any single airport project included in this subdivision may not exceed three hundred thousand dollars ($300,000).

e.   The State-maintained ferry system, excluding passenger vessel replacement.

f.   Rail lines that span two or more counties not included in subdivision (4) of this section. This sub-subdivision does not include short-line railroads.

g.   Public transportation service that spans two or more counties and that serves more than one municipality. Programmed funds pursuant to this sub-subdivision shall not exceed ten percent (10%) of any distribution region allocation. This sub-subdivision includes commuter rail, intercity rail, and light rail.

(4)   Statewide strategic mobility projects. - Includes only the following:

a.   Interstate highways and future interstate highways approved by the federal government.

b.   Routes on the National Highway System as of July 1, 2012, excluding intermodal connectors.

c.   Highway routes on the United States Department of Defense Strategic Highway Network (STRAHNET).

d.   Highway toll routes designated by State law or by the Department of Transportation, pursuant to its authority under State law.

e.   Highway projects listed in G.S. 136-179, as it existed on July 1, 2012, that are not authorized for construction as of July 1, 2015.

f.   Appalachian Development Highway System.

g.   Commercial service airports included in the Federal Aviation Administration's National Plan of Integrated Airport Systems (NPIAS) that provide international passenger service or 375,000 or more enplanements annually, provided that the State's annual financial participation in any single airport project included in this subdivision may not exceed five hundred thousand dollars ($500,000).

h.   Freight capacity and safety improvements to Class I freight rail corridors. (2013-183, s. 1.1(a); 2013-410, s. 38(a).)

30

§ 136-189.11. Transportation Investment Strategy Formula.

(a)   Funds Subject to Formula. - The following sources of funds are subject to this section:

(1)   Highway Trust Fund funds, in accordance with G.S. 136-176.

(2)   Federal aid funds.

(b)   Funds Excluded From Formula. - The following funds are not subject to this section:

(1)   Federal congestion mitigation and air quality improvement program funds appropriated to the State by the United States pursuant to 23 U.S.C. § 104(b)(2) and 23 U.S.C. § 149.

(2)   Funds received through competitive awards or discretionary grants through federal appropriations either for local governments, transportation authorities, transit authorities, or the Department.

(3)   Funds received from the federal government that under federal law may only be used for Appalachian Development Highway System projects.

(4)   Funds used in repayment of "GARVEE" bonds related to Phase I of the Yadkin River Veterans Memorial Bridge project.

(5)   Funds committed to gap funding for toll roads funded with bonds issued pursuant to G.S. 136-176.

(6)   Funds obligated for projects in the State Transportation Improvement Program that are scheduled for construction as of October 1, 2013, in State fiscal year 2012-2013, 2013-2014, or 2014-2015.

(7)   Toll collections from a turnpike project under Article 6H of this Chapter and other revenue from the sale of the Authority's bonds or notes or project loans, in accordance with G.S. 136-89.192.

(8)   Toll collections from the State-maintained ferry system collected under the authority of G.S. 136-82.

(9)   Federal State Planning and Research Program funds (23 U.S.C. § 505) and Metropolitan Planning funds (23 U.S.C. §§ 104 and 134).

(b1)   Funds Excluded From Regional Impact Project Category. - Federal Surface Transportation Program-Direct Attributable funds expended on eligible projects in the Regional Impact Project category are excluded from that category.

(c)   Funds With Alternate Criteria. - The following federal program activities shall be included in the applicable category of the Transportation Investment Strategy Formula set forth in subsection (d) of this section but shall not be subject to the prioritization criteria set forth in that subsection:

(1)   Bridge replacement.

(2)   Interstate maintenance.

(3)   Highway safety improvement.

(d)   Transportation Investment Strategy Formula. - Funds subject to the Formula shall be distributed as follows:

(1)   Statewide Strategic Mobility Projects. - Forty percent (40%) of the funds subject to this section shall be used for Statewide Strategic Mobility Projects:

a.   Criteria. - Transportation-related quantitative criteria shall be used by the Department to rank highway projects that address cost-effective Statewide Strategic Mobility needs and promote economic and employment growth. The criteria for selection of Statewide Strategic Mobility Projects shall utilize a numeric scale of 100 points, based on consideration of the following quantitative criteria:

1.   Benefit cost.

2.   Congestion.

3.   Safety.

4.   Economic competitiveness.

5.   Freight.

32

6.   Multimodal.

7.   Pavement condition.

8.   Lane width.

9.   Shoulder width.

b.   Project cap. - No more than ten percent (10%) of the funds projected to be allocated to the Statewide Strategic Mobility category over any five-year period may be assigned to any contiguous project or group of projects in the same corridor within a Highway Division or within adjoining Highway Divisions.

(2)   Regional Impact Projects. - Thirty percent (30%) of the funds subject to this section shall be used for Regional Impact Projects and allocated by population of Distribution Regions based on the most recent estimates certified by the Office of State Budget and Management:

a.   Criteria. - A combination of transportation-related quantitative criteria, qualitative criteria, and local input shall be used to rank Regional Impact Projects involving highways that address cost-effective needs from a region-wide perspective and promote economic growth. Local input is defined as the rankings identified by the Department's Transportation Division Engineers, Metropolitan Planning Organizations, and Rural Transportation Planning Organizations. Transportation Division Engineer local input scoring shall take into account public comments. The Department shall ensure that the public has a full opportunity to submit public comments, by widely available notice to the public, an adequate time period for input, and public hearings. Board of Transportation input shall be in accordance with G.S. 136-189.11(g)(1) and G.S. 143B-350(g). The criteria utilized for selection of Regional Impact Projects shall be based thirty percent (30%) on local input and seventy percent (70%) on consideration of a numeric scale of 100 points based on the following quantitative criteria:

1.   Benefit cost.

2.   Congestion.

3.   Safety.

4.   Freight.

5.   Multimodal.

6.   Pavement condition.

7.   Lane width.

8.   Shoulder width.

9.   Accessibility and connectivity to employment centers, tourist destinations, or military installations.

(3)   Division Need Projects. - Thirty percent (30%) of the funds subject to this section shall be allocated in equal share to each of the Department divisions, as defined in G.S. 136-14.1, and used for Division Need Projects.

a.   Criteria. - A combination of transportation-related quantitative criteria, qualitative criteria, and local input shall be used to rank Division Need Projects involving highways that address cost-effective needs from a Division-wide perspective, provide access, and address safety-related needs of local communities. Local input is defined as the rankings identified by the Department's Transportation Division Engineers, Metropolitan Planning Organizations, and Rural Transportation Planning Organizations. Transportation Division Engineer local input scoring shall take into account public comments. The Department shall ensure that the public has a full opportunity to submit public comments, by widely available notice to the public, an adequate time period for input, and public hearings. Board of Transportation input shall be in accordance with G.S. 136-189.11(g)(1) and G.S. 143B-350(g). The criteria utilized for selection of Division Need Projects shall be based fifty percent (50%) on local input and fifty percent (50%) on consideration of a numeric scale of 100 points based on the following quantitative criteria, except as provided in sub-subdivision b. of this subdivision:

1.   Benefit cost.

2.   Congestion.

3.   Safety.

4.   Freight.

5.   Multimodal.

34

6.   Pavement condition.

7.   Lane width.

8.   Shoulder width.

9.   Accessibility and connectivity to employment centers, tourist destinations, or military installations.

b.   Alternate criteria. - Funding from the following programs shall be included in the computation of each of the Department division equal shares but shall be subject to alternate quantitative criteria:

1.   Federal Surface Transportation Program-Direct Attributable funds expended on eligible projects in the Division Need Projects category.

2.   Federal Transportation Alternatives funds appropriated to the State.

3.   Federal Railway-Highway Crossings Program funds appropriated to the State.

4.   Projects requested from the Department in support of a time-critical job creation opportunity, when the opportunity would be classified as transformational under the Job Development Investment Grant program established pursuant to G.S. 143B-437.52, provided that the total State investment in each fiscal year for all projects funded under this sub-subdivision shall not exceed ten million dollars ($10,000,000) in the aggregate and five million dollars ($5,000,000) per project.

5.   Federal funds for municipal road projects.

c.   Bicycle and pedestrian limitation. - The Department shall not provide financial support for independent bicycle and pedestrian improvement projects, except for federal funds administered by the Department for that purpose. This sub-subdivision shall not apply to funds allocated to a municipality pursuant to G.S. 136-41.1 that are committed by the municipality as matching funds for federal funds administered by the Department and used for bicycle and pedestrian improvement projects. This limitation shall not apply to funds authorized for projects in the State Transportation Improvement Program that are scheduled for construction as of October 1, 2013, in State fiscal year 2012-2013, 2013-2014, or 2014-2015.

(4)   Criteria for nonhighway projects. - Nonhighway projects subject to this subsection shall be evaluated through a separate prioritization process established by the Department that complies with all of the following:

a.   The criteria used for selection of projects for a particular transportation mode shall be based on a minimum of four quantitative criteria.

b.   Local input shall include rankings of projects identified by the Department's Transportation Division Engineers, Metropolitan Planning Organizations, and Rural Transportation Planning Organizations. Transportation Division Engineer local input scoring shall take into account public comments. The Department shall ensure that the public has a full opportunity to submit public comments, by widely available notice to the public, an adequate time period for input, and public hearings. Board of Transportation input shall be in accordance with G.S. 136-189.11(g)(1) and G.S. 143B-350(g).

c.   The criteria shall be based on a scale not to exceed 100 points that includes no bonus points or other alterations favoring any particular mode of transportation.

(e)   Authorized Formula Variance. - The Department may vary from the Formula set forth in this section if it complies with the following:

(1)   Limitation on variance. - The Department, in obligating funds in accordance with this section, shall ensure that the percentage amount obligated to Statewide Strategic Mobility Projects, Regional Impact Projects, and Division Need Projects does not vary by more than five percent (5%) over any five-year period from the percentage required to be allocated to each of those categories by this section. Funds obligated among distribution regions or divisions pursuant to this section may vary up to ten percent (10%) over any five-year period.

(2)   (Effective until July 1, 2019) Calculation of variance. - Each year the Secretary shall calculate the amount of Regional Impact and Division Need funds allocated in that year to each division and region, the amount of funds obligated, and the amount the obligations exceeded or were below the allocation. In the first variance calculation under this subdivision following the end of fiscal year 2015-2016, the target amounts obtained according to the Formula set forth in this section shall be adjusted to account for any differences between allocations and obligations reported for the previous year. In the first variance calculation under this subdivision following the end of fiscal year 2016-2017, the target amounts obtained according to the Formula set forth in this

36

section shall be adjusted to account for any differences between allocations and obligations reported for the previous two fiscal years. In the first variance calculation under this subdivision following the end of fiscal year 2017-2018, the target amounts obtained according to the Formula set forth in this section shall be adjusted to account for any differences between allocations and obligations reported for the previous three fiscal years. In the first variance calculation under this subdivision following the end of fiscal year 2018-2019, the target amounts obtained according to the Formula set forth in this section shall be adjusted to account for any differences between allocations and obligations reported for the previous four fiscal years. The new target amounts shall be used to fulfill the requirements of subdivision (1) of this subsection for the next update of the Transportation Improvement Program. The adjustment to the target amount shall be allocated by Distribution Region or Division, as applicable.

(2)   (Effective July 1, 2019) Calculation of Variance. - Each year, the Secretary shall calculate the amount of Regional Impact and Division Need funds allocated in that year to each division and region, the amount of funds obligated, and the amount the obligations exceeded or were below the allocation. The target amounts obtained according to the Formula set forth in this section shall be adjusted to account for any differences between allocations and obligations reported for the previous five fiscal years. The new target amounts shall be used to fulfill the requirements of subdivision (1) of this subsection for the next update of the Transportation Improvement Program. The adjustment to the target amount shall be allocated by Distribution Region or Division, as applicable.

(f)   Incentives for Local Funding and Highway Tolling. - The Department may revise highway project selection ratings based on local government funding initiatives and capital construction funding directly attributable to highway toll revenue. Projects authorized for construction after November 1, 2013, and contained in the 10-year Department of Transportation work program are eligible for a bonus allocation under this subsection:

(1)   Definitions. - The following definitions apply in this subsection:

a.   Bonus allocation. - The allocation obtained as a result of local government funding participation or highway tolling.

b.   Local funding participation. - Non-State or nonfederal funds committed by local officials to leverage the commitment of State or federal transportation funds towards construction.

(2)   Funds obtained from local government funding participation. - Upon authorization to construct a project with funds obtained by local government funding participation, the Department shall make available for allocation as set forth in subdivision (4) of this section an amount equal to one-half of the local funding commitment for other eligible highway projects that serve the local entity or entities that provided the local funding.

(3)   Funds obtained through highway tolling. - Upon authorization to construct a project with funding from toll revenue, the Department shall make available for allocation an amount equal to one-half of the project construction cost derived from toll revenue bonds. The amount made available for allocation to other eligible highway projects shall not exceed two hundred million dollars ($200,000,000) of the capital construction funding directly attributable to the highway toll revenues committed in the Investment Grade Traffic and Revenue Study, for a project for which funds have been committed on or before July 1, 2015. The amount made available for allocation to other eligible highway projects shall not exceed one hundred million dollars ($100,000,000) of the capital construction funding directly attributable to the highway toll revenues committed in the Investment Grade Traffic and Revenue Study, for a project for which funds are committed after July 1, 2015. If the toll project is located in one or more Metropolitan Planning Organization or Rural Transportation Planning Organization boundaries, based on the boundaries in existence at the time of letting of the project construction contract, the bonus allocation shall be distributed proportionately to lane miles of new capacity within the Organization's boundaries. The Organization shall apply the bonus allocation only within those counties in which the toll project is located.

(4)   Use of bonus allocation. - The Metropolitan Planning Organization, Rural Transportation Planning Organization, or the local government may choose to apply its bonus allocation in one of the three categories or in a combination of the three categories as provided in this subdivision:

a.   Statewide Strategic Mobility Projects category. - The bonus allocation shall apply over the five-year period in the State Transportation Improvement Program in the cycle following the contractual obligation.

b.   Regional Impact Projects category. - The bonus allocation is capped at ten percent (10%) of the regional allocation, or allocation to multiple regions, made over a five-year period and shall be applied over the five-year period in the State Transportation Improvement Program in the cycle following the contractual obligation.

c.   Division Needs Projects category. - The bonus allocation is capped at ten percent (10%) of the division allocation, or allocation to multiple divisions, made over a five-year period and shall be applied over the five-year period in the State Transportation Improvement Program in the cycle following the contractual obligation.

(g)   Reporting. - The Department shall publish on its Web site, in a link to the "Strategic Transportation Investments" Web site linked directly from the Department's home page, the following information in an accessible format as promptly as possible:

(1)   The quantitative criteria used in each highway and nonhighway project scoring, including the methodology used to define each criteria, the criteria presented to the Board of Transportation for approval, and any adjustments made to finalize the criteria.

(2)   The quantitative and qualitative criteria in each highway or nonhighway project scoring that is used in each region or division to finalize the local input score and shall include distinctions between the Department Division scoring and methodologies and Metropolitan Planning Organization and Rural Transportation Planning Organization scoring and methodologies.

(3)   Notification of changes to the methodologies used to calculate quantitative criteria.

(4)   The final quantitative formulas, including the number of points assigned to each criteria, used in each highway and nonhighway project scoring used to obtain project rankings in the Statewide, Regional, and Division categories. If the Department approves different formulas or point assignments regionally or by division, the final scoring for each area shall be noted.

(5)   The project scorings associated with the release of the draft and final State Transportation Improvement Program, including Division Engineer, Metropolitan Planning Organization, and Rural Transportation Planning Organization scoring and ranking.

(h)   Improvement of Prioritization Process. - The Department shall endeavor to continually improve the methodology and criteria used to score highway and non-highway projects pursuant to this Article, including the use of normalization techniques, and methods to strengthen the data collection process. The Department is directed to continue the use of a workgroup process to develop improvements to the prioritization process. Workgroup participants shall include, but not be limited to, the North Carolina League of Municipalities, the North Carolina Association of County Commissioners, the North Carolina Metropolitan Mayors Coalition, and the North Carolina Council of Regional Governments. The workgroup, led by the Prioritization Office, shall contain a minimum of four representatives each from the North Carolina Association of Municipal Planning Organizations and the North Carolina Association of Rural Planning Organizations, and these members will be selected by a vote of each organization. Department participants in the workgroup shall not exceed half of the total group. Beginning December 1, 2016, the Department shall report annually to the Joint Legislative Transportation Oversight Committee on any changes made to the highway or non-highway prioritization process and the resulting impact to the State Transportation Improvement Program. The General Assembly members and staff may attend all workgroup meetings related to the prioritization process, all subgroup meetings of the workgroup, and have access to all related workgroup or subgroup documents. (2013-183, s. 1.1(a), (b); 2013-410, s. 38(b), (c), (d), (h).)

Article 15.

Railroads.

§ 136-190. Powers of railroad corporations.

Every railroad corporation shall have power:

(1)   To Survey and Enter on Land. - To cause such examination and surveys for its proposed railroad to be made as may be necessary to the selection of the most advantageous route; and for such purpose, by its officers or agents and servants, to enter upon the lands or waters of any person, but subject to responsibility for all damages which shall be done thereto.

(2)   To Condemn Land under Eminent Domain. - To appropriate land and rights therein by condemnation, as provided in the Chapter Eminent Domain.

(3)   To Take Property by Grant. - To take and hold such voluntary grants of real estate and other property as shall be made to it to aid in the construction, maintenance and accommodation of its railroad; but the real estate received by voluntary grant shall be held and used for the purposes of such grant only.

(4)   To Purchase and Hold Property. - To purchase, hold and use all such real estate and other property as may be necessary for the construction and maintenance of its railroad, the stations and other accommodations necessary to accomplish the object of its incorporation.

(5)   To Grade and Construct Road. - To lay out its road, not exceeding 100 feet in width, and to construct the same; to take, for the purpose of cuttings and embankments, as much more land as may be necessary for the proper construction and security of the road; and to cut down any standing trees that may be in danger of falling on the road, making compensation therefor as provided in the Chapter Eminent Domain.

(6)   To Intersect with Highways and Waterways. - To construct its road across, along or upon any stream, watercourse, street, highway, turnpike, railroad or canal which the route of its road shall intersect or touch; but the company shall restore the stream, watercourse, street, highway or turnpike, thus intersected or touched, to its former state or to such state as not unnecessarily to impair its usefulness. Nothing in this Chapter shall be construed to authorize the erection of any bridge or any other construction across, in or over any stream or lake navigated by motor boats commensurate in size to sailboat, or sailboats or vessels, at the place where any bridge or other obstructions may be proposed to be placed, nor to authorize the construction of any railroad not already located in, upon or across any streets in any municipality without the assent of such municipality.

(7)   To Intersect with Other Railroads. - To cross, intersect, join and unite its railroad with any other railroad at any point on its route and upon the grounds of such other railroad, with the necessary turnouts, sidings, switches and other conveniences in furtherance of the object of its connections. Every company whose railroad is or shall be hereafter intersected by any other railroad shall unite with the owners of such other railroad in forming such intersections and connections and grant the facilities aforesaid, and if the two corporations cannot agree upon the amount of compensation to be made therefor, or the points and manner of such crossings and connections, the same shall be ascertained and determined by the Commission.

41

(8)   To Transport Persons and Property. - To take and convey persons and property on its railroad or by water by the power or force of steam, electricity, or by any other power, and to receive compensation therefor.

(9)   To Erect Stations and Other Buildings. - To erect and maintain all necessary and convenient buildings, stations, fixtures and machinery for the accommodation and use of its passengers, freight and business.

(10)   To Borrow Money, Issue Bonds and Execute Mortgages. - From time to time to borrow such sums of money as may be necessary for completing and finishing or operating its railroad, to issue and dispose of its bonds for any amount so borrowed, to mortgage its corporate property and franchises and to secure the payment of any debt contracted by the company for the purposes aforesaid; and the directors of the company may confer on any holder of any bond issued for money borrowed, as aforesaid, the right to convert the principal due or owing thereon into stock of such company at any time under such regulations as the directors may see fit to adopt.

(11)   To Lease Rails. - To lease iron rails to any person for such time and upon such terms as may be agreed on by the contracting parties, and upon the termination of the lease by expiration, forfeiture or surrender, to take possession of and remove the rails so leased as if they had never been laid.

(12)   To Establish Hotels and Eating Houses. - To purchase, lease, hold, operate or maintain eating houses, hotels and restaurants for the accommodation of the traveling public along the line of its road. (1871-2, c. 138, s. 29; Code, s. 1957; 1887, c. 341; 1889, c. 518; Rev., ss. 2567, 2575; C.S., s. 3444; 1953, c. 675, ss. 6, 7; 1963, c. 1165, s. 1; 1998-128, s. 14.)

§ 136-191. Intersection with highways.

Whenever the track of a railroad shall cross a highway or turnpike, such highway or turnpike may be carried under or over the track, as may be found most expedient; and in cases where an embankment or cutting shall make a change in the line of such highway or turnpike desirable, then the railroad company may take such additional lands for the construction of the road, highway or turnpike on such new line as may be deemed requisite. Unless the land so taken shall be purchased for the purposes aforesaid, compensation therefor shall be ascertained in the manner prescribed in the Chapter Eminent

42

Domain, and duly made by such corporation to the owners and persons interested in such land. The same when so taken shall become a part of such intersecting highway or turnpike in such manner and by such tenure as the adjacent parts of the same highway or turnpike may be held for highway purposes. (1871-2, c. 138, s. 26; Code, s. 1954; Rev., s. 2568; C.S., s. 3448; 1963, c. 1165, s. 1; 1998-128, s. 14.)

§ 136-192. Obstructing highways; defective crossings; notice; failure to repair after notice misdemeanor.

(a)   Whenever, in their construction, the works of any railroad corporation shall cross established roads or ways, the corporation shall so construct its works as not to impede the passage or transportation of persons or property along the same. If any railroad corporation shall so construct its crossings with public streets, thoroughfares or highways, or keep, allow or permit the same at any time to remain in such condition as to impede, obstruct or endanger the passage or transportation of persons or property along, over or across the same, the governing body of the county, city or town, or other public road authority having charge, control or oversight of such roads, streets or thoroughfares may give to such railroad notice, in writing, directing it to place any such crossing in good condition, so that persons may cross and property be safely transported across the same.

(b)   The notice may be served upon the agent of the offending railroad located nearest to the defective or dangerous crossing about which the notice is given, or it may be served upon the section master whose section includes such crossing. Such notice may be served by delivering a copy to such agent or section master, or by registered or certified mail addressed to either of such persons.

(c)   If the railroad corporation shall fail to put such crossing in a safe condition for the passage of persons and property within 30 days from and after the service of the notice, it shall be guilty of a Class 1 misdemeanor. Each calendar month which shall elapse after the giving of the notice and before the placing of such crossing in repair shall be a separate offense.

(d)   This section shall in nowise be construed to abrogate, repeal or otherwise affect any existing law now applicable to railroad corporations with respect to highway and street crossings; but the duty imposed and the remedy

43

given by this section shall be in addition to other duties and remedies now prescribed by law. (R.C., c. 61, s. 30; 1874-5, c. 83; Code, s. 1710; Rev., s. 2569; 1915, c. 250, ss. 1, 2; C.S., ss. 3449, 3450; 1963, c. 1165, s. 1; 1993, c. 539, s. 480; 1994, Ex. Sess., c. 24, s. 14(c); 1998-128, s. 14.)

§ 136-193. Joint construction of railroads having same location.

Whenever two railroad companies shall, for a portion of their respective lines, embrace the same location of line, they may by agreement provide for the construction of so much of said line as is common to both of them, by one of the companies, and for the manner and terms upon which the business thereon shall be performed. (1871-2, c. 138, s. 46; Code, s. 1983; Rev., s. 2602; C.S., s. 3473; 1963, c. 1165, s. 1; 1998-128, s. 14.)

§ 136-194. Cattle guards and private crossings; failure to erect and maintain misdemeanor.

Every company owning, operating or constructing any railroad passing through and over the enclosed land of any person shall, at its own expense, construct and constantly maintain, in good and safe condition, good and sufficient cattle guards at the points of entrance upon and exit from such enclosed land and shall also make and keep in constant repair crossings to any private road thereupon. Every railroad corporation which shall fail to erect and constantly maintain the cattle guards and crossings provided for by this section shall be liable to an action for damages to any party aggrieved, and shall be guilty of a Class 3 misdemeanor and only fined in the discretion of the court. Any cattle guard approved by the Commission shall be deemed a good and sufficient guard under this section. (1883, c. 394, ss. 1, 2, 3; Code, s. 1975; Rev., ss. 2601, 3753; 1915, c. 127; C.S., s. 3454; 1933, c. 134, s. 8; 1941, c. 97, s. 5; 1963, c. 1165, s. 1; 1993, c. 539, s. 481; 1994, Ex. Sess., c. 24, s. 14(c); 1998-128, s. 14.)

§ 136-195. To regulate crossings and to abolish grade crossings.

The Department may require the raising or lowering of any tracks or roadway at any grade crossing in a road or street not forming a link in or part of the State highway system and designate who shall pay for the same by partitioning the cost of said work and the maintenance of such crossing among the railroads and municipalities interested in accordance with the formula provided for grade crossing alterations or eliminations on the State highway system in G.S. 136-20(b). (1899, c. 164, s. 2, subsec. 13; Rev., s. 1097; 1907, c. 469, s. 1c; 1911, c. 197, s. 1; C.S. ss. 1041, 1048; 1933, c. 134; s. 8; 1941, c. 97; 1963, c. 1165, s. 1; 1998-128, ss. 14, 15.)

§ 136-196. Injury to passenger while in prohibited place.

If any passenger on any railroad is injured in any portion of a train where passengers are prohibited by notice conspicuously posted in its passenger cars, such railroad shall not be liable for the injury, provided the railroad has furnished sufficient room within its passenger cars for the proper accommodation of all passengers on the train. (1871-2, c. 138, s. 42; Code, s. 1978; Rev., s. 2628; C.S., s. 3509; 1963, c. 1165, s. 1; 1998-128, s. 14.)

§ 136-197. Ticket may be refused intoxicated person; penalty for prohibited entry.

The ticket agent of a passenger train shall at all times have the power to refuse to sell a ticket to a person wanting to purchase a ticket who may at the time be intoxicated. The conductor in charge of the train shall at all times have the power to prevent an intoxicated person from boarding the train. An intoxicated person who boards a train after being forbidden by the conductor to do so is guilty of a Class 1 misdemeanor. (1998-128, s. 16.)

§ 136-198. Passenger refusing to pay fare or violating rules may be ejected.

If a passenger shall refuse to pay the fare, be or become intoxicated, or violate the rules of a passenger train, it shall be lawful for the conductor of the train to stop the train at any station or at any regular stop, and to put the passenger and the passenger's baggage out of the train, using no unnecessary force. (1998-128, s. 16.)

§ 136-199. Reserved for future codification purposes.

Article 16.

Planning.

§ 136-200. Definitions.

As used in this Article:

(1)   "Conformity" means the extent to which transportation plans, programs, and projects conform to federal air quality requirements as specified in 40 Code of Federal Regulations, Part 93, Subpart A (1 July 1998 Edition).

(1a)   "Consolidated Metropolitan Planning Organization" means a metropolitan planning organization created on or after January 1, 2001, through a memorandum of understanding by the consolidation of two or more metropolitan planning organizations in existence prior to January 1, 2001, and in accordance with 23 U.S.C. § 134.

(2)   "Department" means the North Carolina Department of Transportation.

(3)   "Interface" means a relationship between streams of traffic that efficiently and safely maximizes the mobility of people and goods within and through urbanized areas and minimizes transportation-related fuel consumption and air pollution.

(4)   "Metropolitan Planning Organization" or "MPO" means an agency that is designated or redesignated by a memorandum of understanding as a Metropolitan Planning Organization in accordance with 23 U.S.C. § 134.

(5)   "Regionally significant project" has the same meaning as under 40 Code of Federal Regulations 93.101 (1 July 1998 Edition).

(6)   "Regional travel demand model" means a model of a region, defined in the model, that is approved by the Department and each Metropolitan Planning Organization whose boundaries include any part of the region and that uses socioeconomic data and projections to predict demands on a transportation network. (1999-328, s. 4.10; 2000-80, ss. 1-3.)

§ 136-200.1. Metropolitan planning organizations recognized.

Metropolitan planning organizations established pursuant to the provisions of 23 U.S.C. § 134 are hereby recognized under the law of the State. Metropolitan planning organizations in existence on the effective date of this section continue unaffected until redesignated or restructured in accordance with the provisions of and according to the procedures established by 23 U.S.C. § 134 and this Article. The provisions of this Article are intended to supplement the provisions of 23 U.S.C. § 134. In the event any provision of this Article is deemed inconsistent with the requirements of 23 U.S.C. § 134, the provisions of federal law shall control. (2000-80, s. 4.)

§ 136-200.2. Decennial review of metropolitan planning organization boundaries, structure, and governance.

(a)   Evaluation. - Following each decennial census, and more frequently if requested by an individual metropolitan planning organization, the Governor and the Secretary of Transportation, in cooperation with the affected metropolitan planning organization or organizations, shall initiate an evaluation of the boundaries, structure, and governance of each metropolitan planning organization in the State. The goal of the evaluation shall be to examine the need for and to make recommendations for adjustments to metropolitan planning organization boundaries, structure, or governance in order to ensure compliance with the objectives of 23 U.S.C. § 134. The Secretary shall submit a report of the evaluation process to the Governor and to the Joint Legislative Transportation Oversight Committee.

(b)   Factors for Evaluation. - The evaluation of the area, structure, and governance of each metropolitan planning organization shall include all of the following factors:

(1)   Existing and projected future commuting and travel patterns and urban growth projections.

(2)   Integration of planning with existing regional transportation facilities, such as airports, seaports, and major interstate and intrastate road and rail facilities.

(3)   Conformity with and support for existing or proposed regional transit and mass transportation programs and initiatives.

(4)   Boundaries of existing or proposed federally designated air quality nonattainment areas or air-quality management regions.

(5)   Metropolitan Statistical Area boundaries.

(6)   Existing or proposed cooperative regional planning structures.

(7)   Administrative efficiency, availability of resources, and complexity of management.

(8)   Feasibility of the creation of interstate metropolitan planning organizations.

(9)   Governance structures, as provided in subsection (c) of this section.

(c)   Metropolitan Planning Organization Structures. - The Governor and Secretary of Transportation, in cooperation with existing metropolitan planning organizations and local elected officials, may consider the following changes to the structure of existing metropolitan planning organizations:

(1)   Expansion of existing metropolitan planning organization boundaries to include areas specified in 23 U.S.C. § 134(c).

(2)   Consolidation of existing contiguous metropolitan planning organizations in accordance with the redesignation procedure specified in 23 U.S.C. § 134(b).

(3)   Creation of metropolitan planning organization subcommittees with responsibility for matters that affect a limited number of constituent jurisdictions, as specified in a memorandum of understanding redesignating a metropolitan planning organization in accordance with the provisions of 23 U.S.C. § 134.

(4)   Formation of joint committees or working groups among contiguous nonconsolidated metropolitan planning organizations, with such powers and responsibilities as may be delegated to such joint committees pursuant to their respective memoranda of understanding.

(5)   Creation of interstate compacts pursuant to 23 U.S.C. § 134(d) to address coordination of planning among metropolitan planning organizations located in this State and contiguous metropolitan planning organizations located in adjoining states.

(6)   Delegation by the governing board of a metropolitan planning organization of part or all of its responsibilities to a regional transportation authority created under Article 27 of Chapter 160A of the General Statutes, if the regional transportation authority is eligible to exercise that authority under 23 U.S.C. § 134.

(d)   Optional Governance Provisions. - In addition to any other provisions permitted or required pursuant to 23 U.S.C. § 134, the memorandum of understanding, creating, enlarging, modifying, or restructuring a metropolitan planning organization may also include any of the following provisions relating to governance:

(1)   Distribution of voting power among the constituent counties, municipal corporations, and other participating organizations on a basis or bases other than population.

(2)   Membership and representation of regional transit or transportation authorities or other regional organizations in addition to membership of counties and municipal corporations.

(3)   Requirements for weighted voting or supermajority voting on some or all issues.

(4)   Provisions authorizing or requiring the delegation of certain decisions or approvals to less than the full-voting membership of the metropolitan planning

organization in matters that affect only a limited number of constituent jurisdictions.

(5)   Requirements for rotation and sharing of officer positions and committee chair positions in order to protect against concentration of authority within the metropolitan planning organization.

(6)   Any other provision agreed to by the requisite majority of jurisdictions constituting the metropolitan planning organization.

(e)   Effect of Evaluation. - Upon completion of the evaluation required under this section, a metropolitan planning organization may be restructured in accordance with the procedure contained in 23 U.S.C. § 134(b)(5).

(f)   Assistance. - The Department may provide staff assistance to metropolitan planning organizations in existence prior to January 1, 2001, that are considering consolidation on or after January 1, 2001. In addition, the Department may provide funding assistance to metropolitan planning organizations considering consolidation, upon receipt of a letter of intent from jurisdictions representing seventy-five percent (75%) of the affected population, including the central city, in each metropolitan planning organization considering consolidation.

(g)   Ethics Provisions. - All individuals with voting authority serving on a metropolitan planning organization who are not members of the Board of Transportation shall do all of the following:

(1)   Except as permitted under this subdivision, no MPO member acting in that capacity shall participate in an action if the member knows the member, the member's extended family, or any business with which the member is associated may incur a reasonably foreseeable financial benefit from the matter under consideration, which financial benefit would impair the MPO member's independence of judgment or from which it could reasonably be inferred that the financial benefit would influence the member's participation in the action. An MPO member may participate in an action of the MPO under any of the following circumstances:

a.   When action is ministerial only and does not require the exercise of discretion.

b.   When the committee records in its minutes that it cannot obtain a quorum in order to take the action because the MPO member is disqualified from acting, the MPO member may be counted for purposes of a quorum but shall otherwise abstain from taking any further action.

(2)   An MPO member shall have an affirmative duty to promptly disclose in writing to the MPO any conflict of interest or potential conflict of interest under subdivision (1) of this subsection. All written disclosures shall be a public record under Chapter 132 of the General Statutes and attached to the minutes of the meeting in which any discussion or vote was taken by the MPO related to that disclosure.

(3)   File a statement of economic interest with the State Ethics Commission in accordance with Article 3 of Chapter 138A of the General Statutes, for which the State Ethics Commission shall prepare a written evaluation relative to conflicts of interest and potential conflicts of interest and provide a copy of that evaluation to the MPO member. All statements of economic interest and all written evaluations by the Commission of those statements are public records as provided in G.S. 138A-23. The penalties for failure to file shall be as set forth in G.S. 138A-25(a) and (b).

(4)   File, with and in the same manner as the statement of economic interest filed under subdivision (3) of this subsection, an additional disclosure of a list of all real estate owned wholly or in part by the MPO member, the MPO member's extended family, or a business with which the MPO member is associated within the jurisdiction of the MPO on which the MPO member is serving. All additional disclosures of real estate filed by MPO members are public records under Chapter 132 of the General Statutes.

(h)   Confidential Information. - An MPO member shall not use or disclose any nonpublic information gained in the course of or by reason of serving as a member of the MPO in a way that would affect a personal financial interest of the MPO member, the MPO member's extended family, or a business with which the MPO member is associated.

(i)   Definitions. - For purposes of this section, "extended family" shall have the same meaning as in G.S. 138A-3(13), "business with which associated" shall have the same meaning as in G.S. 138A-3(3), and "financial benefit" shall mean a direct pecuniary gain or loss or a direct pecuniary loss to a business competitor.

(j)   Violations. - A violation of subdivision (1) of subsection (g) of this section shall be a Class 1 misdemeanor. An MPO member who knowingly conceals or knowingly fails to disclose information that is required to be disclosed on a required filing under subdivisions (3) or (4) of subsection (g) of this section shall be guilty of a Class 1 misdemeanor. An MPO member who provides false information on a required filing under subdivisions (3) or (4) of subsection (g) of this section knowing that the information is false is guilty of a Class H felony.

(k)   All individuals with voting authority serving on an MPO who are members of the Board of Transportation shall comply with Chapter 138A of the General Statutes and G.S. 143A-350 while serving on the MPO. (2000-80, s. 5; 2013-156, s. 1(b).)

§ 136-200.3. Additional provisions applicable to consolidated metropolitan planning organizations.

(a)   Limit on Basis for Project Objection. - Beginning with the 2004 State Transportation Improvement Program, neither the State nor a consolidated metropolitan planning organization shall have a basis to object to a project that is proposed for funding in the Transportation Improvement Program, provided that the project does not affect projects previously programmed, if the project is included in a mutually adopted plan developed pursuant to G.S. 136-66.2, and is consistent with the project selection criteria contained in the memorandum of understanding creating the consolidated metropolitan planning organization.

(b)   Project Ranking Priorities. - Beginning with the 2004 State Transportation Improvement Program, and subject to the availability of funding, the Department of Transportation, when developing the Transportation Improvement Program, shall abide by the project ranking priorities approved by a:

(1)   Consolidated metropolitan planning organization for any project within its jurisdiction, if the project is not a National Highway System or bridge and Interstate maintenance program project.

(2)   Regional transportation authority created pursuant to Article 27 of Chapter 160A of the General Statutes, for any project that all metropolitan planning organizations within the authority's jurisdiction have delegated

responsibility, if the project is not a National Highway System or bridge and Interstate maintenance program project. (2000-80, s. 6.)

§ 136-200.4. Additional requirements for metropolitan planning organizations located in nonattainment areas.

(a)   Consultation and Single Conformity Plan Required. - When an area of the State is designated as non-attainment under the federal Clean Air Act (42 U.S.C. § 7401, et seq.) all metropolitan planning organizations with at least twenty-five percent (25%) of their area of jurisdiction located within the boundaries of the nonattainment area shall consult on appropriate emissions reduction strategies and shall adopt a single, unified plan for achieving conformity. The strategies set forth in the unified plan shall be incorporated by each affected metropolitan planning organization into its respective long range transportation plan developed pursuant to 23 U.S.C. § 134(g).

(b)   Effect of Failure to Adopt Required Plan. - If a metropolitan planning organization does not comply with the provisions of subsection (a) of this section within one year after designation of at least twenty-five percent (25%) of the metropolitan planning organization's area of jurisdiction as nonattainment under the federal Clean Air Act (42 U.S.C. § 7401, et seq.), the Department shall not allocate any of the following funds to projects within the metropolitan planning organization's area of jurisdiction:

(1)   One hundred percent (100%) State-funded road construction funds.

(2)   State matching funds for any road construction or transit capital project.

(3)   Federal congestion mitigation and air quality improvement program funds.

(c)   Mandatory Evaluation and Report. - Each metropolitan planning organization located in whole or in part in areas designated as nonattainment under the federal Clean Air Act (42 U.S.C. § 7401 et seq.) shall complete the evaluation process provided for in G.S. 136-200.2 and submit its findings and recommendations to the Department of Transportation within one year of the effective date of designation as nonattainment. A metropolitan planning organization may request and be granted by the Department an extension if the metropolitan planning organization can show cause for the extension.

Extensions shall be granted in no more than one year increments. (2000-80, s. 7.)

§ 136-200.5. Matching funds for Metropolitan Planning Organizations located in nonattainment areas or maintenance areas.

(a)   Application. - The lead planning agency for any Metropolitan Planning Organization located in an area designated as a nonattainment or maintenance area under the federal Clean Air Act (42 U.S.C. § 7401, et seq.) may apply to the Department of Transportation for funds to avoid a plan conformity lapse.

(b)   Matching Required. - Funds provided under this section shall be matched one-for-one by the local applicant agency.

(c)   Use of Funds. - Funds provided under this section shall be used by the local applicant agency only to avoid a plan conformity lapse.

(d)   Limit on Funds. - The Department shall not provide more than one million dollars ($1,000,000) per fiscal year to any lead planning organization of a Metropolitan Planning Organization pursuant to this section.

(e)   Payback Required. - Any funds provided to a lead planning organization of a Metropolitan Planning Organization under this section shall be repaid within five years, either from local sources or as an offset against planning funds that might otherwise have been made available from the Department to the lead planning organization. (2003-284, s. 29.14(b).)

§ 136-200.6. Funds for local transportation planning efforts in areas designated nonattainment areas or maintenance areas.

(a)   Application. - A regional transportation planning agency in an area designated as a nonattainment or maintenance area under the federal Clean Air Act (42 U.S.C. § 7401, et seq.) that has policy-setting authority for the entire designated area and that is representative of all local governments within the area, may apply to the Department of Transportation for funds to support local transportation planning efforts in that local government's region.

54

(b)   Matching Required. - Funds provided under this section shall be matched one-for-one by the applicant agency.

(c)   Use of Funds. - Funds provided under this section shall only be used by the local applicant agency to support regional transportation planning within the designated area.

(d)   Local Staff Required. - Funds shall be provided under this section only if local governments in the designated area support and supply staff to the regional transportation planning agency.

(e)   Limit on Funds. - The Department shall not provide more than two hundred fifty thousand dollars ($250,000) in any fiscal year to any agency pursuant to this section. (2003-284, s. 29.14(c).)

§ 136-201. Plan for intermodal interface.

When planning a regionally significant transportation project, the Department shall consider design alternatives that will facilitate the cost-effective interface of the project with other existing or planned transportation projects, including highway, airport, rail, bus, bicycle, and pedestrian facilities. The Department of Transportation shall record its consideration of these design alternatives in the planning documents for the project. (1999-328, s. 4.10.)

§ 136-202. Metropolitan planning organizations.

(a)   Each Metropolitan Planning Organization shall base all transportation plans, metropolitan transportation improvement programs, and conformity determinations on the most recently completed regional travel demand model.

(b)   Each Metropolitan Planning Organization shall update its transportation plans in accordance with the scheduling requirements stated in 23 Code of Federal Regulations 450.322 (1 April 1999 Edition).

(c)   The Department, the metropolitan planning organizations, and the Department of Environment and Natural Resources shall jointly evaluate and adjust the regions defined in each regional travel demand model at least once every five years and no later than October 1 of the year following each decennial federal census. The evaluation and adjustment shall be based on decennial census data and the most recent populations estimates certified by the State Budget Officer. The adjustment of these boundaries shall reflect current and projected patterns of population, employment, travel, congestion, commuting, and public transportation use and the effects of these patterns on air quality.

(d)   The Department shall report on the evaluation and adjustment of the boundaries of the area served by each Metropolitan Planning Organization to the Joint Legislative Transportation Oversight Committee and the Environmental Review Commission no later than November 1 of each year in which the regions are evaluated and adjusted.

(e)   Repealed by Session Laws 2013-156, s. 1(a), effective June 19, 2013. (1999-328, s. 4.10; 2004-203, s. 5(k); 2012-142, s. 24.16(a); 2013-156, s. 1(a).)

§ 136-203: Repealed by Session Laws 2002-148, s. 1, effective October 9, 2002.

§§ 136-204 through 136-209. Reserved for future codification purposes.

Article 17.

Rural Transportation Planning Organizations.

§ 136-210. Definitions.

As used in this Article, "Rural Transportation Planning Organization" means a voluntary organization of local elected officials or their designees and representatives of local transportation systems formed by a memorandum of understanding with the Department of Transportation to work cooperatively with the Department to plan rural transportation systems and to advise the Department on rural transportation policy. (2000-123, s. 2.)

§ 136-211. Department authorized to establish Rural Transportation Planning Organizations.

(a)   Authorization. - The Department of Transportation is authorized to form Rural Transportation Planning Organizations.

(b)   Area Represented. - Rural Transportation Planning Organizations shall include representatives from contiguous areas in three to fifteen counties, or a total population of the entire area represented of at least 50,000 persons according to the latest population estimate of the Office of State Budget and Management. Noncontiguous counties adjacent to the same Metropolitan Planning Organization may form a Rural Transportation Planning Organization. Areas already included in a Metropolitan Planning Organization shall not be included in the area represented by a Rural Transportation Planning Organization.

(c)   Membership. - The Rural Transportation Planning Organization shall consist of local elected officials or their designees and representatives of local transportation systems in the area as agreed to by all parties in a memorandum of understanding.

(d)   Formation; Memorandum of Understanding. - The Department shall notify local elected officials and representatives of local transportation systems around the State of the opportunity to form Rural Transportation Planning Organizations. The Department shall work cooperatively with interested local elected officials, their designees, and representatives of local transportation systems to develop a proposed area, membership, functions, and responsibilities of a Rural Transportation Planning Organization. The agreement of all parties shall be included in a memorandum of understanding approved by the membership of a proposed Rural Transportation Planning Organization and the Secretary of the Department of Transportation.

(e)   Repealed by Session Laws 2013-156, s. 1(a), effective June 19, 2013.

(f)   Ethics Provisions. - All individuals with voting authority serving on a rural transportation planning organization who are not members of the Board of Transportation shall do all of the following:

(1)   Except as permitted under this subdivision, no rural transportation planning organization member acting in that capacity shall participate in an action of the rural transportation planning organization if the rural transportation

planning organization member knows the rural transportation planning organization member, the rural transportation planning organization member's extended family, or any business with which the rural transportation planning organization member is associated may incur a reasonably foreseeable financial benefit from the matter under consideration, which financial benefit would impair the rural transportation planning organization member's independence of judgment or from which it could reasonably be inferred that the financial benefit would influence the rural transportation planning organization member's participation in the action of the rural transportation planning organization. [A member may participate in an action of the rural transportation planning organization under any of the following circumstances:]

a.   When action is ministerial only and does not require the exercise of discretion.

b.   When the committee records in its minutes that it cannot obtain a quorum in order to take the action because the rural transportation planning organization member is disqualified from acting, the rural transportation planning organization member may be counted for purposes of a quorum but shall otherwise abstain from taking any further action.

(2)   A rural transportation planning organization member shall have an affirmative duty to promptly disclose in writing to the rural transportation planning organization any conflict of interest or potential conflict of interest under subdivision (1) of this subsection. All written disclosures shall be a public record under Chapter 132 of the General Statutes and attached to the minutes of the meeting in which any discussion or vote was taken by the rural transportation planning organization related to that disclosure.

(3)   File a statement of economic interest with the State Ethics Commission in accordance with Article 3 of Chapter 138A of the General Statutes for which the State Ethics Commission shall prepare a written evaluation relative to conflicts of interest and potential conflicts of interest and provide a copy of that evaluation to the rural transportation planning organization member. All statements of economic interest and all written evaluations by the Commission of those statements are public records as provided in G.S. 138A-23. The penalties for failure to file shall be as set forth in G.S. 138A-25(a) and (b).

(4)   File, with and in the same manner as the statement of economic interest filed under subdivision (3) of this subsection, an additional disclosure of a list of all real estate owned wholly or in part by the rural transportation planning

organization member, the rural transportation planning organization member's extended family, or a business with which the rural transportation planning organization member is associated within the jurisdiction of the rural transportation planning organization on which the rural transportation planning organization member is serving. All additional disclosures of real estate filed by members are public records under Chapter 132 of the General Statutes.

(g)   Confidential Information. - A rural transportation planning organization member shall not use or disclose any nonpublic information gained in the course of or by reason of serving as a member of the rural transportation planning organization in a way that would affect a personal financial interest of the rural transportation planning organization member, the rural transportation planning organization member's extended family, or a business with which the rural transportation planning organization member is associated.

(i)   Definitions. - For purposes of this section, "extended family" shall have the same meaning as in G.S. 138A-3(13), "business with which associated" shall have the same meaning as in G.S. 138A-3(3), and "financial benefit" shall mean a direct pecuniary gain or loss or a direct pecuniary loss to a business competitor.

(j)   Violations. - A violation of subdivision (1) of subsection (f) of this section shall be a Class 1 misdemeanor. A rural transportation planning organization member who knowingly conceals or knowingly fails to disclose information that is required to be disclosed on a required filing under subdivisions (3) or (4) of subsection (f) of this section shall be guilty of a Class 1 misdemeanor. A rural transportation planning organization member who provides false information on a required filing under subdivisions (3) or (4) of subsection (f) of this section knowing that the information is false is guilty of a Class H felony.

(k)   All individuals with voting authority serving on a rural transportation planning organization who are members of the Board of Transportation shall comply with Chapter 138A of the General Statutes and G.S. 143A-350 while serving on the rural transportation planning organization. (2000-123, s. 2; 2002-170, s. 2; 2012-44, s. 1; 2012-142, s. 24.16(b); 2013-156, s. 2(a), (b).)

§ 136-212. Duties of Rural Transportation Planning Organizations.

The duties of a Rural Transportation Planning Organization shall include, but not be limited to:

(1)   Developing, in cooperation with the Department, long-range local and regional multimodal transportation plans.

(2)   Providing a forum for public participation in the transportation planning process.

(3)   Developing and prioritizing suggestions for transportation projects the organization believes should be included in the State's Transportation Improvement Program.

(4)   Providing transportation-related information to local governments and other interested organizations and persons. (2000-123, s. 2.)

§ 136-213. Administration and staff.

(a)   Administrative Entity. - Each Rural Transportation Planning Organization, working in cooperation with the Department, shall select an appropriate administrative entity for the organization. Eligible administrative entities include, but are not limited to, regional economic development agencies, regional councils of government, chambers of commerce, and local governments.

(b)   Professional Staff. - The Department, each Rural Transportation Planning Organization, and any adjacent Metropolitan Planning Organization shall cooperatively determine the appropriate professional planning staff needs of the organization.

(c)   Funding. - If funds are appropriated for that purpose, the Department may make grants to Rural Transportation Planning Organizations to carry out the duties listed in G.S. 136-212. The members of the Rural Transportation Planning Organization shall contribute at least twenty percent (20%) of the cost of any staff resources employed by the organization to carry out the duties listed in G.S. 136-212. The Department may make additional planning grants to economically distressed counties, as designated by the North Carolina Department of Commerce. (2000-123, s. 2; 2002-170, s. 3.)

§ 136-214: Reserved for future codification purposes.

§ 136-215: Reserved for future codification purposes.

§ 136-216: Reserved for future codification purposes.

§ 136-217: Reserved for future codification purposes.

§ 136-218: Reserved for future codification purposes.

§ 136-219: Reserved for future codification purposes.

Article 18.

Virginia-North Carolina Interstate High-Speed Rail Compact.

§ 136-220. Compact established.

Pursuant to the invitation in 49 U.S.C. § 24101 (Interstate Compacts), in which the United States Congress grants consent to states with an interest in a specific form, route, or corridor of intercity passenger rail service (including high-speed rail service) to enter into interstate compacts, there is hereby established the Virginia-North Carolina Interstate High-Speed Rail Compact. (2004-114, s. 1.)

§ 136-221. Agreement.

The Commonwealth of Virginia and the State of North Carolina agree, upon adoption of this compact:

(1)   To study, develop, and promote a plan for the design, construction, financing, and operation of interstate high-speed rail service through and between points in the Commonwealth of Virginia and the State of North Carolina, and adjacent states.

(2)   To coordinate efforts to establish high-speed rail service at the federal, State, and local governmental levels.

(3)   To advocate for federal funding to support the establishment of high-speed interstate rail service within and through Virginia and North Carolina and to receive federal funds made available for rail development.

(4)   To provide funding and resources to the Virginia-North Carolina High-Speed Rail Compact Commission from funds that are or may become available and are appropriated for that purpose. (2004-114, s. 1.)

§ 136-222. Commission established; appointment and terms of members; chairman; reports; commission funds; staff.

(a)   Commission established. - The Virginia-North Carolina High-Speed Rail Compact Commission is hereby established as a regional instrumentality and a common agency of each signatory party, empowered in a manner hereinafter to carry out the purposes of the Compact.

(b)   Members, terms. - The Virginia members of the Commission shall be appointed as follows: three members of the House of Delegates, appointed by the Speaker of the House of Delegates, and two members of the Senate, appointed by the Senate Committee on Rules. The North Carolina members of the Commission shall be composed of five members as follows: two members of the Senate appointed by the General Assembly upon recommendation of the President Pro Tempore of the Senate, two members of the House of Representatives appointed by the General Assembly upon recommendation of the Speaker of the House of Representatives, and one appointed by the Governor.

(c)   Chair. - The chair of the Commission shall be chosen by the members of the Commission from among its membership for a term of one year and shall alternate between the member states.

(d)   Meetings and reports. - The Commission shall meet at least twice each year, at least once in Virginia and once in North Carolina, and shall issue a report of its activities each year.

(e)   Funds. - The Commission may utilize, for its operation and expenses, funds appropriated to it therefore by the legislatures of Virginia and North Carolina, or received from federal sources.

(f)   Expenses of Members. - Virginia members of the Commission shall receive compensation and reimbursement for expenses in accordance with the applicable laws of that state. North Carolina members of the Commission shall receive per diem, subsistence, and travel allowances in accordance with G.S. 120-31, 138-5, or 138-6, as appropriate.

(g)   Staff. - Primary staff to the Commission shall be provided by the Virginia Department of Rail and Public Transportation and the North Carolina Department of Transportation. (2004-114, s. 1.)

§§ 136-223 through 136-249. Reserved for future codification purposes.

Article 19.

Congestion Relief and Intermodal 21st Century Transportation Fund.

§ 136-250. Congestion Relief and Intermodal Transportation 21st Century Fund.

There is established in the State treasury the Congestion Relief and Intermodal Transportation 21st Century Fund, hereinafter referred to as the Fund. The Fund shall consist of all revenues appropriated and allocated to it. Interest on earnings of the Fund shall remain within the Fund. (2009-527, s. 1.)

§ 136-251. Findings of fact.

The General Assembly finds that:

(1)   Increased use of rail for transport of freight will reduce highway congestion as well as allow economic expansion in a way that lessens the impact on the State highway system.

(2)   Public transportation, in addition to a program of urban loops and toll roads, will enable North Carolina to have a balanced 21st century transportation system.

(3)   As part of its initial program of internal improvements, the State capitalized the North Carolina Railroad in the 1840s and invested in other railroads, and those internal improvements led to North Carolina's rapid economic development. The North Carolina Railroad, with a 317-mile corridor from Charlotte to Morehead City, is still owned by the State.

(4)   Improved rail facilities and restoration of abandoned rail lines can allow increased access to the North Carolina State ports and military installations located within the State.

(5)   Session Law 2005-222 found that expanding and upgrading passenger, freight, commuter, and short-line rail service is important to the economy of North Carolina; and provided that the State would seek to provide matching funds partly so it can leverage the maximum federal and private participation to fund needed rail initiatives, such as the restoration of the rail corridor from Wallace to Castle Hayne and a rail connection between north-south and east-west routes in the vicinity of Pembroke.

(6)   Rail freight plays a vital role in economic development throughout the State. Intermodal service depends on partnerships with railroads, trucking companies, seaports, and others in the transportation logistics chain. North Carolina has 3,250 mainline miles of track, with Class I railroads holding seventy-nine percent (79%) of the trackage rights, the remainder controlled by local railroads and switching and terminal railroads. The 2006 Mid-Cycle Update to the North Carolina Statewide Intermodal Transportation Plan identified seven hundred ninety-nine million dollars ($799,000,000) in freight rail needs over the next 25 years, including maintenance and preservation, modernization, and expansion.

(7)   North Carolina's short-line railroads play a key role in the State's economic development and transportation service and are needed to provide essential services to other modes of transportation and the North Carolina port system. North Carolina agriculture is dependent upon essential service by short-line railroads. State funds are needed to maintain short-line railroads as viable contributors to economic development, agriculture, and transportation in this State in order to prevent the loss of regional rail service. The Department of Transportation reported that 44,992 rail cars handled by short-lines kept 179,688 trucks off North Carolina highways. Short-line railroads are essential to preserve and develop jobs in rural and small urban areas of North Carolina.

(8)   Intermodal facilities and inland ports can greatly reduce freight traffic on North Carolina's highway system, reducing demand, congestion, and damage.

(9)   The proposed North Carolina International Terminal will need high-capacity intermodal access.

(10)   Most of North Carolina's growth is in its urban regions. According to the State Data Center, during the first decade of the 21st century, sixty-six percent (66%) of the projected 1,270,000 growth in population is in 15 urban counties surrounding Charlotte, Raleigh, and the Triad, while forty percent (40%) is in just six counties: Mecklenburg, Wake, Durham, Orange, Forsyth, and Guilford.

(11)   This large urban population growth greatly taxes resources. Despite the visionary creation of the Highway Trust Fund by the 1989 General Assembly and the funding of urban loop highways, congestion continues to worsen. Creation of a special fund to help meet urban transportation needs with alternatives such as rail transit and buses, coupled with land-use planning, will spur and guide economic development in a more economically and environmentally sound manner. Investment in public transportation facilitates economic opportunity to the State through job creation, access to employment, and residential and commercial development. Public transportation also protects the public health by decreasing air pollution and reducing carbon emissions. It reduces traffic congestion, road expenditures, public and private parking costs, and the number of traffic accidents. Charlotte's recent success in opening the first phase of its light rail system, with ridership significantly over projections, shows that North Carolinians are willing to use transportation alternatives.

(12)   Significant local revenues are needed to match State funds so that a major portion of the expenses is borne by the localities receiving the majority of the benefits. A local option sales tax for public transportation was approved by a fifty-eight percent (58%) favorable vote in Mecklenburg County in 1998 and reaffirmed by a seventy percent (70%) favorable vote in 2007. Extending this authority to additional jurisdictions, along with other revenue options, will enable localities to demonstrate local support for additional transit options.

(13)   Surveys have indicated broad public support for providing additional public transportation options and for allowing localities to generate revenue to match State grants. (2009-527, s. 1.)

§ 136-252. Grants to local governments and transportation authorities.

(a) Eligible Entities. - The following entities are eligible to receive grants under this section from the Fund for public transportation purposes, which includes planning and engineering:

(1) Cities.

(2) Counties.

(3) Public transportation authorities under Article 25 of Chapter 160A of the General Statutes.

(4) Regional public transportation authorities under Article 26 of Chapter 160A of the General Statutes.

(5) Regional transportation authorities under Article 27 of Chapter 160A of the General Statutes.

(b) Requirements. - A grant may be approved from the Fund only if all of the following conditions are met:

(1) The application is approved by all Metropolitan Planning Organizations under Article 16 of this Chapter whose jurisdiction includes any of the service area of the grant applicant.

(2) The applicant has approved a transit plan that includes the following:

a. Relief of anticipated traffic congestion.

b. Improvement of air quality.

c. Reduction in anticipated energy consumption.

d. Promotion of a pedestrian- and bike-friendly environment around and connected to transit stations.

e. Promotion of mixed-use and transit-oriented developments and other land-use tools that encourage multimodal mobility.

f.   Coordination with the housing needs assessment and plan provided in subdivision (3) of this subsection.

g.   Promotion of access to public transportation for individuals who reside in areas with a disproportionate number of households below the area median income.

h.   Coordination and planning with local education agencies to reduce transportation costs.

i.   Coordination with local governments with zoning jurisdiction to carry out elements of the plan.

The applicant may also include plans for new public transportation services and public transportation alternatives beyond those required by the Americans with Disabilities Act of 1990 (42 U.S.C. § 12101, et seq.) that assist individuals with disabilities with transportation, including transportation to and from jobs and employment support services.

(3)   The applicant has approved a housing needs assessment and plan, or includes with its application such assessment and plan (or assessments and plans) approved by another unit or units of local government within its service area, that includes the following:

a.   A housing inventory of market rate, assisted housing units, and vacant residential parcels.

b.   An analysis of existing housing conditions, affordable housing needs, and housing needs for specific population groups, such as people who are elderly, are disabled, have special needs, or are homeless.

c.   A catalogue of available resources to address housing needs.

d.   Identification of potential resources and a strategy to provide replacement housing for low-income residents displaced by transit development and to create incentives for the purpose of increasing the stock of affordable housing to at least fifteen percent (15%) within a one-half mile radius of each transit station and bus hub to be affordable to families with income less than sixty percent (60%) of area median income.

e.   Goals, strategies, and actions to address housing needs over a five-year period.

(4)   The applicant has an adequate and sustainable source of funding established for its share of project costs.

(5)   The applicant agrees to submit to both the Secretary and each Metropolitan Planning Organization that approved the application a periodic update of the implementation of both the transit plan and the housing needs assessment and plan. Each Metropolitan Planning Organization receiving such update shall afford interested parties the opportunity to comment on the update.

(c)   Multiyear Allotments. - Grants from the Fund may be committed for a multiyear basis to stabilize the phased implementation of a plan, including multiyear allotments. The Secretary of Transportation, after consultation with the Board of Transportation, shall approve, and amend from time to time, a rolling multiyear projection of up to 15 years for allocation of funds under this section. No applicant is eligible under the 15-year plan projection for more than one-third of the total funds to be granted under this Article during that 15-year period.

(d)   Cap; Matching Requirement. - A grant under this section may not exceed twenty-five percent (25%) of the cost of the project and must be matched by an equal or greater amount of funds by the applicant. In evaluating projects, qualification for federal funding shall be considered. (2009-527, s. 1.)

§ 136-253. Grants to other units.

(a)   Eligible Entities; Purposes. - State agencies and railroads are eligible to receive grants under this section from the Fund for any of the following purposes:

(1)   Assistance to short-line railroads to continue and enhance rail service in the State so as to assist in economic development and access to ports and military installations. This may involve both the Rail Industrial Access Program and the Short Line Infrastructure Access Program, as well as other innovative programs. Grants under this subdivision shall not exceed fifty percent (50%) of the nonfederal share and must be matched by equal or greater funding from the applicant. Total grants under this subdivision may not exceed five million dollars ($5,000,000) per fiscal year.

68

(2)   Assistance to any railroad in the construction of rail improvements, intermodal or multimodal facilities or restorations to (i) serve ports, military installations, inland ports or (ii) improve rail infrastructure to reduce or mitigate truck traffic on the highway system. Grants under this subdivision shall not exceed fifty percent (50%) of the nonfederal share and must be matched by equal or greater funding from the applicant. Total grants under this subdivision may not exceed ten million dollars ($10,000,000) per fiscal year.

(3)   Assistance (i) to the State ports in terminal railroad facilities and operations, (ii) to improve access to military installations, and (iii) to the North Carolina International Terminal. Grants under this subdivision shall not exceed fifty percent (50%) of the nonfederal share and must be matched by equal or greater funding from the applicant. Total grants under this subdivision may not exceed ten million dollars ($10,000,000) per fiscal year.

(4)   Expansion of intercity passenger rail service, including increased frequency and additional cities serviced. Routes under this subdivision must extend beyond the territorial jurisdiction of a transportation authority.

(b)   Commuter Rail Service Grants. - State agencies, railroads, transportation authorities under Article 25 of Chapter 160A of the General Statutes, regional public transportation authorities under Article 26 of Chapter 160A of the General Statutes, and regional transportation authorities under Article 27 of Chapter 160A of the General Statutes are eligible to receive grants under this section from the Fund for the introduction of commuter rail service. Routes under this subsection must extend beyond the territorial jurisdiction of a transportation authority. (2009-527, s. 1.)

§ 136-254. Grant approval.

All grants made under this Article are subject to approval of the Secretary of Transportation after consultation with the Board of Transportation. The Fund may be administered in conjunction with G.S. 136-44.20 and G.S. 136-44.36, but any funds allocated under those sections shall continue to be available as provided therein. (2009-527, s. 1.)

§ 136-255. Expenditure.

69

No monies shall be expended from the Fund until appropriated by the General Assembly. (2009-527, s. 1.)

§ 136-256. Funds remain available until expended.

Appropriations to the Fund remain available until expended. (2009-527, s. 1.)

§ 136-257: Reserved for future codification purposes.

§ 136-258: Reserved for future codification purposes.

§ 136-259: Reserved for future codification purposes.

Article 20.

North Carolina State Ports Authority.

§ 136-260. Creation of Authority - membership; appointment, terms and vacancies; officers; meetings and quorum; compensation.

(a)   The North Carolina State Ports Authority is hereby created within the Department of Transportation and shall be subject to and under the direct supervision of the Secretary of Transportation. It shall be governed by a board composed of nine members and hereby designated as the Authority. Effective July 1, 1983, it shall be governed by a board composed of 11 members and hereby designated as the Authority. The General Assembly suggests and recommends that no person be appointed to the Authority who is domiciled in the district of the North Carolina House of Representatives or the North Carolina Senate in which a State port is located. Members of the North Carolina Board of Transportation may be appointed to the Authority. The Governor shall appoint seven members to the Authority, and the General Assembly shall appoint two members of the Authority. Effective July 1, 1983, the Authority shall consist of seven persons appointed by the Governor, and four persons appointed by the General Assembly. Effective July 1, 2011, the Governor shall appoint six members to the Authority, in addition to the Secretary of Transportation, who shall serve as a voting member of the Authority by virtue of his office. The Secretary of Transportation shall fill the first vacancy occurring after July 1, 2011, in a position on the Authority over which the Governor has appointive power.

(b)   The initial appointments by the Governor shall be made on or after March 8, 1977, two terms to expire July 1, 1979; two terms to expire July 1, 1981; and three terms to expire July 1, 1983. Thereafter, at the expiration of each stipulated term of office all appointments made by the Governor shall be for a term of six years.

(c)   To stagger further the terms of members:

(1)   Of the members appointed by the Governor to replace the members whose terms expire on July 1, 1991, one member shall be appointed to a term of five years, to expire on June 30, 1996; the other member shall be appointed for a term of six years, to expire on June 30, 1997;

(2)   Of the members appointed by the Governor to replace the members whose terms expire on July 1, 1993, one member shall be appointed to a term of five years, to expire on June 30, 1998; the other member shall be appointed to a term of six years, to expire on June 30, 1999;

(3)   Of those members appointed by the Governor to replace the members whose terms expire on July 1, 1995, one member shall be appointed to a term of five years, to expire on June 30, 2000; the other member shall be appointed to a term of six years, to expire on June 30, 2001.

Thereafter, at the expiration of each stipulated term of office all appointments made by the governor shall be for a term of six years.

(d)   The members of the Authority appointed by the Governor shall be selected from the State-at-large and insofar as practicable shall represent each section of the State in all of the business, agriculture, and industrial interests of the State. At least one member appointed by the Governor shall be affiliated with a major exporter or importer currently using the State Ports. Any vacancy occurring in the membership of the Authority appointed by the Governor shall be filled by the Governor for the unexpired term. The Governor may remove a member appointed by the Governor only for reasons provided by G.S. 143B-13.

(e)   The General Assembly shall appoint two persons to serve terms expiring June 30, 1983. The General Assembly shall appoint four persons to serve terms beginning July 1, 1983, to serve until June 30, 1985, and successors shall serve for two-year terms. Of the two appointments to be made in 1982, one shall be made upon the recommendation of the Speaker, and one shall be made upon the recommendation of the President of the Senate. Of the four appointments made in 1983 and biennially thereafter, two shall be made upon the recommendation of the President of the Senate, and two shall be made upon the recommendation of the Speaker. To stagger further the terms of members:

(1)   Of the members appointed upon the recommendation of the Speaker to replace the members whose terms expire on June 30, 1991, one member shall be appointed to a term of one year, to expire on June 30, 1992; the other member shall be appointed to a term of two years, to expire on June 30, 1993;

(2)   Of the members appointed upon the recommendation of the President of the Senate to replace the members whose terms expire on June 30, 1991, one member shall be appointed to a term of one year, to expire on June 30, 1992; the other member shall be appointed to a term of two years, to expire on June 30, 1993. Successors to these persons for terms beginning on or after January 1, 1997, shall be appointed by the General Assembly upon the recommendation of the President Pro Tempore of the Senate.

Thereafter, at the expiration of each stipulated term of office all appointments made by the General Assembly shall be for terms of two years.

(f)   Appointments by the General Assembly shall be made in accordance with G.S. 120-121, and vacancies in those appointments shall be filled in accordance with G.S. 120-122. Members appointed by the General Assembly may be removed only for reasons provided by G.S. 143B-13.

(g)   The Governor shall appoint from the members of the Authority the chairman and vice-chairman of the Authority. The members of the Authority shall appoint a treasurer and secretary of the Authority.

(h)   The Authority shall meet once in each 60 days at such regular meeting time as the Authority by rule may provide and at any place within the State as the Authority may provide, and shall also meet upon the call of its chairman or a majority of its members. A majority of its members shall constitute a quorum for the transaction of business. The members of the Authority shall not be entitled to compensation for their services, but they shall receive per diem and necessary travel and subsistence expense in accordance with G.S. 138-5. No member of the Authority may participate in any discussion or vote on any matter before the Authority on which the member has a conflict of interest. (1945, c. 1097, s. 1; 1949, c. 892, s. 1; 1953, c. 191, s. 1; 1959, c. 523, s. 1; 1961, c. 242; 1975, c. 716, s. 2; 1977, c. 65, s. 1; c. 198, s. 9; 1981 (Reg. Sess., 1982), c.

1191, ss. 69-71; 1983, c. 717, s. 2.1; 1989, c. 273, s. 2; c. 751, s. 8(25); 1989 (Reg. Sess., 1990), c. 1072; 1991 (Reg. Sess., 1992), c. 959, s. 70; 1995, c. 490, s. 54; 1997-235, s. 1; 1997-456, s. 27; 2011-145, s. 14.6(b), (h).)

§ 136-261. Purposes of Authority.

Through the Authority hereinbefore created, the State of North Carolina may engage in promoting, developing, constructing, equipping, maintaining and operating the harbors and seaports within the State, or within the jurisdiction of the State, and works of internal improvements incident thereto, including the acquisition or construction, maintenance and operation at such seaports or harbors of watercraft and highways and bridges thereon or essential for the proper operation thereof. Said Authority is created as an instrumentality of the State of North Carolina for the accomplishment of the following general purposes:

(1)   To develop and improve the harbors or seaports at Wilmington, Morehead City and Southport, North Carolina, and such other places, including inland ports and facilities, as may be deemed feasible for a more expeditious and efficient handling of waterborne commerce from and to any place or places in the State of North Carolina and other states and foreign countries.

(2)   To acquire, construct, equip, maintain, develop and improve the port facilities at said ports and to improve such portions of the waterways thereat as are within the jurisdiction of the federal government.

(3)   To foster and stimulate the shipment of freight and commerce through said ports, whether originating within or without the State of North Carolina, including the investigation and handling of matters pertaining to all transportation rates and rate structures affecting the same.

(4)   To cooperate with the United States of America and any agency, department, corporation or instrumentality thereof in the maintenance, development, improvement and use of said harbors and seaports in connection with and in furtherance of the war operations and needs of the United States.

(5)   To accept funds from any of said counties or cities wherein said ports are located and to use the same in such manner, within the purposes of said Authority, as shall be stipulated by the said county or city, and to act as agent or

73

instrumentality, of any of said counties or cities in any matter coming within the general purposes of said Authority.

(6)   To act as agent for the United States of America, or any agency, department, corporation or instrumentality thereof, in any matter coming within the purposes or powers of the Authority.

(7)   And in general to do and perform any act or function which may tend or be useful toward the development and improvement of harbors, seaports and inland ports of the State of North Carolina, and to increase the movement of waterborne commerce, foreign and domestic, to, through, and from such harbors and ports.

The enumeration of the above purposes shall not limit or circumscribe the broad objective of developing to the utmost the port possibilities of the State of North Carolina. (1945, c. 1097, s. 2; 1953, c. 191, ss. 3, 4; 1977, c. 198, s. 9; 1979, c. 159, s. 2; 2011-145, s. 14.6(b).)

§ 136-262. Powers of Authority.

(a)   In order to enable it to carry out the purposes of this Article, the said Authority shall:

(1)   Have the powers of a body corporate, including the power to sue and be sued, to make contracts, and to adopt and use a common seal and to alter the same as may be deemed expedient;

(2)   Have the authority to make all necessary contracts and arrangements with other port authorities of this and other states for the interchange of business, and for such other purposes as will facilitate and increase the business of the North Carolina State Ports Authority;

(3)   Be authorized and empowered to rent, lease, buy, own, acquire, mortgage, otherwise encumber, and dispose of such property, real or personal, as said Authority may deem proper to carry out the purposes and provisions of this Article, all or any of them;

(4)   Be authorized and empowered to acquire, construct, maintain, equip and operate any wharves, docks, piers, quays, elevators, compresses,

refrigeration storage plants, warehouses and other structures, and any and all facilities needful for the convenient use of the same in the aid of commerce, including the dredging of approaches thereto, and the construction of beltline roads and highways and bridges and causeways thereon, and other bridges and causeways necessary or useful in connection therewith, and shipyards, shipping facilities, and transportation facilities incident thereto and useful or convenient for the use thereof, and to acquire, construct, and maintain, but not operate, such rail facilities as may be necessary or useful in connection with the operation of the State Ports, provided that nothing in this subdivision shall be construed as requiring or allowing the North Carolina State Ports Authority to become a carrier by rail subject to the federal laws regulating those carriers;

(5)   The Authority shall appoint an Executive Director, whose salary shall be fixed by the Authority, to serve at its pleasure. The Executive Director or his designee shall appoint, employ, dismiss and, within the limits of available funding, fix the compensation of such other employees as he deems necessary to carry out the purposes of this Article. There shall be an executive committee consisting of the chairman of the Authority and two other members elected annually by the Authority. The executive committee shall be vested with authority to do all acts which are authorized by the bylaws of the Authority. Members of the executive committee shall serve until their successors are elected;

(6)   Establish an office for the transaction of its business at such place or places as, in the opinion of the Authority, shall be advisable or necessary in carrying out the purposes of this Article;

(7)   Be authorized and empowered to create and operate such agencies and departments as said board may deem necessary or useful for the furtherance of any of the purposes of this Article;

(8)   Be authorized and empowered to pay all necessary costs and expenses involved in and incident to the formation and organization of said Authority, and incident to the administration and operation thereof, and to pay all other costs and expenses reasonably necessary or expedient in carrying out and accomplishing the purposes of this Article;

(9)   Be authorized and empowered to apply for and accept loans and grants of money from any federal agency or the State of North Carolina or any political subdivision thereof or from any public or private sources available for any and all of the purposes authorized in this Article, and to expend the same in

75

accordance with the directions and requirements attached thereto, or imposed thereon by any such federal agency, the State of North Carolina, or any political subdivision thereof, or any public or private lender or donor, and to give such evidences of indebtedness as shall be required, provided, however, that no indebtedness of any kind incurred or created by the Authority shall constitute an indebtedness of the State of North Carolina, or any political subdivision thereof, and no such indebtedness shall involve or be secured by the faith, credit or taxing power of the State of North Carolina, or any political subdivision thereof;

(10)   Be authorized and empowered to act as agent for the United States of America, or any agency, department, corporation, or instrumentality thereof, in any matter coming within the purposes or powers of the Authority;

(11)   Have power to adopt, alter or repeal its own bylaws, rules and regulations governing the manner in which its business may be transacted and in which the power granted to it may be enjoyed, and may provide for the appointment of such committees, and the functions thereof, as the Authority may deem necessary or expedient in facilitating its business. The Authority may establish fees for its services. In establishing these fees, the Authority shall consider the cost of providing service, revenue requirements, the cost of similar services at other seaports in the South Atlantic region, and any other factors it considers relevant. The Authority shall report the establishment or increase of any fee to the Joint Legislative Commission on Governmental Operations no later than 30 business days after it establishes or increases the fee.

(12)   Be authorized and empowered to do any and all other acts and things in this Article authorized or required to be done, whether or not included in the general powers in this section mentioned; and

(13)   Be authorized and empowered to do any and all things necessary to accomplish the purposes of this Article: Provided, that said Authority shall not engage in shipbuilding.

The property of the Authority shall not be subject to any taxes or assessments thereon.

(b)   In order to execute the powers enumerated in subsection (a), the Authority shall determine the policies of the North Carolina State Ports Authority by majority vote of all members of the Authority present and voting. Once a policy is determined, the Authority shall communicate it to the Executive Director, who shall have the sole and exclusive authority to execute the policy of the Authority. No member of the Authority shall have responsibility or authority to give operational directives to any employee of the North Carolina State Ports Authority other than the Executive Director. (1945, c. 1097, s. 3; 1949, c. 892, s. 2; 1953, c. 191, s. 5; 1959, c. 523, ss. 3-5; 1975, c. 716, s. 2; 1977, c. 65, s. 2; c. 198, ss. 7, 9; c. 802, s. 50.45; 1979, c. 159, s. 3; 1981 (Reg. Sess., 1982), c. 1181, s. 2; 1983, c. 717, s. 84; 1985, c. 479, s. 219; 1985 (Reg. Sess., 1986), c. 955, ss. 102, 103; 1987, c. 275, ss. 1, 2; 1989, c. 273, s. 1; 2002-99, s. 7(a); 2002-126, s. 6.6(c); 2006-203, s. 109; 2011-145, s. 14.6(b), (k).)

§ 136-263. Container shipping.

The State Ports Authority shall provide at the ports of Morehead City and Wilmington adequate equipment and facilities including container cranes at each port as needed, in order to maintain existing and future levels of containerized cargo shipping at both ports and provide and encourage growth in handling of containerized cargoes at both ports. (1979, c. 934; 2011-145, s. 14.6(b).)

§ 136-264. Approval of acquisition and disposition of real property.

Any transactions relating to the acquisition or disposition of real property or any estate or interest in real property, by the North Carolina State Ports Authority, shall be subject to prior review by the Governor and Council of State, and shall become effective only after the same has been approved by the Governor and Council of State. Upon the acquisition of real property or other estate therein, by the North Carolina State Ports Authority, the fee title or other estate shall vest in and the instrument of conveyance shall name the "North Carolina State Ports Authority" as grantee, lessee, or transferee. Upon the disposition of real property or any interest or estate therein, the instrument of conveyance or transfer shall be executed by the North Carolina State Ports Authority. The approval of any transaction by the Governor and Council of State may be evidenced by a duly certified copy of excerpt of minutes of the meeting of the Governor and Council of State, attested by the private secretary to the Governor or the Governor, reciting such approval, affixed to the instrument of acquisition or transfer, and said certificate may be recorded as a part thereof, and the same shall be conclusive evidence of review and approval of the subject transaction by the Governor and Council of State. The Governor, acting with the approval of the Council of State, may delegate the review and approval of such classes of lease, rental, easement, or right-of-way transactions as he deems advisable, and he may likewise delegate the review and approval of the severance of buildings and timber from the land. (1959, c. 523, s. 6; 1977, c. 198, s. 9; 2011-145, s. 14.6(b).)

§ 136-265. Issuance of bonds and notes.

(a)   As a means of raising the funds needed from time to time in the acquisition, construction, equipment, maintenance or operation of any facility, building, structure or any other matter or thing which the Authority is authorized to acquire, construct, equip, maintain, or operate, all or any of them, including authorized special user projects, the Authority is hereby authorized, at one time or from time to time, to borrow money and in evidence thereof to issue bonds, notes and other obligations of the Authority as provided in this Article. Bonds, notes and other obligations may also be issued to (i) establish such reserves as the Authority may determine to be desirable including, without limitation, a debt service reserve fund, and (ii) provide for interest during the estimated period of construction and for a reasonable period thereafter and to provide for working capital.

The principal of and the interest on such bonds or notes shall be payable solely from the funds herein provided for such payment. Any such notes may be made payable from the proceeds of bonds or renewal notes or, in the event bond or renewal note proceeds are not available, such notes may be paid from any available revenues, income or assets of the Authority. The bonds or notes of each issue shall be dated and may be made redeemable before maturity at the option of the Authority at such price or prices and under such terms and conditions as may be determined by the Authority. Any such bonds or notes shall bear interest at such rate or rates, including variable rates, as may be determined by the Authority. Such bonds or notes shall mature at such time or times not exceeding 40 years from their date or dates, as may be determined by the Authority.

(b)   Prior to the sale and delivery of any bonds or notes by the Authority, the Governor shall approve the general purposes of and the general security provisions for any such bonds or notes. Such bonds or notes may be sold in such manner, either at public or private sale, and for such price as the Authority shall determine. Bonds or notes may be issued under the provisions of this

Article without obtaining, except as otherwise expressly provided in this Article, the consent of any department, division, commission, board, body, bureau or agency of the State, and without any other proceedings or the happening of any conditions or things other than those proceedings, conditions or things which are specifically required by this Article and the provisions of the resolution authorizing the issuance of such bonds or notes or the trust agreement securing the same.

(c)   In the discretion of the Authority any obligations issued under the provisions of this Article may be secured by a trust agreement by and between the Authority and a corporate trustee, which may be any trust company or bank having the powers of a trust company within or without the State and, in the case of an authorized special user project, a deed of trust of which the trustee may be an individual who is a resident of the State. It shall be lawful for any bank or trust company incorporated under the laws of the State which may act as depository of the proceeds of obligations, revenues or other money under this Article to furnish such indemnifying bonds or to pledge such securities as may be required by the Authority. The pledge of any assets, income or revenues of the Authority to the payment of the principal of or the interest on any obligations of the Authority shall be valid and binding from the time when the pledge is made and any such assets, income or revenues shall immediately be subject to the lien of such pledge without any physical delivery thereof or further act, and the lien of any such pledge shall be valid and binding as against all parties having claims of any kind in tort, contract or otherwise against the Authority, irrespective of whether such parties have notice thereof.

(d)   The resolution authorizing any obligations or the trust agreement securing the same may provide that any moneys held pursuant thereto may be temporarily invested pending the disbursement thereof and shall provide that any officer with whom, or any bank or trust company with which, such moneys shall be deposited shall act as trustee of such moneys and shall hold and apply the same for the purposes hereof, subject to such regulations as this Article and such resolution or trust agreement may provide. Any such moneys or any other moneys of the Authority may be invested as provided in G.S. 159-30 or any successor provision thereof.

(e)   Obligations issued under the provisions of this Article are hereby made securities in which all public officers and public bodies of the State and its political subdivisions, all insurance companies, trust companies, banking associations, investment companies, executors, administrators, trustees and other fiduciaries may properly and legally invest funds, including capital in their

79

control or belonging to them. Such obligations are hereby made securities which may properly and legally be deposited with and received by any State or municipal officer or any agency or political subdivision of the State for any purpose for which the deposit of bonds, notes or obligations of the State is now or may hereafter be authorized by law.

(f)   The Authority is hereby authorized to provide for the issuance of refunding obligations for the purpose of refunding any obligations then outstanding which shall have been issued under the provisions of this Article, including the payment of any redemption premium thereon and any interest accrued or to accrue to the date of redemption of such obligations and, if deemed advisable by the Authority, for any corporate purpose of the Authority. The issuance of such obligations, the maturities and other details thereof, the rights of the holders thereof, and the rights, duties and obligations of the Authority in respect of the same shall be governed by the provisions of this Article which relate to the issuance of obligations, insofar as such provisions may be appropriate therefor.

Refunding obligations may be sold or exchanged for outstanding obligations issued under this Article and, if sold, the proceeds thereof may be applied, in addition to any other authorized purposes, to the purchase, redemption or payment of such outstanding obligations.

(g)   Any obligations issued by the Authority under the provisions of this Article shall at all times be free from taxation by the State or any local unit or political subdivision or other instrumentality of the State, excepting inheritance or gift taxes, income taxes on the gain from the transfer of the obligations, and franchise taxes. The interest on the obligations is not subject to taxation as income.

(h)   Obligations issued under the provisions of this Article shall not be deemed to constitute a debt, liability or obligation of the State or of any other public body in the State secured by a pledge of the faith and credit of the State or of any other public body in the State, respectively, but shall be payable solely from the revenues, income or assets of the Authority pledged thereto. Each obligation issued under this Article shall contain on the face thereof a statement to the effect that the Authority shall not be obligated to pay the same or the interest thereon except from the revenues, income or assets pledged therefor and that neither the faith and credit nor the taxing power of the State or of any other public body in the State is pledged to the payment of the principal of or the interest on such obligation. (1945, c. 1097, s. 4; 1975, c. 716, s. 2; 1977, c.

80

198, s. 9; 1979, c. 159, s. 4; 1981, c. 856, s. 1; 1981 (Reg. Sess., 1982), c. 1181, s. 1; 1985 (Reg. Sess., 1986), c. 955, ss. 104, 105; 1987, c. 275, s. 3; 1995, c. 46, s. 16; 2006-203, s. 110; 2011-145, s. 14.6(b), (k).)

§ 136-266. Bonds and notes for special user projects.

(a) The Authority is also hereby authorized, subject to the provisions of this section, to issue, at one time or from time to time, bonds and notes to finance special user projects. The term "special user project" shall mean any land, equipment or any one or more buildings or other structures, whether or not on the same site or sites, and any rehabilitation, improvement, renovation or enlargement of, or any addition to, any building or structure for use as or in connection with any commercial, industrial, manufacturing, processing, mining, transportation, distribution, storage, marine or environmental facility or improvement primarily for the use of one or more private parties. Any such special user project may include all appurtenances and incidental facilities such as land, headquarters or office facilities, restaurant and lodging facilities, warehouses, distribution centers, pollution control facilities, access roads, sidewalks, utilities, railway sidings, trucking and similar facilities, parking facilities, waterways, docks, wharves and other improvements necessary or convenient for ships, tugboats, barges or other vessels or for the construction, maintenance and operation of any building or structure, or addition thereto.

(b) Bonds and notes may be sold to finance special user projects irrespective of the interest limitations set forth in G.S. 24-1.1, as amended, and successor provisions.

(c) The bonds or notes of each issue of the Authority under this section shall be special, limited obligations of the Authority payable solely from such other revenues, income or assets of the Authority as the Authority shall specifically assign or pledge and such funds, collateral and undertakings as any private parties may assign or pledge therefor.

The financing agreement may provide the Authority with rights and remedies in the event of a default by the obligor thereunder including, without limitation, reentry and repossession or leasing or sale or foreclosure of the special user project to others.

The Authority's interest in a special user project may be that of owner, lessor, operator, lessee, conditional or installment vendor, mortgagor, mortgagee, secured party or otherwise, but the Authority need not have any ownership or possessory interest in the project, and if that of lessor, the lessee may have an option or an obligation to purchase the special user project upon the expiration or termination of the lease.

(d)   Bonds and notes issued under the provisions of this section may be secured by one or more agreements, including forecloseable deeds of trust and other trust instruments, which may pledge and assign to the trustee or the holders of its obligations the assets, revenues, and income provided for the security of the bonds or notes, including proceeds from the sale of any special user project, or part thereof, insurance proceeds and condemnation awards, and third-party agreements, and may convey or mortgage the project and other property and collateral to secure a bond issue.

The Authority may subordinate the bonds or notes or its rights, assets, revenues and income derived from any special user project to any prior, contemporaneous or future securities or obligations or lien, mortgage or other security interest.

(e)   Notwithstanding any other provision of law, the Authority may agree that all contracts relating to the acquisition, construction, installation and equipping of the special user project shall be solicited, negotiated, awarded and executed by the private party or parties for which the Authority is financing the special user project or their agents subject only to such approvals by the Authority as the Authority may require. The Authority may, out of the proceeds of bonds or notes, make advances to or reimburse such private parties or such agents for all or a portion of the costs incurred in connection with such contracts. The provisions of G.S. 136-271 of this Article shall have no application to funds and moneys derived pursuant to this section.

(f)   Repealed by Session Laws 2001-218, s. 5, effective July 1, 2001. (1981, c. 856, s. 2; 2000-169, s. 41; 2001-218, s. 5; 2001-487, s. 33; 2011-145, s. 14.6(b), (k).)

§ 136-267. Power of eminent domain.

For the acquiring of rights-of-way and property necessary for the construction of structures, including railroad crossings, airports, seaplane bases, naval bases, wharves, piers, ships, docks, quays, elevators, compresses, refrigerator storage plants, warehouses and other riparian and littoral terminals and structures and approaches thereto and transportation facilities needful for the convenient use of same, and belt line roads and highways and causeways and bridges and other bridges and causeways, the Authority shall have the right and power to acquire the same by purchase, by negotiation, or by condemnation, and should it elect to exercise the right of eminent domain, condemnation proceedings shall be maintained by and in the name of the Authority, and it may proceed in the manner provided by the general laws of the State of North Carolina for the procedure by any county, municipality or authority organized under the laws of this State, or by the Board of Transportation, or in any other manner provided by law, as the Authority may, in its discretion, elect. The power of eminent domain shall not apply to property of persons, State agency or corporations already devoted to public use. (1945, c. 1097, s. 5; 1973, c. 507, s. 5; 1977, c. 198, s. 9; 1979, c. 159, s. 5; 2011-145, s. 14.6(b).)

§ 136-268. Exchange of property; removal of buildings, etc.

The Authority may exchange any property or properties acquired under the authority of this Chapter for other property, or properties usable in carrying out the powers hereby conferred, and also may remove from lands needed for its purposes and reconstruct on other locations, buildings, terminals, or other structures, upon the payment of just compensation, if in its judgment, it is necessary or expedient so to do in order to carry out any of its plans for port development, under the authorization of this Article. (1945, c. 1097, s. 6; 1977, c. 198, s. 9; 1979, c. 159, s. 6; 2011-145, s. 14.6(b).)

§ 136-269. Jurisdiction of the Authority; application of Chapter 20; appointment and authority of special police.

(a)   The jurisdiction of the Authority in any of said harbors or seaports within the State shall extend to all properties owned by or under control of the Authority and shall also extend over the waters and shores of such harbors or seaports and over that part of all tributary streams flowing into such harbors or seaports in which the tide ebbs and flows, and shall extend to the outer edge of the outer bar at such harbors or seaports.

(b)   All the provisions of Chapter 20 of the General Statutes relating to the use of the highways of the State and the operation of motor vehicles thereon are hereby made applicable to the streets, alleys and driveways on the properties owned by or under the control of the North Carolina State Ports Authority. Any person violating any of the provisions of said Chapter in or on such streets, alleys or driveways shall, upon conviction thereof, be punished as therein prescribed. Nothing herein contained shall be construed as in any way interfering with the ownership and control of such streets, alleys and driveways on the properties of said Authority as is now vested by law in the said Authority.

(c)   The North Carolina State Ports Authority is hereby authorized to make such reasonable rules, regulations, and adopt such additional ordinances with respect to the use of the streets, alleys, driveways and to the establishment of parking areas on the properties of the Authority and relating to the safety and welfare of persons using the property of the Authority. All rules, regulations and ordinances adopted pursuant to the authority of this subsection shall be recorded in the proceedings of the Authority and printed and copy of such rules, regulations and ordinances shall be filed in the office of the Attorney General of North Carolina and the Authority shall cause to be posted, at appropriate places on the properties of the Authority, notice to the public of applicable rules, regulations and ordinances as may be adopted under the authority of this subsection. Any person violating any such rules, regulations or ordinances shall, upon conviction thereof, be guilty of a Class 3 misdemeanor.

(d)   The Executive Director of the Authority is authorized to appoint such number of employees of the Authority as he may think proper as special policemen, who, when so appointed, shall have all the powers of policemen of incorporated towns. Such policemen shall have the power of arrest of persons committing violations of State law or any reasonable rules, regulations and ordinances lawfully adopted by the Authority as herein authorized. Employees appointed as such special policemen shall take the general oath of office prescribed by G.S. 11-11. (1945, c. 1097, s. 9; 1959, c. 523, s. 7; 1965, c. 1074; 1975, 2nd Sess., c. 983, s. 83; 1977, c. 198, ss. 8, 9; 1987, c. 275, s. 5; 1993, c. 539, s. 1041; 1994, Ex. Sess., c. 24, s. 14(c); 2011-145, s. 14.6(b).)

§ 136-270. Treasurer of the Authority.

The Authority shall select its own treasurer. The Authority shall require a surety bond of such appointee in such amount as the Authority may fix, and the premium or premiums thereon shall be paid by said Authority as a necessary expense of said Authority. (1945, c. 1097, s. 10; 1959, c. 523, s. 8; 1977, c. 198, s. 9; 2011-145, s. 14.6(b).)

§ 136-271. Deposit and disbursement of funds.

All Authority funds shall be deposited in a bank or banks to be designated by the Authority. Funds of the Authority shall be paid out only upon warrants signed by the treasurer or assistant treasurer of the Authority and countersigned by the chairman, the acting chairman or the executive director. No warrants shall be drawn or issued disbursing any of the funds of the Authority except for a purpose authorized by this Article and only when the account or expenditure for which the same is to be given in payment has been audited and approved by the Authority or its executive director. (1945, c. 1097, s. 11; 1951, c. 1088, s. 1; 1977, c. 198, s. 9; 1981, c. 856, s. 3; 2011-145, s. 14.6(b).)

§ 136-272. Audit.

The operations of the State Ports Authority shall be subject to the oversight of the State Auditor pursuant to Article 5A of Chapter 147 of the General Statutes. The State Ports Authority shall reimburse the State Auditor the cost of any audit. (1945, c. 1097, s. 12; 1951, c. 1088, s. 2; 1957, c. 269, s. 1; 1977, c. 198, s. 9; 1983, c. 913, s. 43; 2010-31, s. 21.2; 2011-145, s. 14.6(b).)

§ 136-273. Purchase of supplies, material and equipment and building contracts.

(a)   All of the provisions of Article 3 of Chapter 143 of the General Statutes relating to the purchase of supplies, material and equipment by the State government are hereby made applicable to the North Carolina State Ports Authority.

(b)   All of the provisions of Chapter 143 of the General Statutes relating to public building contracts are hereby made applicable to the North Carolina State Ports Authority for those construction projects which may be funded, in whole or in part, by appropriations from the General Assembly.

(c)   Notwithstanding subsections (a) and (b) of this section, if the North Carolina State Ports Authority finds that the delivery of a particular port facility must be expedited for good cause, the Authority shall be exempt from the following statutes, and rules implementing those statutes, to the extent necessary to expedite delivery: G.S. 133-1.1(g), G.S. 143-128(a) through (e), G.S. 143-132, and G.S. 143-135.26. Prior to exercising an exemption authorized under this subsection, the North Carolina State Ports Authority, through its Executive Director, shall give notice in writing of the Authority's intent to exercise the exemption to the Secretary of Administration. The notice shall contain, at a minimum, the following information: (i) the specific statutory requirement or requirements from which the Authority intends to exercise an exemption; (ii) the reason the exemption is necessary to expedite delivery of a port facility; and (iii) the way the Authority anticipates the exemption will expedite the delivery of a port facility. The Authority shall report quarterly to the Joint Legislative Commission on Governmental Operations on any building contracts exceeding two hundred fifty thousand dollars ($250,000) to which an exemption authorized by this subsection is applied. (1953, c. 191, s. 6; 1977, c. 198, s. 9; 1987, c. 275, s. 6; 1997-331, s. 1; 1999-368, s. 2; 2011-145, s. 14.6(b).)

§ 136-274. Liberal construction of Article.

It is intended that the provisions of this Article shall be liberally construed to accomplish the purposes provided for, or intended to be provided for, herein, and where strict construction would result in the defeat of the accomplishment of any of the acts authorized herein, and a liberal construction would permit or assist in the accomplishment thereof, the liberal construction shall be chosen. (1945, c. 1097, s. 13; 1977, c. 198, s. 9; 2011-145, s. 14.6(b).)

§ 136-275. Warehouses, wharves, etc., on property abutting navigable waters.

The powers, authority and jurisdiction granted to the North Carolina State Ports Authority under this Article and Chapter shall not be construed so as to prevent other persons, firms and corporations, including municipalities, from owning, constructing, leasing, managing and operating warehouses, structures and other improvements on property owned, leased or under the control of such other persons, firms and corporations abutting upon and adjacent to navigable waters and streams in this State, nor to prevent such other persons, firms and corporations from constructing, owning, leasing and operating in connection therewith wharves, docks and piers, nor to prevent such other persons, firms and corporations from encumbering, leasing, selling, conveying or otherwise dealing with and disposing of such properties, facilities, lands and improvements after such construction. (1955, c. 727; 1977, c. 198, s. 9; 2011-145, s. 14.6(b).)

Chapter 137.

Rural Rehabilitation.

Article 1.

State Rural Rehabilitation Law.

§§ 137-1 through 137-30: Repealed by Session Laws 1955, c. 190.

Article 2.

North Carolina Rural Rehabilitation Corporation.

§§ 137-31 through 137-43: Repealed by Session Laws 2001-424, s. 17.2(b).

Chapter 138.

Salaries, Fees and Allowances.

§ 138-1. Annual salaries payable at periodic intervals.

All annual salaries shall be paid at least monthly and may be paid twice a month, every two weeks, or weekly. A unit of State government whose payroll is processed through the central payroll disbursing account of the Office of the

State Controller must obtain the approval of the State Controller to pay annual salaries on any basis other than a monthly basis. (Code, s. 3731; 1893, c. 54; Rev., s. 2772; C.S., s. 3847; 1925, c. 230; 1928, c. 100; 1973, c. 1430; 1991, c. 542, s. 3.)

§ 138-2. Payment of fees; when to be paid in advance.

All public officers shall receive the fees prescribed for them respectively, from the persons for whom, or at whose instance, the service shall be performed, except persons suing as paupers, and no officer shall be compelled to perform any service, unless his fee be paid or tendered, except in criminal actions. The said officers shall receive no extra allowance or other compensation whatever, unless the same shall be expressly authorized by statute. In case the service shall be ordered by any proper officer of the State, or of a county, for the benefit of the State or county, the fees need not be paid in advance; but if for the State, shall be paid by the State, as other claims against it are; if for a county, by the board of commissioners, out of the county funds. The fees in criminal cases are not demandable in advance. (Code, ss. 1173, 3758; Rev., s. 2804; C.S., s. 3849.)

§ 138-3. Compensation limited to that fixed by law.

No officer or employee of the State shall receive any compensation other than the salaries fixed by law, except as provided by way of fees or by special appropriation or from any departmental funds. (1907, c. 830, s. 1; c. 994, s. 1; C.S., s. 3850; 1925, c. 128, s. 1.)

§ 138-4. Governor to set salaries of administrative officers; exceptions; longevity pay.

The salaries of all State administrative officers not subject to the North Carolina Human Resources Act shall be set by the Governor, unless a law provides otherwise.

Whenever by law it is provided that a salary shall be fixed or set by the General Assembly in the Current Operations Appropriations Act, and that office or position is filled by appointment of the Governor, or the appointment is subject to the approval of the Governor, or is made by a commission a majority of whose members are appointed by the Governor, then the Governor may, increase or decrease the salary of a new appointee by a maximum of ten percent (10%) over or under the salary of that position as provided in the Current Operations Appropriations Act, such increased or decreased salary to remain in effect until changed by the General Assembly or until the end of the fiscal year, whichever occurs first. The Governor under this paragraph may not increase the salary of any nonelected official above the level set in the Current Operations Appropriations Act for any member of the Council of State. This section does not apply to any office filled by election by the people, and does not apply to any office in the legislative or judicial branches.

Officials whose salaries are covered by the provisions of this section shall be eligible for longevity pay on the same basis as is provided to employees of the State who are subject to the State Personnel Act. (1947, c. 898; 1957, c. 541, s. 1; 1983, c. 717, s. 49; 1983 (Reg. Sess., 1984), c. 1034, ss. 164, 216; 1985 (Reg. Sess., 1986), c. 955, ss. 51-53; 1987, c. 738, s. 32(a); 1991, c. 542, s. 4; 2006-203, s. 79; 2013-382, s. 9.1(c).)

§ 138-5. Per diem and allowances of State boards, etc.

(a)   Except as provided in subsections (c) and (f) of this section, members of State boards, commissions, committees and councils which operate from funds deposited with the State Treasurer shall be compensated for their services at the following rates:

(1)   Except as otherwise provided by this subdivision, compensation at the rate of fifteen dollars ($15.00) per diem for each day of service. Members of the North Carolina Vocational Rehabilitation Council, the Statewide Independent Living Council, and the Commission for the Blind who are unemployed or who shall forfeit wages from other employment to attend Council or Commission meetings or to perform related duties, may receive compensation not to exceed fifty dollars ($50.00) per diem for attending these meetings or performing related duties, as authorized by sections 105 and 705 of the Rehabilitation Act of 1973, P.L. 102-569, 42 U.S.C. § 701, et seq., as amended.

(2)   Reimbursement of subsistence expenses at the rates allowed to State officers and employees by subdivision (3) of G.S. 138-6(a).

(3)   Reimbursement of travel expenses at the rates allowed to State officers and employees by subdivisions (1) and (2) of G.S. 138-6(a).

(4)   For convention registration fees, the actual amount expended, as shown by receipt.

(b)   Except as provided in subsections (c) and (f) of this section, the schedules of per diem, subsistence, and travel allowances established in this section shall apply to members of all State boards, commissions, committees and councils which operate from funds deposited with the State Treasurer, excluding those boards, commissions, committees and councils the members of which are now serving without compensation and excluding occupational licensing boards as defined in G.S. 93B-1; and all special statutory provisions relating to per diem, subsistence, and travel allowances are hereby amended to conform to this section.

(c)   Repealed by Session Laws 1979, 2nd Session, c. 1137, s. 29.

(d)   The subsistence reimbursement for actual lodging expenses provided in this section must be documented by a receipt of lodging expenses from a commercial establishment.

(e)   Out-of-state travel on official business by members of State boards, commissions, committees and councils which operate from funds deposited with the State Treasurer shall be reimbursed only upon authorization obtained in the manner prescribed by the Director of the Budget.

(f)   Members of all State boards, commissions and councils whose salaries or any portion of whose salaries are paid from State funds shall receive no per diem compensation from State funds for their services; provided, however, that members of State boards, commissions and councils who are also members of the General Assembly shall receive, when the General Assembly is not in session, subsistence and travel allowances at the rate set forth in G.S. 120-3.1(a)(2) through (a)(4). (1961, c. 833, s. 5; 1963, c. 1049, s. 1; 1965, c. 169; 1971, c. 1139; 1973, c. 1397; 1979, c. 838, s. 18; 1979, 2nd Sess., c. 1137, s. 29; 1983, c. 761, s. 24; c. 923, s. 217; 1983 (Reg. Sess., 1984), c. 1034, s. 185; 1985, c. 757, s. 201(b); 1985 (Reg. Sess., 1986), c. 1014, s. 39(a); 1987, c. 738, s. 58(a), (b); 1999-237, s. 11.49.)

§ 138-6. Travel allowances of State officers and employees.

(a)   Travel on official business by the officers and employees of State departments, institutions and agencies which operate from funds deposited with the State Treasurer shall be reimbursed at the following rates:

(1)   For transportation by privately owned automobile, the business standard mileage rate set by the Internal Revenue Service per mile of travel and the actual cost of tolls paid. Any other law which sets a mileage rate by referring to the rate set herein, instead establishes a rate of twenty-five cents (25¢) per mile. No reimbursement shall be made for the use of a personal car in commuting from an employee's home to his duty station in connection with regularly scheduled work hours.

(2)   For bus, railroad, Pullman, or other conveyance, actual fare.

(3)   For expenses incurred for subsistence, payment of eighty-one dollars ($81.00) per day when traveling in-state or ninety-three dollars ($93.00) per day when traveling out-of-state. Payment of sales tax, lodging tax, local tax, or service fees applied to the cost of lodging are to be paid in addition to the daily subsistence amount. The employee may exceed the part of the ceiling allocated for lodging without approval for overexpenditure provided that the total lodging and food reimbursement does not exceed the maximum provided by this subdivision. When travel involves less than a full day (24-hour period), a reasonable prorated amount shall be paid in accordance with regulations and criteria which shall be promulgated and published by the Director of the Budget. Reimbursement to State employees for lunches eaten while on official business may be made only in the following circumstances:

a.   When an overnight stay is required reimbursement is allowed while an employee is in travel status;

b.   When the cost of the lunch is included as part of a registration fee for a formal congress, conference, assembly, or convocation, by whatever name called. Such assembly must involve the active participation of persons other than the employees of a single State department, institution, or agency and must be necessary for conducting official State business; or

c.   When the State employee is a member of, or providing staff assistance to, a State board, commission, committee, or council which operates from funds deposited with the State Treasurer, and the lunch is preplanned as part of the meeting for the entire board, commission, committee, or council.

(4)   For convention registration fees not to exceed the actual amount expended as shown by a valid receipt or invoice.

(5)   Effective July 1, 2001, and effective July 1 of each odd-numbered year thereafter, the Director of the Budget shall revise the amounts of payment of subsistence per day when traveling in-State and out-of-state by an amount equal to the percentage increase in the Consumer Price Index for All Urban Consumers for the most recent 24-month period.

(b)   Out-of-state travel on official business by the officers and employees of State departments, institutions, and agencies which operate from funds deposited with the State Treasurer shall be reimbursed only upon authorization obtained in the manner prescribed by the Director of the Budget.

(c)   Reimbursement of actual costs of overnight lodging, whether in-state or out-of-state, must be documented by a receipt of actual lodging expenses from a commercial establishment. This documentation shall be attached to the reimbursement request. All reimbursement requests shall be filed for approval and payment within 30 days after the travel period for which the reimbursement is being requested. (1961, c. 833, s. 6; 1963, c. 1049, s. 2; 1965, c. 1089; 1969, c. 1153; 1971, c. 881, ss. 1, 2; 1973, c. 595, s. 1; c. 1456; 1975, c. 892, s. 1; 1977, c. 928; 1977, 2nd Sess., c. 1136, s. 38.1; c. 1237, ss. 1, 2; 1979, c. 34, s. 1; c. 1002, s. 1; c. 1050, s. 1; 1979, 2nd Sess., c. 1137, s. 26; 1981, c. 859, ss. 57-59; 1983, c. 761, s. 22; c. 913, s. 27; c. 923, s. 217; 1985, c. 757, s. 201(a); 1985 (Reg. Sess., 1986), c. 1014, s. 39(b); 1987, c. 738, ss. 58(c), 58(d), 60; 1987 (Reg. Sess., 1988), c. 1086, s. 30(a); c. 1100, s. 38(a); 1993, c. 321, s. 24(a); 1993 (Reg. Sess., 1994), c. 769, s. 7.27A; 1998-212, s. 28.20(a); 1999-237, s. 28.20; 2000-140, s. 93.1(a); 2001-424, s. 12.2(b); 2007-322, s. 8.)

§ 138-7. Exceptions to §§ 138-5 and 138-6.

Expenditures in excess of the maximum amounts set forth in G.S. 138-5 and 138-6 for travel and subsistence may be reimbursed if the prior approval of the department head is obtained. The Director of the Budget shall establish and publish uniform standards and criteria under which actual expenses in excess of the travel and subsistence allowances and convention registration fees as

92

prescribed in G.S. 138-5 and 138-6 may be authorized by department heads for extraordinary charges for hotel, meals, and registration, whenever such charges are the result of required official business. (1961, c. 833, s. 6.1; 1965, c. 1089; 1969, c. 1153; 1971, c. 881, s. 3; 1973, c. 595, s. 2; 1979, c. 838, s. 17.)

§ 138-8. Moving expenses of State employees.

Subject to the rules and regulations promulgated by the Office of State Budget and Management and approved by the Director of the Budget, any department, institution or agency of the State is hereby authorized to pay, from funds available to it, reasonable expenses for transporting the household goods of an employee and members of his household when the transfer of the employee is considered by the Director of the Budget to be in the best interests of the State. (1977, c. 802, s. 15; 1979, 2nd Sess., c. 1137, s. 27; 2000-140, s. 93.1(a); 2001-424, s. 12.2(b).)

Chapter 138A.

State Government Ethics Act.

Article 1.

General Provisions.

§ 138A-1. Title.

This Chapter shall be known and may be cited as the "State Government Ethics Act". (2006-201, s. 1.)

§ 138A-2. Purpose.

The purpose of this Chapter is to ensure that elected and appointed State agency officials exercise their authority honestly and fairly, free from impropriety, threats, favoritism, and undue influence. To this end, it is the intent of the General Assembly in this Chapter to ensure that standards of ethical conduct and standards regarding conflicts of interest are clearly established for elected and appointed State agency officials, that the State continually educates these officials on matters of ethical conduct and conflicts of interest, that potential and actual conflicts of interests are identified and resolved, and that violations of standards of ethical conduct and conflicts of interest are investigated and properly addressed. (2006-201, s. 1.)

§ 138A-3. Definitions.

The following definitions apply in this Chapter:

(1) Blind trust. - A trust established by or for the benefit of a covered person or a member of the covered person's immediate family for divestiture of all control and knowledge of assets. A trust qualifies as a blind trust under this subdivision if the covered person or a member of the covered person's immediate family has no knowledge of the holdings and sources of income of the trust, the trustee of the trust is independent of and not associated with or employed by the covered person or a member of the covered person's immediate family and is not a member of the covered person's extended family, and the trustee has sole discretion as to the management of the trust assets.

(1c) Board. - Any State board, commission, council, committee, task force, authority, or similar public body, however denominated, created by statute or executive order, as determined and designated by the Commission, except for those public bodies that have only advisory authority.

(2) Business. - Any of the following organized for profit:

a. Association.

b. Business trust.

c. Corporation.

d. Enterprise.

e. Joint venture.

f. Organization.

94

g.   Partnership.

h.   Proprietorship.

i.   Vested trust.

j.   Every other business interest, including ownership or use of land for income.

(3)   Business with which associated. - A business in which the covered person or filing person or any member of that covered person's or filing person's immediate family does any of the following:

a.   Is an employee.

b.   Holds a position as a director, officer, partner, proprietor, or member or manager of a limited liability company, irrespective of the amount of compensation received or the amount of the interest owned.

c.   Owns a legal, equitable, or beneficial interest of ten thousand dollars ($10,000) or more in the business or five percent (5%) of the business, whichever is less, other than as a trustee on a deed of trust.

d.   Is a lobbyist registered under Chapter 120C of the General Statutes.

For purposes of this subdivision, the term "business" shall not include a widely held investment fund, including a mutual fund, regulated investment company, or pension or deferred compensation plan, if all of the following apply:

1.   The covered person, filing person, or a member of the covered person's or filing person's immediate family neither exercises nor has the ability to exercise control over the financial interests held by the fund.

2.   The fund is publicly traded, or the fund's assets are widely diversified.

(4)   Commission. - The State Ethics Commission.

(5)   Committee. - The Legislative Ethics Committee as created in Part 3 of Article 14 of Chapter 120 of the General Statutes.

(6)   Compensation. - Any money, thing of value, or economic benefit conferred on or received by any covered person or filing person in return for services rendered or to be rendered by that covered person or filing person or another. This term does not include campaign contributions properly received and, reported as required by Article 22A of Chapter 163 of the General Statutes.

(7)   Confidential information. - Information defined as confidential by the law.

(8)   Constitutional officers of the State. - Officers whose offices are established by Article III of the North Carolina Constitution.

(9)   Contract. - Any agreement, including sales and conveyances of real and personal property, and agreements for the performance of services.

(10)   Covered person. - A legislator, public servant, or judicial officer, as identified by the Commission under G.S. 138A-11.

(11)   Repealed by Session Laws 2008-213, s. 84(c), effective August 15, 2008.

(12)   Employing entity. - For public servants, any of the following bodies of State government of which the public servant is an employee or a member, or over which the public servant exercises supervision: agencies, authorities, boards, commissions, committees, councils, departments, offices, institutions and their subdivisions, and constitutional offices of the State. For legislators, it is the house of which the legislator is a member. For legislative employees, it is the authority that hired the individual. For judicial employees, it is the Chief Justice.

(13)   Extended family. - Spouse, lineal descendant, lineal ascendant, sibling, spouse's lineal descendant, spouse's lineal ascendant, spouse's sibling, and the spouse of any of these individuals.

(14)   Filing person. - An individual required to file a statement of economic interest under G.S. 138A-22.

(14a),   (14b) Reserved for future codification purposes.

(14c)   Financial benefit. - A direct pecuniary gain or loss to the legislator, the public servant, or a person with which the legislator or public servant is associated, or a direct pecuniary loss to a business competitor of the legislator, the public servant, or a person with which the legislator or public servant is associated.

(15)   Gift. - Anything of monetary value given or received without valuable consideration by or from a lobbyist, lobbyist principal, liaison personnel, or a person described under G.S. 138A-32(d)(1), (2), or (3). The following shall not be considered gifts under this subdivision:

a.   Anything for which fair market value, or face value if shown, is paid by the covered person or legislative employee.

b.   Commercially available loans made on terms not more favorable than generally available to the general public in the normal course of business if not made for lobbying.

c.   Contractual arrangements or commercial relationships or arrangements made in the normal course of business if not made for lobbying.

d.   Academic or athletic scholarships based on the same criteria as applied to the public.

e.   Anything of value properly reported as required under Article 22A of Chapter 163 of the General Statutes.

f.   Expressions of condolence related to a death of an individual, sent within a reasonable time of the death, if the expression is one of the following:

1.   A sympathy card, letter, or note.

2.   Flowers.

3.   Food or beverages for immediate consumption.

4.   Donations to a religious organization, charity, the State or a political subdivision of the State, not to exceed a total of two hundred dollars ($200.00) per death per donor.

(15a)   through (15c) Reserved for future codification purposes.

(15d)   Governmental unit. - A political subdivision of the State, and any other entity or organization created by a political subdivision of the State.

(16)   Honorarium. - Payment for services for which fees are not legally or traditionally required.

(17)   Immediate family. - An unemancipated child of the covered person residing in the household and the covered person's spouse, if not legally separated. A member of a covered person's extended family shall also be considered a member of the immediate family if actually residing in the covered person's household.

(18)   Judicial employee. - The director and assistant director of the Administrative Office of the Courts and any other individual, designated by the Chief Justice, employed in the Judicial Department whose annual compensation from the State is sixty thousand dollars ($60,000) or more.

(19)   Judicial officer. - Justice or judge of the General Court of Justice, district attorney, clerk of court, or any individual elected or appointed to any of these positions prior to taking office.

(20)   Legislative action. - As the term is defined in G.S. 120C-100.

(21)   Legislative employee. - As the term is defined in G.S. 120C-100.

(22)   Legislator. - A member or presiding officer of the General Assembly, or an individual elected or appointed a member or presiding officer of the General Assembly before taking office.

(23)   Lobbying. - As the term is defined in G.S. 120C-100.

(24)   Nonprofit corporation or organization with which associated. - Any not for profit corporation, organization, or association, incorporated or otherwise, that is organized or operating in the State primarily for religious, charitable, scientific, literary, public health and safety, or educational purposes and of which the covered person, filing person, or any member of the covered person's or filing person's immediate family is a director, officer, governing board member, employee, lobbyist registered under Chapter 120C of the General Statutes, or independent contractor. Nonprofit corporation or organization with which associated shall not include any board, entity, or other organization created by this State or by any political subdivision of this State.

(25)   Official action. - Any decision, including administration, approval, disapproval, preparation, recommendation, the rendering of advice, and

98

investigation, made or contemplated in any proceeding, application, submission, request for a ruling or other determination, contract, claim, controversy, investigation, charge, or rule making.

(26)   Participate. - To take part in, influence, or attempt to influence, including acting through an agent or proxy.

(26c)   Permanent designee. - An individual designated by a public servant to serve and vote in the absence of the public servant on a regular basis on a board on which the public servant serves.

(27)   Person. - Any individual, firm, partnership, committee, association, corporation, business, or any other organization or group of persons acting together. The term "person" does not include the State, a political subdivision of the State, a board, or any other entity or organization created by the State or a political subdivision of the State.

(27a), (27b) Reserved for future codification purposes.

(27c)   Person with which the legislator is associated. - Any of the following:

a.   A member of the legislator's extended family.

b.   A client of the legislator.

c.   A business with which the legislator or a member of the legislator's immediate family is associated.

d.   A nonprofit corporation or association with which the legislator or a member of the legislator's immediate family is associated.

e.   The State, a political subdivision of the State, a board, or any other entity or organization created by the State or a political subdivision of the State that employs the legislator or a member of the legislator's immediate family.

(27d)   Person with which the public servant is associated. - Any of the following:

a.   A member of the public servant's extended family.

b.   A client of the public servant.

c.   A business with which the public servant or a member of the public servant's immediate family is associated.

d.   A nonprofit corporation or association with which the public servant or a member of the public servant's immediate family is associated.

e.   The State, a political subdivision of the State, a board, or any other entity or organization created by the State or a political subdivision of the State that employs the public servant or a member of the public servant's immediate family.

(28)   Political party. - Either of the two largest political parties in the State based on statewide voter registration at the applicable time.

(29)   Repealed by Session Laws 2008-213, s. 49, effective August 15, 2008.

(30)   Public servants. - All of the following:

a.   Constitutional officers of the State and individuals elected or appointed as constitutional officers of the State prior to taking office.

b.   Employees of the Office of the Governor.

c.   Heads of all principal State departments, as set forth in G.S. 143B-6, who are appointed by the Governor.

d.   The chief deputy and chief administrative assistant of each individual designated under sub-subdivision a. or c. of this subdivision.

e.   Confidential assistants and secretaries as defined in G.S. 126-5(c)(2), to individuals designated under sub-subdivision a., c., or d. of this subdivision.

f.   Employees in exempt positions designated in accordance with G.S. 126-5(d)(1), (2), or (2a) and confidential secretaries to these individuals.

g.   Any other employees or appointees in the principal State departments as may be designated by the Governor to the extent that the designation does not conflict with the State Personnel Act.

h.   Judicial employees.

i.   All voting members of boards, including ex officio members, permanent designees of any voting member, and members serving by executive, legislative, or judicial branch appointment.

j.   For The University of North Carolina, the voting members of the Board of Governors of The University of North Carolina, the president, the vice-presidents, and the chancellors, the vice-chancellors, and voting members of the boards of trustees of the constituent institutions.

k.   For the Community College System, the voting members of the State Board of Community Colleges, the President and the chief financial officer of the Community College System, the president, chief financial officer, and chief administrative officer of each community college, and voting members of the boards of trustees of each community college.

l.   Members of the Commission, the executive director, and the assistant executive director of the Commission.

m.   Individuals under contract with the State working in or against a position included under this subdivision.

n.   The director of the Office of State Human Resources.

o.   The State Controller.

p.   The chief information officer, deputy chief information officers, chief financial officers, and general counsel of the Office of Information Technology Services.

q.   The director of the State Museum of Art.

r.   The executive director of the Agency for Public Telecommunications.

s.   The Commissioner of Motor Vehicles.

t.   The Commissioner of Banks and the chief deputy commissioners of the Banking Commission.

u.   The executive director of the North Carolina Housing Finance Agency.

101

v.   The executive director, chief financial officer, and chief operating officer of the North Carolina Turnpike Authority.

(30a)   through (30j) Reserved for future codification purposes.

(30k)   State agency. - An agency in the executive branch of the government of this State, including the Governor's Office, a board, a department, a division, and any other unit of government in the executive branch.

(31)   Vested trust. - A trust, annuity, or other funds held by a trustee or other third party for the benefit of the covered person or a member of the covered person's immediate family, except a blind trust. A vested trust shall not include a widely held investment fund, including a mutual fund, regulated investment company, or pension or deferred compensation plan, if:

a.   The covered person or a member of the covered person's immediate family neither exercises nor has the ability to exercise control over the financial interests held by the fund; and

b.   The fund is publicly traded, or the fund's assets are widely diversified. (2006-201, s. 1; 2007-347, ss. 7, 8; 2007-348, ss. 19-26; 2008-187, s. 44; 2008-213, ss. 40-54, 84(c); 2010-169, ss. 10, 17(n), (o); 2010-170, s. 14; 2013-382, s. 9.1(c).)

§ 138A-4. Application to Lieutenant Governor.

For purposes of this Chapter, the Lieutenant Governor shall be considered a legislator when carrying out the Lieutenant Governor's duties under Sec. 13 of Article II of the Constitution, and a public servant for all other purposes. (2006-201, s. 1.)

§ 138A-5. Reserved for future codification purposes.

Article 2.

State Ethics Commission.

§ 138A-6. State Ethics Commission established.

There is established the State Ethics Commission. (2006-201, s. 1.)

§ 138A-7. Membership.

(a)   The Commission shall consist of eight members. Four members shall be appointed by the Governor, of whom no more than two shall be of the same political party. Four members shall be appointed by the General Assembly, two upon the recommendation of the Speaker of the House of Representatives, neither of whom shall be of the same political party, and two upon the recommendation of the President Pro Tempore of the Senate, neither of whom shall be of the same political party. Members shall serve for four-year terms, beginning January 1, 2007, except for the initial terms that shall be as follows:

(1)   Two members appointed by the Governor shall serve an initial term of one year.

(2)   Two members appointed by the General Assembly, one upon the recommendation of the Speaker of the House of Representatives and one upon the recommendation of the President Pro Tempore of the Senate, shall serve initial terms of two years.

(3)   Two members appointed by the Governor shall serve initial terms of three years.

(4)   Two members appointed by the General Assembly, one upon the recommendation of the Speaker of the House of Representatives and one member upon the recommendation of the President Pro Tempore of the Senate, shall serve initial terms of four years.

(b)   Members shall be removed from the Commission only for misfeasance, malfeasance, or nonfeasance. Members appointed by the Governor may be removed by the Governor. Members appointed by the General Assembly upon the recommendation of the Speaker of the House of Representatives shall be removed by the Governor upon the recommendation of the Speaker. Members appointed by the General Assembly upon the recommendation of the President Pro Tempore of the Senate shall be removed by the Governor upon the recommendation of the President Pro Tempore.

(c)   Vacancies in appointments made by the Governor shall be filled by the Governor for the remainder of any unfulfilled term. Vacancies in appointments made by the General Assembly shall be filled in accordance with G.S. 120-122 for the remainder of any unfulfilled term.

(d)   No member while serving on the Commission or employee while employed by the Commission shall:

(1)   Hold or be a candidate for any other office or place of trust or profit under the United States, the State, or a political subdivision of the State.

(2)   Hold office in any political party above the precinct level.

(3)   Participate in or contribute to the political campaign of any covered person or any candidate for a public office as a covered person over which the Commission would have jurisdiction or authority.

(4)   Otherwise be an employee of the State, a community college, or a local school system, or serve as a member of any other State board.

(e)   The Governor shall annually appoint a member of the Commission to serve as chair of the Commission. The Commission shall elect a vice-chair annually from its membership. The vice-chair shall act as the chair in the chair's absence or if there is a vacancy in that position.

(f)   Members of the Commission shall receive no compensation for service on the Commission but shall be reimbursed for subsistence, travel, and convention registration fees as provided under G.S. 138-5 or 138-7, as applicable. (2006-201, s. 1.)

§ 138A-8. Meetings and quorum.

The Commission shall meet at least quarterly and at other times as called by its chair or by four of its members. In the case of a vacancy in the chair, meetings

104

may be called by the vice-chair. Five members of the Commission constitute a quorum. (2006-201, s. 1.)

§ 138A-9. Staff and offices.

The Commission may employ professional and clerical staff, including an executive director. The Commission shall be located within the Department of Administration for administrative purposes only, but shall exercise all of its powers, including the power to employ, direct, and supervise all personnel, independently of the Secretary of Administration, and is subject to the direction and supervision of the Secretary of Administration only with respect to the management functions of coordinating and reporting. (2006-201, s. 1.)

§ 138A-10. Powers and duties.

(a)   In addition to other powers and duties specified in this Chapter, the Commission shall:

(1)   Provide reasonable assistance to covered persons in complying with this Chapter.

(2)   Develop readily understandable forms, policies, and procedures to accomplish the purposes of the Chapter.

(3)   Identify and publish the following:

a.   A list of nonadvisory boards.

b.   The names of individuals subject to this Chapter as covered persons and legislative employees under G.S. 138A-11.

(4)   Receive and review all statements of economic interest filed with the Commission by prospective and actual covered persons as provided in G.S. 138A-28. Pursuant to G.S. 138A-24(e), this subdivision does not apply to statements of economic interest of legislators and judicial officers.

(5)   Conduct inquiries of alleged violations against judicial officers, legislators, and legislative employees in accordance with G.S. 138A-12.

(6)   Conduct inquiries into alleged violations against public servants in accordance with G.S. 138A-12.

(7)   Render advisory opinions in accordance with G.S. 138A-13 and G.S. 120C-102.

(8)   Initiate and maintain oversight of ethics educational programs for public servants and their staffs, and legislators and legislative employees, consistent with G.S. 138A-14.

(9)   Conduct a continuing study of governmental ethics in the State and propose changes to the General Assembly in the government process and the law as are conducive to promoting and continuing high ethical behavior by governmental officers and employees.

(10)   Adopt procedures and guidelines to implement this Chapter.

(11)   Report annually to the General Assembly and the Governor on the Commission's activities and generally on the subject of public disclosure, ethics, and conflicts of interest, including recommendations for administrative and legislative action, as the Commission deems appropriate.

(12)   Publish annually statistics on complaints filed with or considered by the Commission, including the number of complaints filed, the number of complaints referred under G.S. 138A-12(b), the number of complaints dismissed under G.S. 138A-12(c)(4), the number of complaints dismissed under G.S. 138A-12(f), the number of complaints referred for criminal prosecution under G.S. 138A-12, the number of complaints dismissed under G.S. 138A-12(h), the number of complaints referred for appropriate action under G.S. 138A-12(h) or G.S. 138A-12(k)(3), and the number and age of complaints pending action by the Commission.

(13)   Perform other duties as may be necessary to accomplish the purposes of this Chapter.

(b)   The Commission may authorize the Executive Director and other staff of the Commission to evaluate statements of economic interest on behalf of the Commission as authorized under subdivision (a)(4) of this section.

(c)   Except as otherwise provided in this Chapter, the Commission shall be the sole State agency with authority to determine compliance with or violations of this Chapter and to issue interpretations and advisory opinions under this Chapter. Decisions and advisory opinions by the Commission under this Chapter shall be binding on all other State agencies. (2006-201, s. 1; 2008-213, s. 55; 2008-215, s. 7; 2009-549, s. 8; 2013-360, s. 30.4(a).)

§ 138A-11. Identify and publish names of covered persons and legislative employees.

The Commission shall identify and publish at least quarterly a listing of the names and positions of all individuals subject to this Chapter as covered persons or legislative employees. The Commission shall also identify and publish at least annually a listing of all boards to which this Chapter applies. This listing may be published electronically on a public Internet Web site maintained by the Commission. (2006-201, s. 1; 2008-213, s. 56.)

§ 138A-12. Inquiries by the Commission.

(a)   Jurisdiction. - The Commission may receive complaints alleging unethical conduct by covered persons and legislative employees and shall conduct inquiries of complaints alleging unethical conduct by covered persons and legislative employees, as set forth in this section.

(a1)   Notice of Allegation. - Upon receipt by the Commission of a written allegation of unethical conduct by a covered person or legislative employee, or the initiation by the Commission of an inquiry into unethical conduct under subsection (b) of this section, the Commission shall immediately notify the covered person or legislative employee subject to the allegation or inquiry in writing.

(b)   Institution of Proceedings. - On its own motion, in response to a signed and sworn complaint of any individual filed with the Commission, or upon the written request of any public servant or those responsible for the hiring, appointing, or supervising of a public servant, the Commission shall conduct an inquiry into any of the following:

(1)   The application or alleged violation of this Chapter.

(2)   For legislators, the application or alleged violations of Part 1 of Article 14 of Chapter 120 of the General Statutes.

(3)   An alleged violation of the criminal law by a covered person in the performance of that individual's official duties.

(4)   An alleged violation of G.S. 126-14.

Upon receipt of a referral under G.S. 147-64.6B or a report under G.S. 147-64.6(c)(19), the Commission may conduct an inquiry under this section on its own motion. Allegations of violations of the Code of Judicial Conduct shall be referred to the Judicial Standards Commission without investigation.

(b1)   Complaints on Its Own Motion. - An investigation initiated by the Commission on its own motion or upon written request of any public servant or those responsible for the hiring, appointing, or supervising of a public servant instituted under subsection (b) of this section shall be treated as a complaint for purposes of this section and need not be sworn or verified.

(c)   Complaint. -

(1)   A sworn complaint filed under this Chapter shall state the name, address, and telephone number of the individual filing the complaint, the name and job title or appointive position of the covered person or legislative employee against whom the complaint is filed, and a concise statement of the nature of the complaint and specific facts indicating that a violation of this Chapter or Chapter 120 of the General Statutes or G.S. 126-14 or the criminal law in the performance of that individual's official duties has occurred, the date the alleged violation occurred, and either (i) that the contents of the complaint are within the knowledge of the individual verifying the complaint, or (ii) the basis upon which the individual verifying the complaint believes the allegations to be true.

(2)   Except as provided in subsection (d) of this section, a complaint filed under this Chapter must be filed within two years of the date the complainant knew or should have known of the conduct upon which the complaint is based.

(3)   The Commission may decline to accept, refer, or conduct an inquiry into any complaint that does not meet all of the requirements set forth in subdivision (1) of this subsection, or the Commission may, in its sole discretion, request

additional information to be provided by the complainant within a specified period of time of no less than five business days.

(4)   In addition to subdivision (3) of this subsection, the Commission may decline to accept, refer, or conduct an inquiry into a complaint if it determines that any of the following apply:

a.   The complaint is frivolous or brought in bad faith.

b.   The covered person or legislative employee and conduct complained of have already been the subject of a prior complaint.

c.   The conduct complained of is primarily a matter more appropriately and adequately addressed and handled by other federal, State, or local agencies or authorities, including law enforcement authorities. If other agencies or authorities are conducting an investigation of the same actions or conduct involved in a complaint filed under this section, the Commission may stay its complaint inquiry pending final resolution of the other investigation.

(5)   The Commission shall send a copy of the complaint to the covered person or legislative employee who is the subject of the complaint and the employing entity, within 10 business days of the filing.

(d)   Conduct of Inquiry of Complaints by the Commission. - The Commission shall conduct an inquiry into all complaints properly before the Commission in a timely manner. The Commission shall initiate an inquiry into a complaint within 10 business days of the filing of the complaint. The Commission is authorized to initiate inquiries upon request of any member of the Commission if there is reason to believe that a covered person or legislative employee has or may have violated this Chapter. Commission-initiated complaint inquiries under this section shall be initiated within two years of the date the Commission knew of the conduct upon which the complaint is based, except when the conduct is material to the continuing conduct of the duties in office. In determining whether there is reason to believe that a violation has or may have occurred, a member of the Commission may take general notice of available information even if not formally provided to the Commission in the form of a complaint. The Commission may utilize the services of a hired investigator when conducting inquiries.

(e)   Covered Person and Legislative Employees Cooperation With Inquiry. - Covered persons and legislative employees shall promptly and fully cooperate

109

with the Commission in any Commission-related inquiry. Failure to cooperate fully with the Commission in any inquiry shall be grounds for sanctions as set forth in G.S. 138A-45.

(f)   Dismissal of Complaint After Preliminary Inquiry. - The Commission shall conclude the preliminary inquiry within 20 business days. The Commission shall dismiss the complaint, if at the end of its preliminary inquiry the Commission determines that any of the following apply:

(1)   The individual who is the subject of the complaint is not a covered person or legislative employee subject to the Commission's jurisdiction and authority under this Chapter.

(2)   The complaint does not allege facts sufficient to constitute a violation within the jurisdiction of the Commission under subsection (b) of this section.

(3)   The complaint is determined to be frivolous or brought in bad faith.

(g)   Commission Inquiries. - If at the end of its preliminary inquiry, the Commission determines to proceed with further inquiry into the conduct of a covered person or legislative employee, the Commission shall provide written notice to the individual who filed the complaint and the covered person or legislative employee as to the fact of the inquiry and the charges against the covered person or legislative employee. The covered person or legislative employee shall be given an opportunity to file a written response with the Commission.

(h)   Action on Inquiries. - The Commission shall conduct inquiries into complaints to the extent necessary to either dismiss the complaint for lack of probable cause of a violation under this section, or:

(1)   For public servants, decide to proceed with a hearing under subsection (i) of this section.

(2)   For legislators, except the Lieutenant Governor, refer the complaint to the Committee.

(3)   For judicial officers, refer the complaint to the Judicial Standards Commission for complaints against justices and judges, to the senior resident superior court judge of the district or county for complaints against district

110

attorneys, or to the chief district court judge for the district or county for complaints against clerks of court.

(4)   For legislative employees, refer the complaint to the employing entity.

(i)   Hearing. -

(1)   The Commission shall give full and fair consideration to all complaints received against a public servant. If the Commission determines that the complaint cannot be resolved without a hearing, or if the public servant requests a hearing, a hearing shall be held.

(2)   The Commission shall send a notice of the hearing to the complainant, and the public servant. The notice shall contain the time and place for a hearing on the matter, which shall begin no less than 30 days and no more than 90 days after the date of the notice.

(3)   The Commission shall make available to the public servant or that public servant's private legal counsel all documents or other evidence which are intended to be presented at the hearing to the Commission or which a reasonable person would believe might exculpate the accused public servant at least 30 days prior to the date of the hearing held in connection with the investigation of a complaint. Any documents or other evidence discovered within less than 30 days of the hearing shall be furnished as soon as possible after discovery but prior to the hearing.

(4)   At any hearing held by the Commission:

a.   Oral evidence shall be taken only on oath or affirmation.

b.   The hearing shall be open to the public, except for matters involving minors, personnel records, or matters that could otherwise be considered in closed session under G.S. 143-318.11. In any event, the deliberations by the Commission on a complaint may be held in closed session.

c.   The public servant being investigated shall have the right to present evidence, call and examine witnesses, cross-examine witnesses, introduce exhibits, and be represented by counsel.

(j)   Settlement of Inquiries. - The public servant who is the subject of the complaint and the staff of the Commission may meet by mutual consent before

111

the hearing to discuss the possibility of settlement of the inquiry or the stipulation of any issues, facts, or matters of law. Any proposed settlement of the inquiry is subject to the approval of the Commission.

(k)   Disposition of Inquiries. - After hearing, the Commission shall dispose of the matter in one or more of the following ways:

(1)   If the Commission finds substantial evidence of an alleged violation of a criminal statute, the Commission shall refer the matter to the Attorney General for investigation and referral to the district attorney for possible prosecution.

(2)   If the Commission finds that the alleged violation is not established by clear and convincing evidence, the Commission shall dismiss the complaint.

(3)   If the Commission finds that the alleged violation of this Chapter is established by clear and convincing evidence, the Commission shall do one or more of the following:

a.   Issue a private admonishment to the public servant and notify the employing entity, if applicable. Such notification shall be treated as part of the personnel record of the public servant.

b.   Refer the matter for appropriate action to the Governor and the employing entity that appointed or employed the public servant or of which the public servant is a member.

c.   Refer the matter for appropriate action to the Chief Justice for judicial employees.

d.   Refer the matter to the Principal Clerks of the House of Representatives and Senate of the General Assembly for constitutional officers of the State.

e.   Refer the matter for appropriate action to the principal clerk of the house of the General Assembly that elected the public servant for members of the Board of Governors and the State Board of Community Colleges.

(l)   Notice of Dismissal. - Upon the dismissal of a complaint under this section, the Commission shall provide written notice of the dismissal to the individual who filed the complaint and the covered person or legislative employee against whom the complaint was filed. The Commission shall forward copies of complaints and notices of dismissal of complaints against legislators to the Committee, against legislative employees to the employing entity for legislative employees, and against judicial officers to the Judicial Standards Commission for complaints against justices and judges, and the senior resident superior court judge of the district or county for complaints against district attorneys, or the chief district court judge of the district or county for complaints against clerks of court. The Commission shall also forward a copy of the notice of dismissal to the employing entity of the covered person against whom a complaint was filed if the employing entity received a copy of the complaint under subdivision (5) of subsection (c) of this section. Except as provided in subsection (n) of this section, the complaint and notice of dismissal are confidential and not public records.

(m)   Reports and Records. - The Commission shall render the results of its inquiry in writing. When a matter is referred under subdivision (h)(2) and (3), or subsection (k) of this section, the Commission's report shall consist of the complaint, response, and detailed results of its inquiry in support of the Commission's finding of a violation under this Chapter.

(n)   Confidentiality. - Complaints and responses filed with the Commission and reports and other investigative documents and records of the Commission connected to an inquiry under this section, including information provided pursuant to G.S. 147-64.6B or G.S. 147-64.6(c)(19), shall be confidential and not matters of public record, except as otherwise provided in this section or when the covered person or legislative employee under inquiry requests in writing that the complaint, response, and findings be made public. Once a hearing under this section commences, the complaint, response, and all other documents offered at the hearing in conjunction with the complaint, not otherwise privileged or confidential under law, shall be public records. If no hearing is held at such time as the Commission reports to the employing entity a recommendation of sanctions, the complaint and response shall be made public.

(n1)   Staff to the Commission may share with staff to the Committee information connected to an inquiry into the conduct of a legislator under this section. The Commission shall provide to the Committee copies of all reports, investigative documents, information, and other documents used by the Commission when it refers a complaint to the Committee under subdivision (2) of subsection (h) of this section. Upon written request by staff to the Committee, the Commission shall provide copies of all reports, investigative documents, information, and other documents used by the Commission when it dismisses a complaint against a legislator under subsection (l) of this section. The

113

information and documents provided to the Committee and staff to the Committee and the written request provided to the Commission are confidential and are not public records as defined in G.S. 132-1.

(o)   Recommendations of Sanctions. - After referring a matter under subsection (k) of this section, if requested by the entity to which the matter was referred, the Commission may recommend sanctions or issue rulings as it deems necessary or appropriate to protect the public interest and ensure compliance with this Chapter. In recommending appropriate sanctions, the Commission may consider the following factors:

(1)   The public servant's prior experience in an agency or on a board and prior opportunities to learn the ethical standards for a public servant as set forth in Article 4 of this Chapter, including those dealing with conflicts of interest.

(2)   The number of ethics violations.

(3)   The severity of the ethics violations.

(4)   Whether the ethics violations involve the public servant's financial interest.

(5)   Whether the ethics violations were inadvertent or intentional.

(6)   Whether the public servant knew or should have known that the improper conduct was a violation of this Chapter.

(7)   Whether the public servant has previously been advised or warned by the Commission.

(8)   Whether the conduct or situation giving rise to the ethics violation was pointed out to the public servant in the Commission's Statement of Economic Interest evaluation letter issued under G.S. 138A-24(e).

(9)   The public servant's motivation or reason for the improper conduct or action, including whether the action was for personal financial gain versus protection of the public interest.

In making recommendations under this subsection, if the Commission determines, after proper review and investigation, that sanctions are appropriate, the Commission may recommend any action it deems necessary to

114

properly address and rectify any violation of this Chapter by a public servant, including removal of the public servant from the public servant's State position. Nothing in this subsection is intended, and shall not be construed, to give the Commission any independent civil, criminal, or administrative investigative or enforcement authority over covered persons, or other State employees or appointees.

(p)   Authority of Employing Entity. - Any action or failure to act by the Commission under this Chapter, except G.S. 138A-13, shall not limit any authority of any of the applicable employing entities to discipline the covered person or legislative employee.

(q)   Continuing Jurisdiction. - The Commission shall have continuing jurisdiction to investigate possible criminal violations of this Chapter for a period of one year following the date an individual, who was formerly a public servant or legislative employee, ceases to be a public servant or legislative employee for any investigation that commenced prior to the date the public servant or legislative employee ceases to be a public servant or legislative employee.

(r)   Subpoena Authority. - The Commission may petition the Superior Court of Wake County for the approval to issue subpoenas and subpoenas duces tecum as necessary to conduct investigations of alleged violations of this Chapter. The court shall authorize subpoenas under this subsection when the court determines the subpoenas are necessary for the enforcement of this Chapter. Subpoenas issued under this subsection shall be enforceable by the court through contempt powers. Venue shall be with the Superior Court of Wake County for any person or governmental unit covered by this Chapter, and personal jurisdiction may be asserted under G.S. 1-75.4.

(s)   Reports. - The number of complaints referred under this section shall be reported under G.S. 138A-10(a)(12).

(t)   Concurrent Jurisdiction. - Nothing in this section shall limit the jurisdiction of the Committee or the Judicial Standards Commission with regards to legislative or judicial misconduct, and jurisdiction under this section shall be concurrent with the jurisdiction of the Committee and the Judicial Standards Commission. (2006-201, s. 1; 2007-348, ss. 27-30; 2008-187, s. 21; 2008-213, ss. 1(b), 57; 2008-215, ss. 4, 5; 2009-549, ss. 9, 10, 11; 2010-169, s. 23(a)-(e), (h); 2012-182, s. 3.)

§ 138A-13. Request for advice.

(a)   At the request of any public servant or legislative employee, any individual who is responsible for the supervision or appointment of a public servant or legislative employee, legal counsel for any public servant or legislative employee, any ethics liaison under G.S. 138A-14, or any member of the Commission, the Commission shall render advice on specific questions involving the meaning and application of this Chapter and the public servant's or legislative employee's compliance therewith. Requests for advice and advice rendered in response to those requests shall relate prospectively to real or reasonably anticipated fact settings or circumstances.

(a1)   On its own motion, the Commission may render advisory opinions on specific questions involving the meaning and application of this Chapter.

(a2)   A request for a formal advisory opinion under subsection (a) of this section shall be in writing, electronic or otherwise. The Commission shall issue formal advisory opinions having prospective application only. A public servant or legislative employee who relies upon the advice provided to that public servant or legislative employee on a specific matter addressed by the requested formal advisory opinion shall be immune from all of the following:

(1)   Investigation by the Commission, except for an inquiry under G.S. 138A-12(b)(3).

(2)   Any adverse action by the employing entity.

(3)   Investigation by the Secretary of State.

(b)   At the request of a legislator, the Commission shall render advice on specific questions involving the meaning and application of this Chapter and Part 1 of Article 14 of Chapter 120 of the General Statutes, and the legislator's compliance therewith. Requests for advice and advice rendered in response to those requests shall relate prospectively to real or reasonably anticipated fact settings or circumstances.

(b1)   A request by a legislator for a recommended formal advisory opinion shall be in writing, electronic or otherwise. The Commission shall issue recommended formal advisory opinions having prospective application only. Until action is taken by the Committee under G.S. 120-104, a legislator who relies upon the advice provided to that legislator on a specific matter addressed by the requested recommended formal advisory opinion shall be immune from all of the following:

(1)   Investigation by the Committee or Commission, except for an inquiry under G.S. 138A-12(b)(3).

(2)   Any adverse action by the house of which the legislator is a member.

(3)   Investigation by the Secretary of State.

Any recommended formal advisory opinion issued to a legislator under this subsection shall immediately be delivered to the chairs of the Committee, together with a copy of the request. Except for the Lieutenant Governor, the immunity granted under this subsection shall not apply after the time the Committee modifies or overturns the advisory opinion of the Commission in accordance with G.S. 120-104.

(b2)   At the request of the Auditor, the Commission shall render advisory opinions on specific questions involving the meaning and application of this Chapter, Article 14 of Chapter 120 of the General Statutes, and Chapter 120C of the General Statutes and an affected person's compliance therewith. The request shall be in writing, electronic or otherwise, and relate to real fact settings and circumstances. Except when the question involves a question governed by subsection (b) or (b1) of this section, the Commission shall issue an advisory opinion under this subsection within 60 days of the receipt of all information deemed necessary by the Commission to render an opinion. If the question involves a question governed by subsection (b) or (b1) of this section, the Commission shall comply with the provisions of that section prior to responding to the Auditor by delivering the recommended advisory opinion to the Committee within 60 days of the receipt of all information deemed necessary by the Commission to render an opinion. The Committee shall act on the opinion within 30 days of receipt and the Commission shall deliver the opinion to the Auditor. If the Committee fails to act on a recommended advisory opinion under this subsection with 30 days of receipt, the Commission shall deliver its recommended advisory opinion to the Auditor. Notwithstanding G.S. 138A-13(e), the Auditor may only release those portions of the advisory opinion necessary to comply with the requirements of G.S. 147-64.6(c)(1).

(c)   Staff to the Commission may issue advice, but not formal or recommended formal advisory opinions, under procedures adopted by the Commission.

(d)   The Commission shall publish its formal advisory opinions within 30 days of issuance. These formal advisory opinions shall be edited for publication purposes as necessary to protect the identities of the individuals requesting formal advisory opinions. When the Commission issues a recommended formal advisory opinion to a legislator under subsection (b1) of this section, the Commission shall publish only the edited formal advisory opinion of the Committee within 30 days of receipt of the edited opinion from the Committee.

(e)   Except as provided under subsections (b2), (d) and (e1) of this section, a request for advice, any advice provided by Commission staff, any formal or recommended formal advisory opinions, any supporting documents submitted or caused to be submitted to the Commission or Commission staff, and any documents prepared or collected by the Commission or Commission staff in connection with a request for advice are confidential. The identity of the individual making the request for advice, the existence of the request, and any information related to the request may not be revealed without the consent of the requestor. An individual who requests advice or receives advice, including a formal or recommended formal advisory opinion, may authorize the release to any other person, the State, or any governmental unit of the request, the advice, or any supporting documents.

For purposes of this section, "document" is as defined in G.S. 120-129. Requests for advice, any advice, and any documents related to requests for advice are not "public records" as defined in G.S. 132-1.

(e1)   Staff to the Commission may share all information and documents related to requests for advice, made by legislators under this section with staff to the Committee. The information and documents in the possession of staff to the Committee are confidential and are not public records.

(f)   This section shall apply to judicial officers only for advice related to Article 3 of this Chapter.

(g)   Requests for advice may be withdrawn by the requestor at any time prior to the issuance of the advice. (2006-201, s. 1; 2007-348, s. 31; 2008-213, ss. 2(b), 91.5; 2008-215, s. 6; 2009-570, s. 17; 2010-169, s. 17(p).)

§ 138A-14. Ethics education program.

(a)   The Commission shall develop and implement an ethics education and awareness program designed to instill in all covered persons and their immediate staffs, and legislative employees, a keen and continuing awareness of their ethical obligations and a sensitivity to situations that might result in real or potential conflicts of interest.

(b)   The Commission shall offer basic ethics education and awareness presentations to all public servants and their immediate staffs, upon their election, appointment, or employment, and shall offer periodic refresher presentations as the Commission deems appropriate. Every public servant shall participate in an ethics presentation approved by the Commission within six months of the public servant's election, reelection, appointment, or employment, and shall attend refresher ethics education presentations at least every two years thereafter in a manner as the Commission deems appropriate.

(b1)   A public servant appointed to a board determined and designated as nonadvisory under G.S. 138A-10(a)(3) shall attend an ethics presentation approved by the Commission within six months of notification of the designation by the Commission and at least every two years thereafter in a manner as the Commission deems appropriate.

(c)   The Commission, jointly with the Committee, shall make basic ethics education and awareness presentations to all legislators and legislative employees upon their election, reelection, appointment, or employment and shall offer periodic refresher presentations as the Commission and the Committee deem appropriate. Every legislator shall participate in an ethics presentation approved by the Commission and Committee within two months of either the convening of the General Assembly to which the legislator is elected or within two months of the legislator's appointment, whichever is later. Every legislative employee shall participate in an ethics presentation approved by the Commission and Committee within three months of employment, and shall attend refresher ethics education presentations at least every two years thereafter, in a manner as the Commission and Committee deem appropriate.

(d)   Upon request, the Commission shall assist each agency in developing in-house education programs and procedures necessary or desirable to meet the agency's particular needs for ethics education, conflict identification, and conflict avoidance.

(e)   Each agency head shall designate an ethics liaison who shall maintain active communication with the Commission on all agency ethical issues. The

119

ethics liaison shall attend ethics education and awareness programs as provided under this section and lobbying education and awareness programs as provided under G.S. 120C-103 and continuously assess and advise the Commission of any issues or conduct which might reasonably be expected to result in a conflict of interest and seek advice and rulings from the Commission as to their appropriate resolution.

(f)   The Commission shall publish a newsletter containing summaries of the Commission's opinions, policies, procedures, and interpretive bulletins as issued from time to time. The newsletter shall be distributed to all covered persons and legislative employees. Publication under this subsection may be done electronically.

(g)   The Commission shall assemble and maintain a collection of relevant State laws, rules, and regulations that set forth ethical standards applicable to covered persons. This collection shall be made available electronically as resource material to public servants, and ethics liaisons, upon request.

(h)   Repealed by Session Laws 2009-549, s. 12, effective August 28, 2009.

(i)   This section shall not apply to judicial officers. (2006-201, s. 1; 2007-347, s. 9(a); 2008-213, ss. 59, 60; 2009-10, s. 4; 2009-549, s. 12; 2010-169, s. 22(a).)

§ 138A-15. Duties of heads of State agencies.

(a)   The head of each State agency, including the chair of each board subject to this Chapter, shall take an active role in furthering ethics in public service and ensuring compliance with this Chapter. The head of each State agency and the chair of each board shall make a conscientious, good-faith effort to assist public servants within the agency or on the board in monitoring their personal, financial, and professional affairs to avoid taking any action that results in a conflict of interest.

(b)   The head of each State agency, including the chair of each board subject to this Chapter, shall maintain familiarity with and stay knowledgeable of the reports, opinions, newsletters, and other communications from the Commission regarding ethics in general and the interpretation and enforcement of this Chapter. The head of each State agency and the chair of each board

120

shall also maintain familiarity with and stay knowledgeable of the Commission's reports, evaluations, opinions, or findings regarding individual public servants in that individual's agency or on that individual's board, or under that individual's supervision or control, including all reports, evaluations, opinions, or findings pertaining to actual or potential conflicts of interest.

(c)   When an actual or potential conflict of interest is cited by the Commission under G.S. 138A-24(e) with regard to a public servant sitting on a board, the conflict shall be recorded in the minutes of the applicable board and duly brought to the attention of the membership by the board's chair as often as necessary to remind all members of the conflict and to help ensure compliance with this Chapter.

(d)   The head of each State agency, including the chair of each board subject to this Chapter, shall periodically remind public servants under that individual's authority of the public servant's duties to the public under the ethical standards and rules of conduct in this Chapter, including the duty of each public servant to continually monitor, evaluate, and manage the public servant's personal, financial, and professional affairs to ensure the absence of conflicts of interest.

(e)   At the beginning of any meeting of a board, the chair shall remind all members of their duty to avoid conflicts of interest under this Chapter. The chair also shall inquire as to whether there is any known conflict of interest with respect to any matters coming before the board at that time.

(f)   The head of each State agency, including the chair of each board subject to this Chapter, shall ensure that legal counsel employed by or assigned to their agency or board are familiar with the provisions of this Chapter, including the Ethical Standards for Covered Persons set forth in Article 4 of this Chapter, and are available to advise public servants on the ethical considerations involved in carrying out their public duties in the best interest of the public. Legal counsel so engaged may consult with the Commission, seek the Commission's assistance or advice, and refer public servants and others to the Commission as appropriate.

(g)   Taking into consideration the individual autonomy, needs, and circumstances of each agency and board, the head of each State agency, including the chair of each board subject to this Chapter, shall consider the need for the development and implementation of in-house educational programs, procedures, or policies tailored to meet the agency's or board's particular needs for ethics education, conflict identification, and conflict avoidance. This includes the periodic presentation to all agency heads, their chief deputies or assistants, other public servants under their supervision or control, and members of boards, of the basic ethics education and awareness presentation outlined in G.S. 138A-14 and any other workshop or seminar program the agency head or board chair deems necessary in implementing this Chapter. Agency heads and board chairs may request reasonable assistance from the Commission in complying with the requirements of this subsection.

(h)   As soon as reasonably practicable after the designation, hiring, or promotion of their chief deputies, assistants, or other public servants under their supervision or control, or learning of the appointment or election of other public servants to a board covered under this Chapter, all agency heads and board chairs shall (i) notify the Commission of such designation, hiring, promotion, appointment, or election and (ii) provide these public servants with copies of this Chapter and all applicable financial disclosure forms, if these materials and forms have not been previously provided to these public servants in connection with their designation, hiring, promotion, appointment, or election. In order to avoid duplication of effort, agency heads and board chairs shall coordinate this effort with the Commission's staff. (2006-201, s. 1; 2007-347, s. 9(b); 2008-213, ss. 61, 62.)

§ 138A-16. Reserved for future codification purposes.

§ 138A-17. Reserved for future codification purposes.

§ 138A-18. Reserved for future codification purposes.

§ 138A-19. Reserved for future codification purposes.

§ 138A-20. Reserved for future codification purposes.

Article 3.

Public Disclosure of Economic Interests.

§ 138A-21. Purpose.

The purpose of disclosure of the financial and personal interests by covered persons is to assist covered persons and those who appoint, elect, hire,

122

supervise, or advise them identify and avoid conflicts of interest and potential conflicts of interest between the covered person's private interests and the covered person's public duties. It is critical to this process that current and prospective covered persons examine, evaluate, and disclose those personal and financial interests that could be or cause a conflict of interest or potential conflict of interest between the covered person's private interests and the covered person's public duties. Covered persons must take an active, thorough, and conscientious role in the disclosure and review process, including having a complete knowledge of how the covered person's public position or duties might impact the covered person's private interests. Covered persons have an affirmative duty to provide any and all information that a reasonable person would conclude is necessary to carry out the purposes of this Chapter and to fully disclose any conflict of interest or potential conflict of interest between the covered person's public and private interests, but the disclosure, review, and evaluation process is not intended to result in the disclosure of unnecessary or irrelevant personal information. (2006-201, s. 1; 2008-213, s. 63.)

§ 138A-22. Statement of economic interest; filing required.

(a)   Every covered person subject to this Chapter who is elected, appointed, or employed, including one appointed to fill a vacancy in elective office, except for public servants (i) included under G.S. 138A-3(30)b., e., f., or g. whose annual compensation from the State is less than sixty thousand dollars ($60,000), or (ii) who are ex officio student members under Chapters 115D and 116 of the General Statutes, shall file a statement of economic interest with the Commission prior to the covered person's initial appointment, election, or employment and no later than April 15 of every year thereafter, except as otherwise filed under subsections (c1) and (d) of this section. A prospective covered person required to file a statement under this Chapter shall not be appointed, employed, or receive a certificate of election, prior to submission by the Commission of the Commission's evaluation of the statement in accordance with this Article. The requirement for an annual filing under this subsection also shall apply to covered persons whose terms have expired but who continue to serve until the covered person's replacement is appointed. Once a statement of economic interest is properly completed and filed under this Article, the statement of economic interest does not need to be supplemented or refiled prior to the next due date set forth in this subsection.

(b)   Notwithstanding subsection (a) of this section, individuals hired by, and appointees of, constitutional officers of the State may file a statement of economic interest within 30 days after their appointments or employment when the appointment or employment is made during the first 60 days of the constitutional officer's initial term in that constitutional office.

(c)   Notwithstanding subsection (a) of this section, public servants, under G.S. 138A-3(30)j. and k., who have submitted a statement of economic interest under subsection (a) of this section, may be hired, appointed, or elected provisionally prior to submission by the Commission of the Commission's evaluation of the statement in accordance with this Article, subject to dismissal or removal based on the Commission's evaluation.

(c1)   A public servant reappointed to a board between January 1 and April 15 shall file a current statement of economic interest prior to the reappointment.

(c2)   A public servant appointed to a board determined and designated as nonadvisory under G.S. 138A-10(a)(3) shall file the initial statement of economic interest within 60 days of notification of the designation by the Commission and as provided in this section thereafter.

(d)   A candidate for an office subject to this Article shall file the statement of economic interest at the same place and in the same manner as the notice of candidacy for that office is required to be filed under G.S. 163-106 or G.S. 163-323 within 10 days of the filing deadline for the office the candidate seeks. An individual who is nominated under G.S. 163-114 after the primary and before the general election, and an individual who qualifies under G.S. 163-122 as an unaffiliated candidate in a general election, shall file a statement of economic interest with the county board of elections of each county in the senatorial or representative district. An individual nominated under G.S. 163-114 shall file the statement within three days following the individual's nomination, or not later than the day preceding the general election, whichever occurs first. An individual seeking to qualify as an unaffiliated candidate under G.S. 163-122 shall file the statement of economic interest with the petition filed under that section. An individual seeking to have write-in votes counted for that individual in a general election shall file a statement of economic interest at the same time the candidate files a declaration of intent under G.S. 163-123. A candidate of a new party chosen by convention shall file a statement of economic interest at the same time that the president of the convention certifies the names of its candidates to the State Board of Elections under G.S. 163-98.

(d1)   In addition to subsections (a) and (d) of this section, a covered person holding elected office or a former covered person who held elected office subject to this Article shall file a statement of economic interest in all of the following instances, as specified:

(1)   Filed on or before April 15 of the year following the year a covered person or former covered person does not file a notice of candidacy or petition for election, or does not receive a certificate of election, to the position making that individual a covered person, with all information provided in the statement of economic interest current as of the last day of December of the preceding year.

(2)   Filed on or before April 15 of the year following the year the covered person or former covered person resigns from the position making that individual a covered person, with all information provided in the statement of economic interest current as of the last day in the position.

(e)   The State Board of Elections shall provide for notification of the statement of economic interest requirements of this Article to be given to any candidate filing for nomination or election to those offices subject to this Article at the time of the filing of candidacy.

(f)   Within 10 days of the filing deadline for office of a covered person, the executive director of the State Board of Elections shall send to the State Ethics Commission a list of the names and addresses of each candidate who have filed as a candidate for office as a covered person. A county board of election shall forward any statements of economic interest filed with the board under this section to the State Board of Elections. The executive director of the State Board of Elections shall forward a certified copy of the statements of economic interest to the Commission for evaluation upon its filing with the State Board of Elections under this section.

(g)   The Commission shall issue forms to be used for the statement of economic interest and shall revise the forms from time to time as necessary to carry out the purposes of this Chapter. Except as otherwise set forth in this section and in G.S. 138A-15(h), upon notification by the employing entity, the Commission shall furnish to all other covered persons the appropriate forms needed to comply with this Article. (2006-201, s. 1; 2007-29, s. 2; 2007-348, ss. 32, 33; 2008-213, s. 64; 2009-549, s. 13; 2010-169, ss. 12, 22(b).)

§ 138A-23. Statements of economic interest as public records.

(a)   The statements of economic interest filed by prospective public servants under this Article for appointed or employed positions and written evaluations by the Commission of these statements are not public records until the prospective public servant is appointed or employed by the State. All other statements of economic interest and all other written evaluations by the Commission of those statements are public records.

(b)   The statements of economic interest filed by prospective public servants, and the written evaluations by the Commission of those statements, for individuals elected by the General Assembly shall be provided to the chair of the standing committee handling the legislation regarding the election and made available to all members of the General Assembly. The statements of economic interest filed by public servants elected to positions by the General Assembly, and written evaluations by the Commission of those statements, are not public records until the prospective public servant is sworn into office.

(c)   The statements of economic interest filed by prospective public servants, and the written evaluations by the Commission of those statements, for individuals confirmed for appointment as a public servant by the General Assembly shall be provided to the chair of the standing committee handling the legislation regarding the appointment. The statements of economic interest filed by prospective public servants for confirmation for appointment by the General Assembly, and written evaluations by the Commission of those statements, are public records at the time of the announcement of the appointment. (2006-201, s. 1; 2007-347, s. 10; 2008-213, ss. 65, 66.)

§ 138A-24. Contents of statement.

(a)   Any statement of economic interest filed under this Article shall be on a form prescribed by the Commission. Answers must be provided to all questions. The form shall include the following information about the filing person and the filing person's immediate family:

(1)   Except as otherwise provided in this subdivision, the name, current mailing address, occupation, employer, and business of the filing person. Any individual holding or seeking elected office for which residence is a qualification for office shall include a home address. A judicial officer may use a current

mailing address instead of the home address on the form required in this subsection. The filing person may also use the initials instead of the name of any unemancipated child of the filing person who also resides in the household of the filing person. If the filing person provides the initials of an unemancipated child, the filing person shall concurrently provide the name of the unemancipated child to the Commission. The name of an unemancipated child provided by the filing person to the Commission shall not be a public record under Chapter 132 of the General Statutes and is privileged and confidential.

(2)   A list of each asset and liability included in this subdivision of whatever nature (including legal, equitable, or beneficial interest) with a value of at least ten thousand dollars ($10,000) owned by the filing person and the filing person's immediate family, except assets or liabilities held in a blind trust. This list shall include the following:

a.   All real estate located in the State owned wholly or in part by the filing person or the filing person's immediate family, including descriptions adequate to determine the location by city and county of each parcel.

b.   Real estate that is currently leased or rented to or from the State.

c.   Personal property sold to or bought from the State within the preceding two years.

d.   Personal property currently leased or rented to or from the State.

e.   The name of each publicly owned company. For purposes of this subsubdivision, the term "publicly owned company" shall not include a widely held investment fund, including a mutual fund, regulated investment company, or pension or deferred compensation plan, if all of the following apply:

1.   The filing person or a member of the filing person's immediate family neither exercises nor has the ability to exercise control over the financial interests held by the fund.

2.   The fund is publicly traded, or the fund's assets are widely diversified.

f.   The name of each nonpublicly owned company or business entity, including interests in sole proprietorships, partnerships, limited partnerships, joint ventures, limited liability companies, limited liability partnerships, and closely held corporations.

127

g.   For each company or business entity listed under sub-subdivision f. of this subdivision, if known, a list of any other companies or business entities in which the company or business entity owns securities or equity interests exceeding a value of ten thousand dollars ($10,000).

h.   Repealed by Session Laws 2010-169, s. 13(a), effective January 1, 2011, and applicable to statements of economic interest filed on or after that date.

i.   Recodified as subdivision (a)(16) by Session Laws 2010-169, s. 13(c), effective January 1, 2011, and applicable to statements of economic interest filed on or after that date.

j.   For a vested trust created, established, or controlled by the filing person of which the filing person or the members of the filing person's immediate family are the beneficiaries, excluding a blind trust, the name and address of the trustee, a description of the trust, and the filing person's relationship to the trust.

k.   A list of all liabilities, excluding indebtedness on the filing person's primary personal residence, by type of creditor and debtor.

l.   Repealed by Session Laws 2007-348, s. 34. See Editor's note for effective date.

m.   A list of all stock options in a company or business not otherwise disclosed on this statement.

(3)   The name of each source (not specific amounts) of income of more than five thousand dollars ($5,000) received during the previous year by business or industry type, if that source is not listed under subdivision (2) of this subsection. Income shall include salary, wages, professional fees, honoraria, interest, dividends, rental income, and business income from any source other than capital gains, federal government retirement, military retirement, or social security income.

(4)   If the filing person is a practicing attorney, an indication of whether the filing person, or the law firm with which the filing person is affiliated, earned legal fees during the past year in excess of ten thousand dollars ($10,000) from any of the following categories of legal representation:

a.   Administrative law.

128

b.   Admiralty law.

c.   Corporate law.

d.   Criminal law.

e.   Decedents' estates law.

f.   Environmental law.

g.   Insurance law.

h.   Labor law.

i.   Local government law.

j.   Negligence or other tort litigation law.

k.   Real property law.

l.   Securities law.

m.   Taxation law.

n.   Utilities regulation law.

(5)   Except for a filing person in compliance under subdivision (4) of this subsection, if the filing person is a licensed professional or provides consulting services, either individually or as a member of a professional association, a list of categories of business and the nature of services rendered, for which payment for services were charged or paid during the past year in excess of ten thousand dollars ($10,000).

(6)   An indication of whether the filing person, the filing person's employer, a member of the filing person's immediate family, or the immediate family member's employer is licensed or regulated by, or has a business relationship with, the board or employing entity with which the filing person is or will be associated. This subdivision does not apply to a legislator, a judicial officer, or that legislator's or judicial officer's immediate family.

(7)   A list of societies, organizations, or advocacy groups, pertaining to subject matter areas over which the public servant's agency or board may have jurisdiction, in which the public servant or a member of the public servant's immediate family is a director, officer, or governing board member. This subdivision does not apply to a legislator, a judicial officer, or that legislator's or judicial officer's immediate family.

(8)   A list of all things with a total value of over two hundred dollars ($200.00) per calendar quarter given and received without valuable consideration and under circumstances that a reasonable person would conclude that the thing was given for lobbying, if such things were given by a person not required to report under Chapter 120C of the General Statutes, excluding things given by a member of the filing person's extended family. The list shall include only those things received during the 12 months preceding the reporting period under subsection (d) of this section, and shall include the source of those things. The list required by this subdivision shall not apply to things of monetary value received by the filing person prior to the time the filing person filed or was nominated as a candidate for office, as described in G.S. 138A-22, or was appointed or employed as a covered person.

(9)   A list of any felony convictions of the filing person, excluding any felony convictions for which a pardon of innocence or order of expungement has been granted.

(10)   Any other information that the filing person believes may assist the Commission in advising the filing person with regards to compliance with this Chapter.

(11)   A list of any nonprofit corporation or organization with which associated during the preceding calendar year, including a list of which of those nonprofit corporations or organizations with which associated do business with the State or receive State funds and a brief description of the nature of the business, if known or with which due diligence could reasonably be known.

(12)   A statement of whether the filing person or the filing person's immediate family is or has been a lobbyist or lobbyist principal registered under Chapter 120C of the General Statutes within the preceding 12 months.

(13)   A list of all contributions as defined in G.S. 163-278.6(6) with a cumulative total of more than one thousand dollars ($1,000) made by the filing person only, during the preceding calendar year, to the candidate or candidate

campaign committee of the covered person as defined in G.S. 138A-3(30)a. appointing the filing person to the covered board.

(14)   A statement indicating "Yes" or "No" as to whether the filing person engaged in each of the following activities during the preceding calendar year, with respect to or on the behalf of the candidate or candidate campaign committee of the covered person as defined in G.S. 138A-3(30)a. appointing the filing person: (i) collected contributions from multiple contributors, took possession of such multiple contributions, and transferred or delivered those collected multiple contributions, (ii) hosted a fund-raiser in the filing person's residence or place of business, or (iii) volunteered for campaign-related activity. This subdivision only applies to filing persons in the following categories:

a.   A public servant, or a prospective appointee to, as defined in G.S. 138A-3(30)c.

b.   A judicial officer that serves on, or a prospective appointee to, the Supreme Court, the Court of Appeals, the superior court, or the district court.

c.   A covered person serving on, or a prospective appointee to, one of the following panels or boards:

1.   Alcoholic Beverage Control Commission.

2.   Coastal Resources Commission.

3.   State Board of Education.

4.   State Board of Elections.

5.   Division of Employment Security.

6.   Environmental Management Commission.

7.   Industrial Commission.

8.   State Human Resources Commission.

9.   Rules Review Commission.

10.   Board of Transportation.

131

11.   Board of Governors of the University of North Carolina.

12.   Utilities Commission.

13.   Wildlife Resources Commission.

(15)   The name of each business with which associated that the filing person or a member of the filing person's immediate family is an employee, director, officer, partner, proprietor, or member or manager.

(16)   For any company or business entity listed under subdivision (15) of this subsection and sub-subdivisions f. and g. of subdivision (2) of this subsection, if known, a statement whether that company or business entity has any material business dealings or business contracts with the State, or is regulated by the State, including a brief description of the business activity.

(b)   The Supreme Court, the Committee, constitutional officers of the State, heads of principal departments, the Board of Governors of The University of North Carolina, the State Board of Community Colleges, other boards, and the appointing authority or employing entity may require a filing person to file supplemental information in conjunction with the filing of that filing person's statement of economic interest. These supplemental filings requirements shall be filed with the Commission and included on the forms to be filed with the Commission. The Commission shall evaluate the supplemental forms as part of the statement of economic interest. The failure to file supplemental forms shall be subject to the provisions of G.S. 138A-25.

(c)   Each statement of economic interest shall contain a certification by the filing person that the filing person has read the statement and that, to the best of the filing person's knowledge and belief, the statement is true, correct, and complete. The filing person's certification also shall provide that the filing person has not transferred, and will not transfer, any asset, interest, or other property with the intent to conceal it from disclosure while retaining an equitable interest therein.

(c1)   Reserved for future codification purposes.

(c2)   Recodified as G.S. 138A-22(c2) by Session Laws 2010-169, s. 22(b), effective August 2, 2010.

(d)   All information provided in the statement of economic interest shall be current as of the last day of December of the year preceding the date the statement of economic interest was due.

(e)   The Commission shall prepare a written evaluation of each statement of economic interest relative to conflicts of interest and potential conflicts of interest. This subsection does not apply to statements of economic interest of legislators and judicial officers. The Commission shall submit the evaluation to all of the following:

(1)   The filing person who submitted the statement.

(2)   The head of the agency in which the filing person serves.

(3)   The Governor for gubernatorial appointees and employees in agencies under the Governor's authority.

(4)   Repealed by Session Laws 2008-213, s. 74, effective August 15, 2008.

(5)   The appointing or hiring authority for those public servants not under the Governor's authority.

(6)   The State Board of Elections for those filing persons who are elected.

(7)   Repealed by Session Laws 2008-213, s. 74, effective August 15, 2008.

(f)   The Commission shall prepare a written evaluation of each statement of economic interest for nominees of the Board of Governors of The University of North Carolina elected pursuant to G.S. 116-6, and nominees of the State Board of Community Colleges elected pursuant to G.S. 115D-2.1 within seven days of the submission of the completed statement of economic interest to the Commission. (2006-201, s. 1; 2007-29, s. 1; 2007-348, s. 34; 2008-187, s. 32; 2008-213, ss. 67-72(a), 73, 74, 74.5, 91; 2009-549, s. 14; 2009-570, s. 45; 2010-169, ss. 13(a)-(d), 17(q), 22(b); 2011-401, s. 3.18; 2013-382, s. 9.1(c).)

§ 138A-25. Failure to file.

(a)   Within 30 days after the date due under G.S. 138A-22, the Commission shall notify filing persons who have failed to file or filing persons whose statement has been deemed incomplete. For a filing person currently serving as a covered person, the Commission shall notify the filing person and the ethics liaison that if the statement of economic interest is not filed or completed within 30 days of receipt of the notice of failure to file or complete, the filing person shall be subject to a fine as provided for in this section.

(b)   Any filing person who fails to file or complete a statement of economic interest within 30 days of the receipt of the notice, required under subsection (a) of this section, shall be subject to a fine of two hundred fifty dollars ($250.00), to be imposed by the Commission.

(c)   Failure by any filing person to file or complete a statement of economic interest within 60 days of the receipt of the notice, required under subsection (a) of this section, shall be deemed to be a violation of this Chapter and shall be grounds for disciplinary action under G.S. 138A-45. (2006-201, s. 1; 2008-213, s. 75; 2009-549, s. 15.)

§ 138A-26. Concealing or failing to disclose material information.

A filing person who knowingly conceals or knowingly fails to disclose information that is required to be disclosed on a statement of economic interest under this Article shall be guilty of a Class 1 misdemeanor and shall be subject to disciplinary action under G.S. 138A-45. (2006-201, s. 1.)

§ 138A-27. Penalty for false information.

A filing person who provides false information on a statement of economic interest as required under this Article knowing that the information is false is guilty of a Class H felony and shall be subject to disciplinary action under G.S. 138A-45. (2006-201, s. 1.)

§ 138A-28. Review and evaluation of statements of economic interest.

(a)   The Commission shall receive and review all statements of economic interest pursuant to G.S. 138A-10(a)(4) and shall evaluate whether (i) the

134

statements conform to the law and the rules of the Commission, and (ii) the financial interests and other information reported by prospective and actual covered persons reveal actual or potential conflicts of interest.

(b)   Beginning July 1, 2013, the Commission shall establish a biennial cycle for evaluating statements of economic interest. The Commission shall evaluate each initial filing as provided in subsection (a) of this section.

(c)   Notwithstanding subsection (b) of this section, statements filed by the following prospective and actual public servants shall be evaluated on an annual basis:

(1)   The University of North Carolina Board of Governors, subject to G.S. 138A-24(f).

(2)   The State Board of Community Colleges, subject to G.S. 138A-24(f).

(3)   The North Carolina Utilities Commission.

(4)   The North Carolina Industrial Commission.

(5)   Supplemental statements filed pursuant to Chapter 136 of the General Statutes.

(6)   Any other board or commission whose members are elected or confirmed by the General Assembly.

(d)   Notwithstanding subsections (a) and (b) of this section, statements of economic interest filed by Constitutional officers of the State and individuals elected or appointed as Constitutional officers of the State prior to taking office shall be evaluated every four years upon election or appointment to office.

(e)   A public servant who simultaneously serves on more than one covered board may file one statement of economic interest and that statement shall serve as disclosure for all the covered boards. If, during the biennial cycle, a public servant leaves one covered board and begins membership on another covered board, the public servant is not required to file another statement of economic interest, and the Commission is not required to evaluate the statement again in light of the subsequent appointment. The public servant must make subsequent filings pursuant to G.S. 138A-22(a) upon the expiration of the biennial cycle.

(f)   Nothing in this section shall be construed to impair the Commission's duties and authority under G.S. 138A-25 and G.S. 138A-26. (2013-360, s. 30.4(b).)

§ 138A-29: Reserved for future codification purposes.

§ 138A-30: Reserved for future codification purposes.

Article 4.

Ethical Standards for Covered Persons.

§ 138A-31. Use of public position for private gain.

(a)   Except as permitted under G.S. 138A-38, a covered person or legislative employee shall not knowingly use the covered person's or legislative employee's public position in an official action or legislative action that will result in financial benefit to the covered person or legislative employee, a member of the covered person's or legislative employee's extended family, or business with which the covered person or legislative employee is associated. This subsection shall not apply to financial or other benefits derived by a covered person or legislative employee that the covered person or legislative employee would enjoy to an extent no greater than that which other citizens of the State would or could enjoy, or that are so remote, tenuous, insignificant, or speculative that a reasonable person would conclude under the circumstances that the covered person's or legislative employee's ability to protect the public interest and perform the covered person's or legislative employee's official duties would not be compromised.

(b)   A covered person shall not mention or authorize another person to mention the covered person's public position in nongovernmental advertising that advances the private interest of the covered person or others. The prohibition in this subsection shall not apply to any of the following:

(1)   Political advertising.

(2)   News stories and articles.

(3)   The inclusion of a covered person's public position in a directory or a biographical listing.

(4)   The inclusion of a covered person's public position in an agenda or other document related to a meeting, conference, or similar event when the disclosure could reasonably be considered material by an individual attending the meeting, conference, or similar event.

(5)   The inclusion of a covered person's public position in a charitable solicitation for a nonprofit business entity qualifying under 26 U.S.C. § 501(c)(3).

(6)   The disclosure of a covered person's position to an existing or prospective customer, supplier, or client when the disclosure could reasonably be considered material by the customer, supplier, or client.

(c)   Notwithstanding G.S. 163-278.16A, no covered person shall use or permit the use of State funds for any advertisement or public service announcement in a newspaper, on radio, television, magazines, or billboards, that contains that covered person's name, picture, or voice, except in case of State or national emergency and only if the announcement is reasonably necessary to the covered person's official function. This subsection shall not apply to fund-raising on behalf of and aired on public radio or public television. (2006-201, s. 1; 2009-549, s. 16; 2011-393, s. 1.)

§ 138A-32. Gifts.

(a)   A covered person or a legislative employee shall not knowingly, directly or indirectly, ask, accept, demand, exact, solicit, seek, assign, receive, or agree to receive anything of value for the covered person or legislative employee, or for another person, in return for being influenced in the discharge of the covered person's or legislative employee's official responsibilities, other than that which is received by the covered person or the legislative employee from the State for acting in the covered person's or legislative employee's official capacity.

(b)   A covered person may not solicit for a charitable purpose any thing of monetary value from any subordinate State employee. This subsection shall not apply to generic written solicitations to all members of a class of subordinates. Nothing in this subsection shall prohibit a covered person from serving as the honorary head of the State Employees Combined Campaign.

(c)   No public servant, legislator, or legislative employee shall knowingly accept a gift from a lobbyist or lobbyist principal registered under Chapter 120C of the General Statutes. No legislator or legislative employee shall knowingly accept a gift from liaison personnel designated under Chapter 120C of the General Statutes. No public servant, legislator, or legislative employee shall accept a gift knowing all of the following:

(1)   The gift was obtained indirectly from a lobbyist, lobbyist principal, or liaison personnel registered under Chapter 120C of the General Statutes.

(2)   The lobbyist, lobbyist principal, or liaison personnel registered under Chapter 120C of the General Statutes intended for an ultimate recipient of the gift to be a public servant, legislator, or legislative employee as provided in G.S. 120C-303.

(d)   No public servant shall knowingly accept a gift from a person whom the public servant knows or has reason to know any of the following:

(1)   Is doing or is seeking to do business of any kind with the public servant's employing entity.

(2)   Is engaged in activities that are regulated or controlled by the public servant's employing entity.

(3)   Has financial interests that may be substantially and materially affected, in a manner distinguishable from the public generally, by the performance or nonperformance of the public servant's official duties.

(d1)   No public servant shall accept a gift knowing all of the following:

(1)   The gift was obtained indirectly from a person described under subdivision (d)(1), (2), or (3) of this section.

(2)   The person described under subdivision (d)(1), (2), or (3) of this section intended for an ultimate recipient of the gift to be a public servant.

(e)   Subsections (c), (d), and (d1) of this section shall not apply to any of the following:

(1)   Food and beverages for immediate consumption in connection with any of the following:

138

a.   An open meeting of a public body, provided that the open meeting is properly noticed under Article 33C of Chapter 143 of the General Statutes.

b.   A gathering of a person or governmental unit with at least 10 or more individuals in attendance open to the general public, provided that a sign or other communication containing a message that is reasonably designed to convey to the general public that the gathering is open to the general public is displayed at the gathering.

c.   A gathering of a person or governmental unit to which the entire board of which a public servant is a member, at least 10 public servants, all the members of the House of Representatives, all the members of the Senate, all the members of a county or municipal legislative delegation, all the members of a recognized legislative caucus with regular meetings other than meetings with one or more lobbyists, all the members of a committee, a standing subcommittee, a joint committee or joint commission of the House of Representatives, the Senate, or the General Assembly, or all legislative employees are invited, and one of the following applies:

1.   At least 10 individuals associated with the person or governmental unit actually attend, other than the covered person or legislative employee, or the immediate family of the covered person or legislative employee.

2.   All shareholders, employees, board members, officers, members, or subscribers of the person or governmental unit located in North Carolina are notified and invited to attend.

For purposes of this sub-subdivision only, the term "invited" shall mean written notice from at least one host or sponsor of the gathering containing the date, time, and location of the gathering given at least 24 hours in advance of the gathering to the specific qualifying group listed in this sub-subdivision. If it is known at the time of the written notice that at least one sponsor is a lobbyist or lobbyist principal, the written notice shall also state whether or not the gathering is permitted under this section.

(2)   Informational materials relevant to the duties of the covered person or legislative employee.

(3)   Reasonable actual expenditures of the legislator, public servant, or legislative employee for food, beverages, registration, travel, lodging, other incidental items of nominal value, and entertainment, in connection with (i) a

legislator's, public servant's, or legislative employee's attendance at an educational meeting for purposes primarily related to the public duties and responsibilities of the legislator, public servant, or legislative employee; (ii) a legislator's, public servant's, or legislative employee's participation as a speaker or member of a panel at a meeting; (iii) a legislator's or legislative employee's attendance and participation in meetings of a nonpartisan state, regional, national, or international legislative organization of which the General Assembly is a member or that the legislator or legislative employee is a member or participant of by virtue of that legislator's or legislative employee's public position, or as a member of a board, agency, or committee of such organization; or (iv) a public servant's attendance and participation in meetings as a member of a board, agency, or committee of a nonpartisan state, regional, national, or international organization of which the public servant's agency is a member or the public servant is a member by virtue of that public servant's public position, provided the following conditions are met:

a.   The reasonable actual expenditures shall be made by a lobbyist principal, and not a lobbyist.

b.   Any meeting must be attended by at least 10 or more participants, have a formal agenda, and notice of the meeting has been given at least 10 days in advance.

c.   Any food, beverages, transportation, or entertainment must be provided to all attendees or defined groups of 10 or more attendees as part of the meeting or in conjunction with the meeting.

d.   Any entertainment must be incidental to the principal agenda of the meeting.

e.   If the legislator, public servant, or legislative employee is participating as a speaker or member of a panel, then that legislator, public servant, or legislative employee must be a bona fide speaker or participant.

(4)   A plaque or similar nonmonetary memento recognizing individual services in a field or specialty or to a charitable cause.

(5)   Gifts accepted on behalf of the State for use by the State or for the benefit of the State.

(6)   Anything generally made available or distributed to the general public or all other State employees by lobbyists or lobbyist principals, or persons described in subdivisions (d)(1), (2), or (3) of this section.

(7)   Gifts from the covered person's or legislative employee's extended family, or a member of the same household of the covered person or legislative employee.

(8)   Gifts given to a public servant not otherwise subject to an exception under this subsection, where the gift is food and beverages, transportation, lodging, entertainment or related expenses associated with the public business of industry recruitment, promotion of international trade, or the promotion of travel and tourism, and the public servant is responsible for conducting the business on behalf of the State, provided all the following conditions apply:

a.   The public servant did not solicit the gift, and the public servant did not accept the gift in exchange for the performance of the public servant's official duties.

b.   The public servant reports electronically to the Commission within 30 days of receipt of the gift or of the date set for disclosure of public records under G.S. 132-6(d), if applicable. The report shall include a description and value of the gift and a description how the gift contributed to the public business of industry recruitment, promotion of international trade, or the promotion of travel and tourism. This report shall be posted to the Commission's public Web site.

c.   A tangible gift, other than food or beverages, not otherwise subject to an exception under this subsection shall be turned over as State property to the Department of Commerce within 30 days of receipt, except as permitted under subsection (f) of this section.

(9)   Gifts of personal property valued at less than one hundred dollars ($100.00) given to a public servant in the commission of the public servant's official duties if the gift is given to the public servant as a personal gift in another country as part of an overseas trade mission, and the giving and receiving of such personal gifts is considered a customary protocol in the other country.

(10)   Gifts given or received as part of a business, civic, religious, fraternal, personal, or commercial relationship provided all of the following conditions are met:

141

a.   The relationship is not related to the public servant's, legislator's, or legislative employee's public service or position.

b.   The gift is made under circumstances that a reasonable person would conclude that the gift was not given to lobby.

(11)   Food and beverages for immediate consumption and related transportation provided all of the following conditions are met:

a.   The food, beverage, or transportation is given by a lobbyist principal and not a lobbyist.

b.   The food, beverage, or transportation is provided during a conference, meeting, or similar event and is available to all attendees of the same class as the recipient.

c.   The recipient of the food, beverage, or transportation is a director, officer, governing board member, employee, or independent contractor of one of the following:

1.   The lobbyist principal giving the food, beverage, or transportation.

2.   A third party that received the funds to purchase the food, beverages, or transportation.

(12)   Food and beverages for immediate consumption at an organized gathering of a person, the State, or a governmental unit to which a public servant is invited to attend for purposes primarily related to the public servant's public service or position, and to which at least 10 individuals, other than the public servant, or the public servant's immediate family, actually attend, or to which all shareholders, employees, board members, officers, members, or subscribers of the person or governmental unit who are located in a specific North Carolina office or county are notified and invited to attend.

(f)   A prohibited gift that would constitute an expense appropriate for reimbursement by the public servant's employing entity if it had been incurred by the public servant personally shall be considered a gift accepted by or donated to the State, provided the public servant has been approved by the public servant's employing entity to accept or receive such things of value on behalf of the State. The fact that the employing entity's reimbursement rate for the type of

142

expense is less than the value of a particular gift shall not render the gift prohibited.

(g)　　A prohibited gift shall be, and a permissible gift may be, promptly declined, returned, paid for at fair market value, or donated to charity or the State.

(h)　　A covered person or legislative employee shall not accept an honorarium from a source other than the employing entity for conducting any activity where any of the following apply:

(1)　　The employing entity reimburses the covered person or legislative employee for travel, subsistence, and registration expenses.

(2)　　The employing entity's work time or resources are used.

(3)　　The activity would be considered official duty or would bear a reasonably close relationship to the covered person's or legislative employee's official duties.

An outside source may reimburse the employing entity for actual expenses incurred by a covered person or legislative employee in conducting an activity within the duties of the covered person or legislative employee, or may pay a fee to the employing entity, in lieu of an honorarium, for the services of the covered person or legislative employee. An honorarium permissible under this subsection shall not be considered a gift for purposes of subsection (c) of this section.

(i)　　Acceptance or solicitation of a gift in compliance with this section without corrupt intent shall not constitute a violation of the statutes related to bribery under G.S. 14-217, 14-218, or 120-86. (2006-201, s. 1; 2007-347, s. 11; 2007-348, ss. 15(b), 35-41(a); 2008-213, ss. 77(a), 78(a), 79-82, 90; 2009-549, s. 17; 2010-169, ss. 15(b), (c), 17(r).)

§ 138A-33. Other compensation.

A public servant or legislative employee shall not solicit or receive personal financial gain, other than that received by the public servant or legislative employee from the State, or with the approval of the employing entity, for acting in the public servant's or legislative employee's official capacity, or for advice or assistance given in the course of carrying out the public servant's or legislative employee's duties. (2006-201, s. 1.)

§ 138A-34. Use of information for private gain.

A public servant or legislative employee shall not use or disclose nonpublic information gained in the course of, or by reason of, the public servant's or legislative employee's official responsibilities in a way that would affect a personal financial interest of the public servant or legislative employee, a member of the public servant's or legislative employee's extended family, or a person or governmental unit with whom or business with which the public servant or legislative employee is associated. A public servant or legislative employee shall not improperly use or improperly disclose any confidential information. (2006-201, s. 1; 2008-213, s. 83.)

§ 138A-35. Other rules of conduct.

(a)   A public servant shall make a due and diligent effort before taking any action, including voting or participating in discussions with other public servants on a board on which the public servant also serves, to determine whether the public servant has a conflict of interest. If the public servant is unable to determine whether or not a conflict of interest may exist, the public servant has a duty to inquire of the Commission as to that conflict.

(b)   A public servant shall continually monitor, evaluate, and manage the public servant's personal, financial, and professional affairs to ensure the absence of conflicts of interest.

(c)   A public servant shall obey all other civil laws, administrative requirements, and criminal statutes governing conduct of State government applicable to appointees and employees. (2006-201, s. 1.)

§ 138A-36. Public servant participation in official actions.

144

(a)   Except as permitted by subsection (d) of this section and under G.S. 138A-38, no public servant acting in that capacity, authorized to perform an official action requiring the exercise of discretion, shall participate in an official action by the employing entity if the public servant knows the public servant or a person with which the public servant is associated may incur a reasonably foreseeable financial benefit from the matter under consideration, which financial benefit would impair the public servant's independence of judgment or from which it could reasonably be inferred that the financial benefit would influence the public servant's participation in the official action.

(b)   A public servant described in subsection (a) of this section shall abstain from taking any verbal or written action in furtherance of the official action. The public servant shall submit in writing to the employing entity the reasons for the abstention. When the employing entity is a board, the abstention shall be recorded in the employing entity's minutes.

(c)   A public servant shall take appropriate steps, under the particular circumstances and considering the type of proceeding involved, to remove himself or herself to the extent necessary, to protect the public interest and comply with this Chapter, from any proceeding in which the public servant's impartiality might reasonably be questioned due to the public servant's familial, personal, or financial relationship with a participant in the proceeding. A participant includes (i) an owner, shareholder, partner, member or manager of a limited liability company, employee, agent, officer, or director of a business, organization, or group involved in the proceeding, or (ii) an organization or group that has petitioned for rule making or has some specific, unique, and substantial interest in the proceeding. Proceedings include quasi-judicial proceedings and quasi-legislative proceedings. A personal relationship includes one in a leadership or policy-making position in a business, organization, or group.

(d)   If a public servant is uncertain about whether the relationship described in subsection (c) of this section justifies removing the public servant from the proceeding under subsection (c) of this section, the public servant shall disclose the relationship to the individual presiding over the proceeding and seek appropriate guidance. The presiding officer, in consultation with legal counsel if necessary, shall then determine the extent to which the public servant will be permitted to participate. If the affected public servant is the individual presiding, then the vice-chair or any other substitute presiding officer shall make the determination. A good-faith determination under this subsection of the allowable degree of participation by a public servant is presumptively valid and only

145

subject to review under G.S. 138A-12 upon a clear and convincing showing of mistake, fraud, abuse of discretion, or willful disregard of this Chapter.

(e)   This section shall not allow participation in an official action prohibited by G.S. 14-234. (2006-201, s. 1; 2007-347, s. 12; 2007-348, s. 42; 2008-213, s. 84(a).)

§ 138A-37. Legislator participation in legislative actions.

(a)   Except as permitted under G.S. 138A-38, no legislator shall participate in a legislative action if the legislator knows the legislator or a person with which the legislator is associated may incur a reasonably foreseeable financial benefit from the action, and if after considering whether the legislator's judgment would be substantially influenced by the financial benefit and considering the need for the legislator's particular contribution, including special knowledge of the subject matter to the effective functioning of the legislature, the legislator concludes that an actual financial benefit does exist which would impair the legislator's independence of judgment.

(a1)   The legislator shall submit in writing to the principal clerk of the house of which the legislator is a member the reasons for the abstention from participation in the legislative matter.

(b)   If the legislator has a material doubt as to whether the legislator should act, the legislator may submit the question for an advisory opinion to the State Ethics Commission in accordance with G.S. 138A-13 or the Legislative Ethics Committee in accordance with G.S. 120-104. (2006-201, s. 1; 2007-347, s. 13; 2008-213, s. 84(b); 2010-169, s. 22(c).)

§ 138A-38. Permitted participation exception.

(a)   Notwithstanding G.S. 138A-36 and G.S. 138A-37, a covered person may participate in an official action or legislative action under any of the following circumstances except as specifically limited:

(1)   The only interest or reasonably foreseeable benefit or detriment that accrues to the covered person, the covered person's extended family, business

146

with which the covered person is associated, or nonprofit corporation or organization with which the covered person is associated as a member of a profession, occupation, or general class is no greater than that which could reasonably be foreseen to accrue to all members of that profession, occupation, or general class.

(2)   When an official or legislative action affects or would affect the covered person's compensation and allowances as a covered person.

(3)   Before the covered person participated in the official or legislative action, the covered person requested and received from the Commission or Committee a written advisory opinion that authorized the participation. In authorizing the participation under this subdivision, the Commission or Committee shall consider the need for the legislator's particular contribution, such as special knowledge of the subject matter, to the effective functioning of the General Assembly.

(4)   Before participating in an official action, a public servant made full written disclosure to the public servant's employing entity which then made a written determination that the interest or benefit would neither impair the public servant's independence of judgment nor influence the public servant's participation in the official action. The employing entity shall file a copy of that written determination with the Commission.

(5)   When action is ministerial only and does not require the exercise of discretion.

(6)   When a public or legislative body records in its minutes that it cannot obtain a quorum in order to take the official or legislative action because the covered person is disqualified from acting under G.S. 138A-36, G.S. 138A-37, or this section, the covered person may be counted for purposes of a quorum, but shall otherwise abstain from taking any further action.

(7)   When a public servant notifies the Commission in writing that the public servant, or someone whom the public servant appoints to act in the public servant's stead, or both, are the only individuals having legal authority to take an official action, and the public servant discloses in writing the circumstances and nature of the conflict of interest.

(b)   This section shall not allow participation in an official action prohibited by G.S. 14-234.

147

(c)   Notwithstanding G.S. 138A-37, if a legislator is employed or retained by, or is an independent contractor of, a governmental unit, and the legislator is the only member of the house elected from the district where that governmental unit is located, then the legislator may take legislative action on behalf of that governmental unit provided the legislator discloses in writing to the principal clerk the nature of the relationship with the governmental unit prior to, or at the time of, taking the legislative action.

(d)   Notwithstanding G.S. 138A-36, service by the president, chief financial officer, chief administrative officer, or voting member of the board of trustees of a community college as an officer, employee, or member of the board of directors of a nonprofit corporation established under G.S. 115D-20(9) to support the community college shall not constitute a conflict of interest under G.S. 138A-36, provided that the majority of the nonprofit corporation's board of directors is not comprised of the president, chief financial officer, and chief administrative officer, or voting members of the board of trustees of the community college which the nonprofit corporation was created to support. (2006-201, s. 1; 2007-347, s. 14; 2008-213, s. 85; 2010-169, s. 22(d).)

§ 138A-39. Disqualification to serve.

(a)   Within 30 days of notice of the Commission's determination that a public servant has a disqualifying conflict of interest, the public servant shall eliminate the interest that constitutes the disqualifying conflict of interest or resign from the public position.

(b)   Failure by a public servant to comply with subsection (a) of this section is a violation of this Chapter for purposes of G.S. 138A-45.

(c)   A decision under this section shall be considered a final decision for contested case purposes under Article 3 of Chapter 150B of the General Statutes.

(d)   As used in this section, a disqualifying conflict of interest is a conflict of interest of such significance that the conflict of interest would prevent a public servant from fulfilling a substantial function or portion of the public servant's public duties. (2006-201, s. 1.)

§ 138A-40. Employment and supervision of members of covered person's or legislative employee's extended family.

A covered person or legislative employee shall not cause the employment, appointment, promotion, transfer, or advancement of an extended family member of the covered person or legislative employee to a State office, or a position to which the covered person or legislative employee supervises or manages, except for positions at the General Assembly as permitted under G.S. 120-32(2). A public servant or legislative employee shall not supervise, manage, or participate in an action relating to the discipline of a member of the public servant's or legislative employee's extended family, except as specifically authorized by the public servant's or legislative employee's employing entity. (2006-201, s. 1; 2007-347, s. 15.)

§ 138A-41. Other ethics standards.

(a)   Nothing in this Chapter shall prevent the Supreme Court, the Committee, the Legislative Services Commission, constitutional officers of the State, heads of principal departments, the Board of Governors of The University of North Carolina, the State Board of Community Colleges, or other boards from adopting additional or supplemental ethics standards applicable to that public agency's operations.

(b)   The Governor, as a constitutional officer of the State, shall have the authority to adopt additional and supplemental ethics standards applicable to any appointee of the Governor to any State board, commission, council, committee, task force, authority, or similar public body, however denominated, created by statute or executive order, whether advisory or nonadvisory in authority. If the Governor adopts such ethics standards, the standards shall be published in the North Carolina Register and made available to each appointee subject to the ethics standards.

(c)   The Governor, as a constitutional officer of the State, shall have the authority to adopt minimum ethics standards applicable to any employee of a State agency. If the Governor adopts such standards, the ethics standards shall be published in the North Carolina Register and made available to each employee subject to the ethics standards. (2006-201, s. 1; 2010-169, s. 14.)

§ 138A-42. Reserved for future codification purposes.

§ 138A-43. Reserved for future codification purposes.

§ 138A-44. Reserved for future codification purposes.

Article 5.

Violation Consequences.

§ 138A-45. Violation consequences.

(a)   Violation of this Chapter by any covered person or legislative employee is grounds for disciplinary action. Except as specifically provided in this Chapter and for perjury under G.S. 138A-12 and G.S. 138A-24, no criminal penalty shall attach for any violation of this Chapter.

(b)   The willful failure of any public servant serving on a board to comply with this Chapter is misfeasance, malfeasance, or nonfeasance. In the event of misfeasance, malfeasance, or nonfeasance, the offending public servant serving on a board is subject to removal from the board of which the public servant is a member. For appointees of the Governor and members of the Council of State, the appointing authority may remove the offending public servant. For appointees of the Speaker of the House of Representatives, the Speaker of the House of Representatives may remove the offending public servant. For appointees of the General Assembly made upon the recommendation of the Speaker of the House of Representatives, the Governor at the recommendation of the Speaker of the House of Representatives may remove the offending public servant. For appointees of the President Pro Tempore of the Senate, the President Pro Tempore of the Senate may remove the offending public servant. For appointees of the General Assembly made upon the recommendation of the President Pro Tempore of the Senate, the Governor at the recommendation of the President Pro Tempore of the Senate may remove the offending public servant. For public servants elected to a board by either the Senate or House of Representatives, the electing house of the General Assembly shall exercise the discretion of whether to remove the offending public servant. For all other appointees, the Commission shall exercise the discretion of whether to remove the offending public servant.

(c)   The willful failure of any public servant serving as a State employee to comply with this Chapter is a violation of a written work order, thereby permitting disciplinary action as allowed by the law, including termination from employment. For employees of State departments headed by a member of the Council of State, the appropriate member of the Council of State shall make all final decisions on the manner in which the offending public servant shall be disciplined. For public servants who are judicial employees, the Chief Justice shall make all final decisions on the matter in which the offending judicial employee shall be disciplined. For legislative employees, the Legislative Services Commission shall make or refer to the hiring authority all final decisions on the matter in which the offending legislative employee shall be disciplined. For public servants appointed or elected for The University of North Carolina or the Community Colleges System, the appointing or electing authority shall make all final decisions on the matter in which the offending public servant shall be disciplined. For any other public servant serving as a State employee, the Governor shall make all final decisions on the manner in which the offending public servant shall be disciplined.

(d)   The willful failure of any constitutional officer of the State to comply with this Chapter is malfeasance in office for purposes of G.S. 123-5.

(e)   The willful failure of a legislator, other than the Lieutenant Governor, to comply with this Chapter is grounds for sanctions under G.S. 120-103.1.

(f)   Nothing in this Chapter affects the power of the State to prosecute any person for any violation of the criminal law.

(g)   The Commission may seek to enjoin violations of G.S. 138A-34. (2006-201, s. 1.)

Chapter 139.

Soil and Water Conservation Districts.

Article 1.

General Provisions.

§ 139-1. Title of Chapter.

This Chapter may be known and cited as the Soil Conservation Districts Law. (1937, c. 393, s. 1.)

§ 139-2. Legislative determinations, and declaration of policy.

(a)   Legislative Determinations. - It is hereby declared, as a matter of legislative determination:

(1)   The Condition. - The farm, forest and grazing lands of the State of North Carolina are among the basic assets of the State and the preservation of these lands is necessary to protect and promote the health, safety, and general welfare of its people; improper land-use practices have caused and have contributed to, and are now causing and contributing to, a progressively more serious erosion of the farm and grazing lands of this State by wind and water; the breaking of natural grass, plant, and forest cover has interfered with the natural factors of soil stabilization, causing loosening of soil and exhaustion of humus, and developing a soil condition that favors erosion; the topsoil is being blown and washed out of fields and pastures; there has been an accelerated washing of sloping fields; these processes of erosion by wind and water speed up with removal of absorptive topsoil, causing exposure of less absorptive and less protective but more erosive subsoil; failure by any land occupier to conserve the soil and control erosion upon his lands causes a washing and blowing of soil and water from his lands onto other lands and makes the conservation of soil and control of erosion on such other lands difficult or impossible.

(2)   The Consequences. - The consequences of such soil erosion in the form of soil-blowing and soil-washing are the silting and sedimentation of stream channels, reservoirs, dams, ditches, and harbors; the loss of fertile soil material in dust storms; the piling up of soil on lower slopes, and its deposit over alluvial plains; the reduction in productivity or outright ruin of rich bottomlands by overwash of poor subsoil material, sand, and gravel swept out of the hills; deterioration of soil and its fertility, deterioration of crops grown thereon, and declining acre yields despite development of scientific processes for increasing such yields; loss of soil and water which causes destruction of food and cover for wildlife; a blowing and washing of soil into streams which silts over spawning beds, and destroys water plants, diminishing the food supply of fish; a diminishing of the underground water reserve, which causes water shortages, intensifies periods of drought, and causes crop failures; an increase in the

152

speed and volume of rainfall runoff, causing severe and increasing floods, which bring suffering, disease, and death; impoverishment of families attempting to farm eroding and eroded lands; damage to roads, highways, railways, farm buildings, and other property from floods and from dust storms; and losses in navigation, hydroelectric power, municipal water supply, drainage developments, farming, and grazing.

(3)   The Appropriate Corrective Methods. - To conserve soil resources and control and prevent soil erosion and prevent floodwater and sediment damages, and further the conservation, utilization, and disposal of water, and the development of water resources it is necessary that land-use practices contributing to soil wastage and soil erosion be discouraged and discontinued, and appropriate soil-conserving land-use practices and works of improvement for flood prevention or the conservation, utilization, and disposal of water and the development of water resources be adopted and carried out. Among the procedures necessary for widespread adoption, are the carrying on of engineering operations such as the construction of terraces, terrace outlets, check-dams, desilting basins, floodwater retarding structures, channel improvements, floodways, dikes, ponds, ditches, and the like; the utilization of strip cropping, lister furrowing, contour cultivating, contour furrowing, farm drainage, land irrigation; seeding and planting of waste, sloping, abandoned, or eroded lands with water-conserving and erosion-preventing plants, trees, and grasses; forestation and reforestation; rotation of crops; soil stabilization with trees, grasses, legumes, and other thick-growing, soil-holding crops; the addition of soil amendments, manurial materials, and fertilizers for the correction of soil deficiencies and to promote increased growth of soil-protecting crops; retardation of runoff by increasing absorption of rainfall; and retirement from cultivation of steep, highly erosive areas and areas now badly gullied or otherwise eroded.

(b)   Declaration of Policy. - It is hereby declared to be the policy of the legislature to provide for the conservation of the soil and soil resources of this State, and for the control and prevention of soil erosion, and for the prevention of floodwater and sediment damages, and for furthering the conservation, utilization, and disposal of water, and the development of water resources and thereby to preserve natural resources, control floods, prevent impairment of dams and reservoirs, assist in maintaining the navigability of rivers and harbors, preserve wildlife, protect the tax base, protect public lands, and protect and promote the health, safety and general welfare of the people of this State. (1937, c. 393, s. 2; 1947, c. 131, s. 1; 1959, c. 781, ss. 2, 3.)

§ 139-3. Definitions.

Wherever used or referred to in this Chapter, unless a different meaning clearly appears from the context:

(1)   "Agency of this State" includes the government of this State and any subdivision, agency, or instrumentality, corporate or otherwise, of the government of the State.

(2)   "A qualified voter" includes any person qualified to vote in elections by the people under the Constitution of this State.

(3)   "Environmental Management Commission" or "State Environmental Management Commission" means the Environmental Management Commission of the State of North Carolina, or the board, body or commission succeeding to its principal functions, or in whom shall be vested by law the powers herein granted to the said Environmental Management Commission.

(4)   "Commission" or "Soil and Water Conservation Commission" means the Soil and Water Conservation Commission created by G.S. 106-840.

(4a)   "Conservation easement" has the same meaning as provided in G.S. 40A-80.

(5)   "District" or "soil and water conservation district" means a governmental subdivision of this State, and a public body corporate and politic, organized in accordance with the provisions of this Chapter, for the purposes, with the powers, and subject to the restrictions hereinafter set forth.

(6)   "Due notice" means notice given by posting the same at the courthouse door and at three other public places in the county, including those where it may be customary to post notices concerning county or municipal affairs generally, not less than 10 days before the date of the event of which notice is being given. At any hearing held pursuant to such a notice at the time and place designated in such a notice, adjournment may be made from time to time without the necessity of renewing such notice for such adjourned dates.

(7)   "Government" or "governmental" includes the government of this State, the government of the United States, and any subdivision, agency, or instrumentality, corporate or otherwise, of either of them.

(8)   The terms "land occupier" or "occupier of land," and "landowner" or "owner of land" include any person, firm or corporation who shall hold title to or shall have contracted to purchase any lands lying within a soil and water conservation district organized under the provisions of this Chapter.

(9)   "Nominating petition" means a petition filed under the provisions of G.S. 139-6 to nominate candidates for the office of supervisor of a soil and water conservation district.

(10)   Repealed by Session Laws 1993, c. 391, s. 1.

(11)   "Petition" means a petition filed under the provisions of Article 1 of this Chapter for the creation of a soil and water conservation district.

(12)   "State" means the State of North Carolina.

(13)   "Supervisor" means one of the members of the governing body of a district, elected or appointed in accordance with the provisions of this Chapter.

(14)   Repealed by Session Laws 1993, c. 391, s. 1.

(15)   "United States" or "agencies of the United States" includes the United States of America, the Soil Conservation Service of the United States Department of Agriculture, and any other agency or instrumentality, corporate or otherwise, of the United States of America.

(16)   Repealed by Session Laws 1993, c. 391, s. 1.

(17)   A "watershed improvement project" means a project of watershed improvement (whether involving flood prevention, drainage improvement, water supply, soil and water conservation, recreation facilities, fish and wildlife habitat, or other related purposes, singly or in combination) which is undertaken:

a.   Repealed by Session Laws 1993, c. 391, s. 1.

b.   By a soil and water conservation district under the provisions of Article 1 of Chapter 139 of the General Statutes or any local act granting similar powers.

c.   By a drainage district under the provisions of Chapter 156 of the General Statutes or any local act granting similar powers.

155

d.   By a county that is carrying out a county watershed improvement program under the provisions of Article 3 of Chapter 139 of the General Statutes or any local act granting similar powers.

e.   By any combination of the foregoing, acting as joint sponsors of a watershed improvement program.

f.   By any watershed, drainage or flood control project planned or carried out by the Soil Conservation Service, Tennessee Valley Authority or the Army Corps of Engineers.

(18)   A "watershed improvement work" means a single feature or facility or portion of a watershed improvement project, such as a water retarding or impoundment structure for one or more authorized watershed purposes or a section of improved stream channel or the land treatment measures associated with a water retarding structure. (1937, c. 393, s. 3; 1947, c. 131, s. 2; 1959, c. 781, s. 4; 1965, c. 582, s. 1; 1967, c. 987, s. 1; 1971, c. 1138, s. 1A; 1973, c. 1262, s. 38; 1993, c. 391, s. 1; 1995, c. 519, s. 5; 2011-145, s. 13.22A(h); 2011-209, s. 1.)

§ 139-3.1: Repealed by Session Laws 1998-217, s. 14(a).

§ 139-4. Powers and duties of Soil and Water Conservation Commission generally.

(a)   through (c) Repealed by Session Laws 1973, c. 1262, s. 38.

(d)   In addition to the duties and powers hereinafter conferred upon the Soil and Water Conservation Commission, it shall have the following duties and powers:

(1)   To offer such assistance as may be appropriate to the supervisors of soil and water conservation districts, organized as provided hereinafter, in the carrying out of any of their powers and programs.

(2)   To keep the supervisors of each of the several districts organized under the provisions of this Chapter informed of the activities and experience of all other districts organized hereunder, and to facilitate an interchange of advice and experience between such districts and cooperation between them.

156

(3)   To coordinate the programs of the several soil and water conservation districts organized hereunder so far as this may be done by advice and consultation.

(4)   To secure the cooperation and assistance of the United States and any of its agencies, and of agencies of this State, in the work of such districts.

(5)   To disseminate information throughout the State concerning the activities and programs of the soil and water conservation districts organized hereunder, and to encourage the formation of such districts in areas where their organization is desirable.

(6)   Upon the filing of a petition signed by all of the district supervisors of any one or more districts requesting a change in the boundary lines of said district or districts, the Commission may change such lines in such manner as in its judgment would best serve the interests of the occupiers of land in the area affected thereby.

(7)   To receive, review and approve or disapprove applications for planning assistance under the provisions of Public Law 566 (83rd Congress, as amended), and recommend priorities on such applications.

(8)   To supervise and review small watershed work plans pursuant to G.S. 139-41.2 and 139-47.

(9)   To create, implement, and supervise the Agriculture Cost Share Program for Nonpoint Source Pollution Control created pursuant to Article 72 of Chapter 106 of the General Statutes, the Community Conservation Assistance Program created pursuant to Article 73 of Chapter 106 of the General Statutes, and the Agricultural Water Resources Assistance Program created pursuant to Article 5 of this Chapter.

(10)   To review and approve or disapprove the application of a district supervisor for a grant under the Agriculture Cost Share Program for Nonpoint Source Pollution Control, the Community Conservation Assistance Program, or the Agricultural Water Resources Assistance Program as provided by G.S. 139-8(b).

(11)   To develop and implement a program for the approval of water quality and animal waste management systems technical specialists.

(12)   To develop and approve best management practices for the Agriculture Cost Share Program for Nonpoint Source Pollution Control and for use in water quality protection and water use efficiency, availability, and storage programs and to adopt rules that establish criteria governing approval of these best management practices.

(e)   A member of the Commission may apply for and receive a grant under the Agriculture Cost Share Program for Nonpoint Source Pollution Control, the Community Conservation Assistance Program, or the Agricultural Water Resources Assistance Program if:

(1)   The member does not vote on the application or attempt to influence the outcome of any action on the application; and

(2)   The application is approved by the Commissioner of Agriculture. (1937, c. 393, s. 4; 1947, c. 131, s. 3; 1953, c. 255; 1957, c. 1374, s. 1; 1959, c. 781, s. 5; 1961, c. 746, s. 2; 1965, c. 582, s. 2; c. 932; 1971, c. 396; 1973, c. 1262, s. 38; 1981, c. 326, s. 1; 1995, c. 519, s. 1; 1997-443, s. 11A.119(a); 2001-284, s. 1; 2006-78, s. 3; 2011-145, ss. 13.23(c), (d), 13.22A(i), (j); 2012-142, s. 11.6(b); 2012-145, s. 4.3.)

§ 139-5. Creation of soil and water conservation districts.

(a)   Any 25 occupiers of land lying within the limits of the territory proposed to be organized into a district may file a petition with the Soil and Water Conservation Commission asking that a soil and water conservation district be organized to function in the territory described in the petition. Such petition shall set forth:

(1)   The proposed name of said district.

(2)   That there is need, in the interest of the public health, safety, and welfare, for a soil and water conservation district to function in the territory described in the petition.

(3)   A description of the territory proposed to be organized as a district, which description shall not be required to be given by metes and bounds or by legal subdivisions, but shall be deemed sufficient if generally accurate.

(4)   A request that the Soil and Water Conservation Commission duly define the boundaries for such districts; that a referendum be held within the territory so defined on the question of the creation of a soil and water conservation district in such territory; and that the Commission determine that such a district be created.

Where more than one petition is filed covering parts of the same territory, the Soil and Water Conservation Commission may consolidate all or any such petitions.

Town or village lots or government-owned or controlled lands may be included within the boundaries of any district. As used in this subsection: The term "government-owned or controlled land" includes land owned or controlled by any governmental agency or subdivision, federal, State or local; and the term "town and village lots" means parcels or tracts on which no agricultural operations are conducted, or (being less than three acres in extent) whose production of agricultural products for home use or for sale during the immediately preceding calendar year was of less than two hundred and fifty dollars ($250.00) in value. This section applies to existing soil and water conservation districts as well as districts that may hereafter be formed. Insofar as it applies to existing districts it is intended to be declaratory of the present boundaries of such districts as defined by other charters.

(b)   Within 30 days after such a petition has been filed with the Soil and Water Conservation Commission, it shall cause due notice to be given of a proposed hearing upon the question of the desirability and necessity, in the interest of the public health, safety, and welfare, of the creation of such districts, upon the question of the appropriate boundaries to be assigned to such district, upon the propriety of the petition and other proceedings taken under this Chapter, and upon all questions relevant to such inquiries. All occupiers of land within the limits of the territory described in the petition, and of lands within any territory considered for addition to such described territory, and all other interested parties, shall have the right to attend such hearings and to be heard. If it shall appear upon the hearing that it may be desirable to include within the proposed district territory outside the area within which due notice of the hearing has been given, the hearing shall be adjourned and due notice of further hearing shall be given throughout the entire area considered for the inclusion of the district, and such further hearing held. After such hearing, if the Commission shall determine, upon the facts presented at such hearing and upon such other relevant facts and information as may be available, that there is need, in the interest of the public health, safety and welfare, for a soil and water

159

conservation district to function in the territory considered at the hearing, it shall make and record such determination, and shall define, by metes and bounds or by legal subdivisions, the boundaries of such district. In making such determination and in defining such boundaries, the Commission shall give due weight and consideration to the topography or the area considered and of the state and composition of soils therein, the distribution of erosion, the prevailing land-use practices, the desirability and necessity of including within the boundaries the particular lands under consideration and the benefits such lands may receive from being included within such boundaries, the relation of the proposed area to existing watersheds and agricultural regions, and to other soil and water conservation districts already organized or proposed for organization under the provisions of this Chapter, and such other physical, geographical and economic factors as are relevant, having due regard to the legislative determination set forth in G.S. 139-2. The territory to be included within such boundaries need not be contiguous. If the Commission shall determine after such hearing after due consideration of the said relevant facts, that there is no need for a soil and water conservation district to function in the territory considered at the hearing, it shall make and record such determination and shall deny the petition. After six months shall have expired from the date of the denial of any such petition, subsequent petitions covering the same or substantially the same territory may be filed as aforesaid and new hearings held and determinations made thereon.

(c)   After the Commission has made and recorded a determination that there is need, in the interest of the public health, safety and welfare for the organization of a district in a particular territory and has defined the boundaries thereof, it shall consider the question whether the operation of a district within such boundaries with the powers conferred upon soil and water conservation districts in this Chapter is administratively practicable and feasible. To assist the Commission in the determination of such administrative practicability and feasibility, it shall be the duty of the Commission, within a reasonable time after entry of the finding that there is need for the organization of the proposed district and the determination of the boundaries thereof, to hold a referendum within the proposed district upon the proposition of the creation of the district, and to cause due notice of such referendum to be given. The question shall be submitted by ballots upon which the words "For creation of a soil and water conservation district of the lands below described and lying in the county(ies) of ____, ____ and ____." and "Against creation of a soil and water conservation district of the lands below described and lying in the county(ies) of _____ and _____." shall appear with a square before each proposition and a direction to insert an X mark in the square before one or the other of said propositions as the voter may

160

favor or oppose creation of such district. The ballot shall set forth the boundaries of such proposed district as determined by the Commission. All occupiers of land lying within the boundaries of the territory, as determined by the Soil and Water Conservation Commission, shall be eligible to vote in such referendum. Only such land occupiers shall be eligible to vote.

(d)   The Department of Agriculture and Consumer Services shall pay all expenses for the issuance of such notices and the conduct of such hearings and referenda, and shall supervise the conduct of such hearings and referenda. It shall issue appropriate regulations governing the conduct of such hearings and referenda, and providing for the registration prior to the date of the referendum of all eligible voters, or prescribing some other appropriate procedure for the determination of those eligible as voters in such referendum. No informality in the conduct of such referendum or in any matters relating thereto shall invalidate said referendum or the result thereof if notice thereof shall have been given substantially as herein provided and said referendum shall have been fairly conducted.

(e)   The Department of Agriculture and Consumer Services shall publish the results of such referendum and shall thereafter consider and determine whether the operation of the district within the defined boundaries is administratively practicable and feasible. If the Commission shall determine that the operation of such district is not administratively practicable and feasible, it shall record such determination and deny the petition. If the Commission shall determine that the operation of such district is administratively practicable and feasible, it shall record such in the manner hereinafter provided. In making such determination the Commission shall give due regard and weight to the attitudes of the occupiers of lands lying within the defined boundaries, the number of land occupiers eligible to vote in such referendum who shall have voted, the proportion of the votes cast in such referendum in favor of the creation of the district to the total number of votes cast, the approximate wealth and income of the land occupiers of the proposed district, the probable expense of carrying on erosion control operations within such district, and such other economic and social factors as may be relevant to such determination, having due regard to the legislative determination set forth in G.S. 139-2: Provided, however, that the Commission shall not have authority to determine that the operations of the proposed district within the defined boundaries is administratively practicable and feasible unless at least a majority of the votes cast in the referendum upon the proposition of creation of the district shall have been cast in favor of the creation of such district.

(f)   If the Commission shall determine that the operation of the proposed district within the defined boundaries is administratively practicable and feasible, it shall appoint two temporary supervisors to act as the governing body of the district, who shall serve until supervisors are elected or appointed and qualify as provided in G.S. 139-6 and 139-7. Such district shall be a governmental subdivision of this State and a public body corporate and politic, upon the taking of the following proceedings:

The two appointed temporary supervisors shall present to the Secretary of State an application signed by them which shall set forth (and such application need contain no detail other than the mere recitals):

(1)   That a petition for the creation of the district was filed with the Soil and Water Conservation Commission pursuant to the provisions of this Chapter and that the proceedings specified in this Chapter were taken pursuant to such petition; that the application is being filed in order to complete the organization of the district as a governmental subdivision and public body, corporate and politic under this Chapter; and that the Commission has appointed them as supervisors;

(2)   The name and official residence of each of the temporary supervisors, together with a certified copy of the appointment evidencing their right to office;

(3)   The name which is proposed for the district; and

(4)   The location of the principal office of the supervisors of the district.

The application shall be subscribed and sworn to by each of the said temporary supervisors before an officer authorized by the laws of this State to take and certify oaths, who shall certify upon the application that he personally knows the temporary supervisors and knows them to be the officers as affirmed in the application, and that each has subscribed thereto in the officer's presence. The application shall be accompanied by a statement by the Soil and Water Conservation Commission, which shall certify (and such statement need contain no detail other than the mere recitals) that a petition was filed, notice issued, and hearing held as aforesaid, that the Commission did duly determine that there is need, in the interest of the public health, safety and welfare, for a soil and water conservation district to function in the proposed territory and did define the boundaries thereof; that notice was given and a referendum held on the question of the creation of such district, and that the result of such referendum showed a majority of the votes cast in such referendum to be in favor of the creation of the district; that thereafter the Commission did duly determine that the operation of the proposed district is administratively practicable and feasible. The said statement shall set forth the boundaries of the district as they have been defined by the Commission.

The Secretary of State shall examine the application and statement and, if he finds that the name proposed for the district is not identical with that of any other soil and water conservation district of this State or so nearly similar as to lead to confusion or uncertainty, he shall receive and file them and shall record them in an appropriate book of record in his office. If the Secretary of State shall find that the name proposed for the district is identical with that of any other soil and water conservation district of this State, or so nearly similar as to lead to confusion and uncertainty, he shall certify such fact to the Soil and Water Conservation Commission, which shall thereupon submit to the Secretary of State a new name for the said district, which shall not be subject to such defects. Upon receipt of such new name, free of such defects, the Secretary of State shall record the application and statement, with the name so modified, in an appropriate book of record in his office. When the application and statement have been made, filed and recorded, as herein provided, the district shall constitute a governmental subdivision of this State and a public body corporate and politic. The Secretary of State shall make and issue to the said supervisors a certificate, under the seal of the State, of the due organization of the said district, and shall record such certificate with the application and statement. The boundaries of such district shall include the territory as determined by the Soil and Water Conservation Commission as aforesaid, but in no event shall they include any area included within the boundaries of another soil and water conservation district organized under the provisions of this Chapter.

(g)   After six months shall have expired from the date of entry of a determination by the Soil and Water Conservation Commission that operation of a proposed district is not administratively practicable and feasible, and denial of a petition pursuant to such determination, subsequent petitions may be filed as aforesaid, and action taken thereon in accordance with the provisions of this Chapter.

(h)   Petitions for including additional territory within an existing district may be filed with the Soil and Water Conservation Commission, and the proceedings herein provided for in the case of petitions to organize a district shall be observed in the case of petitions for such inclusions. The Commission shall prescribe the form for such petitions, which shall be as nearly as may be in the form prescribed in this Chapter for petitions to organize a district. Where the total number of land occupiers in the area proposed for inclusion shall be less than 25, the petition may be filed when signed by two thirds of the occupiers of such area, and in such case no referendum need be held. In referenda petitions for such inclusion, all occupiers of land lying within the proposed additional area shall be eligible to vote.

(i)   In any suit, action or proceeding involving the validity or enforcement of, or relating to any contract, proceeding or action of the district, the district shall be deemed to have been established in accordance with the provisions of this Chapter upon proof of the issuance of the aforesaid certificate by the Secretary of State. A copy of such certificate duly certified by the Secretary of State shall be admissible in evidence in any such suit, action, or proceeding and shall be proof of the filing and contents thereof. (1937, c. 393, s. 5; 1947, c. 131, s. 4; 1959, c. 781, s. 6; 1965, c. 582, s. 3; 1973, c. 1262, s. 38; 1977, c. 771, s. 4; 1989, c. 727, s. 218(91); 1997-443, s. 11A.119(a); 2011-145, s. 13.22A(k), (l).)

§ 139-6. District board of supervisors - elective members; certain duties.

After the issuance of the certificate of organization of the soil and water conservation district by the Secretary of State, an election shall be held in each county of the district to elect the members of the soil and water conservation district board of supervisors as herein provided.

The district board of supervisors shall consist of three elective members to be elected in each county of the district, and that number of appointive members as provided in G.S. 139-7. Upon the creation of a district, the first election of the members shall be held at the next succeeding election for county officers.

All elections for members of the district board of supervisors shall be held at the same time as the regular election for county officers beginning in November 1974. The election shall be nonpartisan and no primary election shall be held. The election shall be held and conducted by the county board of elections.

Candidates shall file their notice of candidacy on forms prescribed by the county board of elections. The notice of candidacy must be filed no earlier than noon on the second Monday in June and no later than noon on the first Friday in July preceding the election. The candidate shall pay a filing fee of five dollars ($5.00) at the time of filing the notice of candidacy.

Beginning with the election to be held in November 1974, the two candidates receiving the highest number of votes shall be elected for a term of four years, and the candidate receiving the next highest number of votes shall be elected for a term of two years; thereafter, as their terms expire, their successors shall be elected for terms of four years. If the position of district supervisor is not filled by failure to elect, then the office shall be deemed vacant upon the expiration of the term of the incumbent, and the office shall be filled as provided in G.S. 139-7.

The persons elected in 1974 and thereafter shall take office on the first Monday in December following their election.

The terms of the present members of the soil and water conservation districts, both elective and appointive members, are hereby extended to or terminated on the first Monday in December 1974.

All qualified voters of the district shall be eligible to vote in the election. Except as provided in this Chapter, the election shall be held in accordance with the applicable provisions of Articles 23 and 24 of Chapter 163 of the General Statutes.

The district board of supervisors, after the appointment of the appointive members has been made, shall select from its members a chairman, a vice-chairman and a secretary. It shall be the duty of the district board of supervisors to perform those powers, duties, and authority conferred upon supervisors under this Chapter; to develop annual county and district goals and plans for soil conservation work therein; to request agencies, whose duties are such as to render assistance in soil and water conservation, to set forth in writing what assistance they may have available in the county and district. (1937, c. 393, s. 6; 1947, c. 131, s. 5; 1949, c. 268, s. 1; 1957, c. 1374, s. 2; 1963, c. 815; 1973, c. 502, s. 1; 1975, c. 798, s. 4; 1979, c. 519, s. 1; 1981, c. 560, s. 3; 2002-159, s. 55(h).)

§ 139-7. District board of supervisors - appointive members; organization of board; certain powers and duties.

The governing body of a soil and water conservation district shall consist of the three elective supervisors from the county or counties in the district, together with the appointive members appointed by the Soil and Water Conservation

Commission pursuant to this section, and shall be known as the district board of supervisors. When a district is composed of less than four counties, the board of supervisors of each county shall on or before October 31, 1978, and on or before October 31 as the terms of the appointive supervisors expire, recommend in writing two persons from the district to the Commission to be appointed to serve with the elective supervisors. If the names are not submitted to the Commission as required, the office shall be deemed vacant on the date the term is set to expire and the Commission shall appoint two persons of the district to the district board of supervisors to serve with the elected supervisors. The Commission shall make its appointments prior to or at the November meeting of the Commission. Appointive supervisors shall take office on the first Monday in December following their appointment. Such appointive supervisors shall serve for a term of four years, and thereafter, as their terms expire, their successors shall serve for a term of four years. The terms of office of all appointive supervisors who have heretofore been lawfully appointed for terms the final year of which presently extends beyond the first Monday in December are hereby terminated on the first Monday in December of the final year of appointment. Vacancies for any reason in the appointive supervisors shall be filled for the unexpired term by the appointment of a person by the Commission from the district in which the vacancy occurs. Vacancies for any reason in the elected supervisors shall be filled for the unexpired term by appointment by the Commission of a person from the county in the district in which the vacancy occurs.

In those districts composed of four or more counties, the Commission may, but is not required to, appoint two persons from the district without recommendation from the board of supervisors, to serve as district supervisors along with the elected members of the board of supervisors. Such appointments shall be made at the same time other appointments are made under this section, and the persons appointed shall serve for a term of four years.

The supervisors shall designate a chairman and may, from time to time, change such designation. A simple majority of the board shall constitute a quorum for the purpose of transacting the business of the board, and approval by a majority of those present shall be adequate for a determination of any matter before the board, provided at least a quorum is present. Supervisors of soil and water conservation districts shall be compensated for their services at the per diem rate and allowed travel, subsistence and other expenses, as provided for State boards, commissions and committees generally, under the provisions of G.S. 138-5; provided, that when per diem compensation and travel, subsistence, or other expense is claimed by any supervisor for services performed outside the

166

district for which such supervisor ordinarily may be appointed or elected to serve, the same may not be paid unless prior written approval is obtained from the Department of Agriculture and Consumer Services.

The supervisors may employ a secretary, technical experts, whose qualifications shall be approved by the Department, and such other employees as they may require, and shall determine their qualifications, duties and compensation. The supervisors may call upon the Attorney General of the State for such legal services as they may require. The supervisors may delegate to their chairman, to one or more supervisors, or to one or more agents, or employees such powers and duties as they may deem proper. The supervisors shall furnish to the Soil and Water Conservation Commission, upon request, copies of such ordinances, rules, regulations, orders, contracts, forms, and other documents as they shall adopt or employ, and such other information concerning their activities as it may require in the performance of its duties under this Chapter.

The supervisors shall provide for the execution of surety bonds for all employees and officers who shall be entrusted with funds or property; shall provide for the keeping of a full and accurate record of all proceedings and of all resolutions, regulations, and orders issued or adopted; and shall provide for an annual audit of the accounts of receipts and disbursements. In any given year, if the supervisors provide for an internal audit, and the supervisor serving as chairman certifies, under oath, that this internal audit is a true and accurate reflection of the accounts of receipts and disbursements, then the supervisors shall not be required, notwithstanding the provisions of G.S. 159-34, to provide for an audit of the accounts of receipts and disbursements by a certified public accountant or by an accountant certified by the Local Government Commission. Any supervisor may be removed by the Soil and Water Conservation Commission upon notice and hearing, for neglect of duty, incompetence or malfeasance in office, but for no other reason.

The supervisors may invite the legislative body of any municipality or county located near the territory comprised within the district to designate a representative to advise and consult with the supervisors of the district on all questions of program and policy which may affect the property, water supply, or other interests of such municipality or county. (1937, c. 393, s. 7; 1943, c. 481; 1947, c. 31, ss. 6, 7; 1957, c. 1374, s. 3; 1963, c. 563; 1973, c. 502, s. 2; c. 1262, s. 38; 1977, c. 387; c. 771, s. 4; 1979, c. 519, s. 2; 1981, c. 330; 1989, c. 66, s. 1; c. 727, s. 218(92); 1991, c. 689, s. 166; 1997-443, s. 11A.119(a); 2011-145, s. 13.22A(m).)

§ 139-7.1. Special revenue funds for the maintenance of conservation easements.

(a)   Establishing Fund. - The governing body of a soil and water conservation district may establish and maintain a special revenue fund for the purpose of maintaining conservation easements, including maintenance activities such as travel to and observation of easement property, remote monitoring of easement property, and education and ongoing communication with landowners about their easement responsibilities. To establish a special revenue fund under this section, the governing body of a soil and water conservation district shall adopt a resolution or ordinance that includes all of the following provisions:

(1)   The specific purposes of maintaining conservation easements for which the special revenue fund is created.

(2)   The approximate periods of time during which the moneys are to be accumulated for each purpose specified under subdivision (1) of this subsection.

(3)   The approximate amounts to be accumulated for each purpose specified under subdivision (1) of this subsection.

(4)   The sources from which moneys will be derived for each purpose specified under subdivision (1) of this subsection.

(b)   Changes Authorized. - The resolution or ordinance that establishes a special revenue fund under subsection (a) of this section may be amended from time to time in the same manner in which it was adopted. Such amendments may authorize the use of moneys in the special revenue fund for conservation easement maintenance purposes that are not previously provided for by resolution or ordinance.

(c)   Funding. - Any special revenue fund established under this section shall consist of funds received by appropriation from any other fund consistent with the limitations under G.S. 159-13(b); grant moneys; donations; direct appropriations from the State or any of its agencies or political subdivisions; or any other unrestricted funds appropriated to a soil and water conservation district from any source. When the conservation easement maintenance fund receives moneys or investment securities, the use of which is restricted by law, the identity of such moneys or investment securities shall be maintained by appropriate accounting entries.

(d)   Investment of Fund. - All or any part of the cash balances of a special revenue fund established under this section may be deposited at interest or invested as provided by G.S. 159-30.

(e)   Fund Withdrawals When District Adopts Its Own Budget Ordinance. - Withdrawals from a special revenue fund established under this section may be authorized by resolution or ordinance of the governing body of the soil and water conservation district. No withdrawal may be authorized unless it is for a purpose that is specified in the resolution or ordinance under subsection (a) of this section or in a resolution or ordinance under subsection (b) of this section. The resolution or ordinance to authorize a withdrawal under this subsection shall authorize an appropriation from the special revenue fund to one of the funds maintained pursuant to G.S. 159-13(a); however, no withdrawal may be authorized that would result in an appropriation for conservation easement maintenance purposes for which an adequate balance of eligible moneys or investment securities is not available in the special revenue fund at the time the resolution or ordinance under this subsection is adopted.

(f)   Fund Withdrawals When Other Body Adopts District's Budget Ordinance. - If a soil and water conservation district's budget ordinance is subject to adoption by another governing body, then the governing body that is responsible for adopting the soil and water district's budget ordinance must approve the appropriation of moneys from the special revenue fund established under this section to one of the funds maintained pursuant to G.S. 159-13(a), subject to the other limitations provided in subsection (e) of this section. (2011-209, s. 2.)

§ 139-8. Powers of districts and supervisors.

(a)   A soil and water conservation district organized under the provisions of this Article shall constitute a governmental subdivision of this State, and a public body corporate and politic, exercising public powers, and such district, and the supervisors thereof, shall have the following powers in addition to others granted in other sections of this Chapter:

(1)   To conduct surveys and investigations relating to the character of soil erosion and floodwater and sediment damages, and to the conservation, utilization, and disposal of water, the development of water resources, and the preventive and control measures and works of improvement needed, to publish

the results of such surveys and investigations, and to disseminate information concerning such preventive and control measures and works of improvement.

(2)   To carry out preventive and control measures and works of improvement for flood prevention or the conservation, utilization, and disposal of water and development of water resources within the district, including, but not limited to, engineering operations, methods of cultivation, the growing of vegetation, changes in use of land, and the measures listed in subsection (a), subdivision (3) of G.S. 139-2, on lands owned or controlled by this State or any of its agencies, with the cooperation of the agency administering and having jurisdiction thereof, and on any other lands within the district upon obtaining the consent of the occupiers of such lands or the necessary rights or interest in such lands.

(3)   To cooperate, or enter into agreements with, and within the limits or appropriations duly made available to it by law, to furnish financial or other aid to, any agency, governmental or otherwise, or any occupiers of land within the district, in the carrying on of erosion control and prevention operations and works of improvement for flood prevention or the conservation, utilization, and disposal of water and development of water resources within the district, subject to such conditions as the supervisors may deem necessary to advance the purposes of this Chapter.

(4)   To obtain options upon and to acquire by purchase, exchange, lease, gift, grant, devise, or otherwise, any property, real or personal, or rights or interests therein; to maintain, administer, and improve any properties acquired, to receive income from such properties and to expend such income in carrying out the purposes and provisions of this Chapter; and to sell, lease, or otherwise dispose of its property or interests therein in furtherance of the purposes and the provisions of this Chapter.

(5)   To make available, on such terms as it shall prescribe, to land occupiers within the district, agricultural and engineering machinery and equipment, fertilizer, seeds and seedlings, and such other material or equipment as will assist such land occupiers to carry on operations upon their lands for the conservation of soil resources and for the prevention and control of soil erosion and for flood prevention or the conservation, development, utilization, and disposal of water and the development of water resources.

(6)   To construct, improve, operate, and maintain such structures, works and projects as may be necessary or convenient for the performance of any of the

170

operations authorized in this Chapter, including watershed improvement structures, works, and projects as well as any other structures, works, and projects which the district is authorized to undertake.

(7)   To develop comprehensive plans for the conservation of soil resources and for the control and prevention of soil erosion and for flood prevention or the conservation, utilization and disposal of water and development of water resources, within the district, which plans shall specify in such detail as may be possible, the acts, procedures, performances, and avoidances which are necessary or desirable for the effectuation of such plans, including the specification of engineering operations, methods of cultivation, the growing of vegetation, cropping programs, tillage practices, and changes in use of land; and to bring such plans and information to the attention of occupiers of lands within the district.

(8)   To act as agent for the United States, or any of its agencies, in connection with the acquisition, construction, operation, or administration of any project for soil conservation, erosion control, erosion prevention, flood prevention, or for the conservation, utilization, and disposal of water and development of water resources, or combinations thereof, within its boundaries; to accept donations, gifts, and contributions in money, services, materials, or otherwise, from the United States or any of its agencies, or from this State or any of its agencies, and to use or expend such moneys, services, materials, or other contributions in carrying on its operations, except that all forest tree seedlings shall be obtained insofar as available from the Department of Environment and Natural Resources in cooperation with the United States Department of Agriculture.

(9)   To sue and be sued in the name of the district; to have a seal, which seal shall be judicially noticed; to have perpetual succession unless terminated as hereinafter provided; to make and execute contracts and other instruments necessary or convenient to the exercise of its powers; to make, and from time to time amend and repeal, rules and regulations not inconsistent with this Chapter, to carry into effect its purposes and powers.

(10)   As a condition to the extending of any benefits under this Chapter to, or the performance of work upon, any lands not owned or controlled by this State or any of its agencies, the supervisors may require contributions in money, services, materials, or otherwise to any operations conferring such benefits, and may require land occupiers to enter into and perform such agreement or

covenants as to the permanent use of such lands as will tend to prevent or control erosion and prevent floodwater and sediment damages therein.

(11)   No provision with respect to the acquisition, operation, or disposition of property by other public bodies shall be applicable to a district organized hereunder unless the legislature shall specifically so state.

(12)   Nothing contained in this Chapter shall authorize or allow the withdrawal of water from a watershed or stream except to the extent and degree now permissible under the existing common and statute law of this State; nor to change or modify such existing common or statute law with respect to the relative rights of riparian owners or others concerning the use or disposal of water in the streams of this State; nor to authorize a district, its officers or governing body or any other person, firm, corporation (public or private), body politic or governmental agency to utilize or dispose of water except in the manner and to the extent permitted by the existing common and statute law of this State.

(13)   To assist the Commission in the implementation and supervision of the Agriculture Cost Share Program for Nonpoint Source Pollution Control created pursuant to G.S. 106-850 and to assist in the implementation and supervision of any other program intended to protect water quality or quantity administered by the Department of Agriculture and Consumer Services by providing technical assistance, allocating available grant monies, and providing any other assistance that may be required or authorized by any provision of federal or State law.

(b)   A district supervisor may apply for and receive a grant under the Agriculture Cost Share Program for Nonpoint Source Pollution Control created pursuant to Article 72 of Chapter 106 of the General Statutes, the Community Conservation Assistance Program created pursuant to Article 73 of Chapter 106 of the General Statutes, or the Agricultural Water Resources Assistance Program created pursuant to Article 5 of this Chapter if:

1.   The district supervisor does not vote on the application or attempt to influence the outcome of any action on the application; and

2.   The application is approved by the Commission. (1937, c. 398, s. 8; 1939, c. 341; 1959, c. 781, s. 7; 1969, c. 711, s. 1; 1973, c. 1262, s. 38; 1977, c. 771, s. 4; 1989, c. 727, s. 218(93); 1995, c. 519, ss. 2, 3; 1997-443, s. 11A.119(a); 2006-78, s. 4; 2011-145, ss. 13.22A(n), 13.23(e); 2011-284, s. 91.)

§ 139-8.1. Purposes of Chapter.

(a)   It is hereby declared that the provisions of General Statutes Chapter 139 were intended to authorize the maintenance of watershed improvement works and projects, as well as watershed improvement structures. All expenditures heretofore incurred by any local watershed sponsor for any such maintenance of works, projects, or structures are hereby validated and confirmed.

(b)   The proceeds of any tax heretofore approved by the voters of a county for a county watershed improvement program, or authorized by special or local act for a county watershed improvement program, may be expended for such maintenance of works and projects, as well as structures, if the board of county commissioners or other watershed governing body after a public hearing determines that the proceeds should be so expended. Notice of such hearing shall be published as provided for notices under Article 2 of General Statutes Chapter 139.

(c)   The proceeds of any tax hereafter approved by the voters of a county for a watershed improvement program may be expended for such maintenance of works and projects, as well as structures, with or without the holding of a public hearing as designated by subsection (b) of this section, even though any election procedures preliminary to the vote approving the tax may have been initiated prior to the ratification of this section.

(d)   No action based on the alleged invalidity of the expenditures herein confirmed or of the use of tax proceeds herein authorized shall lie after January 1, 1970, to enjoin or contest any such expenditure or any such use of tax proceeds. (1969, c. 711, s. 1.)

§ 139-9. Adoption of land-use regulations.

The supervisors of any district shall have authority to formulate regulations governing the use of lands within the district in the interest of conserving the soil and soil resources and preventing and controlling soil erosion. The supervisors may conduct such public meetings and public hearings upon tentative regulations as may be necessary to assist them in this work. The supervisors shall not have authority to enact such land-use regulations into law until after they shall have caused due notice to be given of their intention to conduct a referendum for submission of such regulations to the occupiers of lands lying

173

within the boundaries of the district for their indication of approval or disapproval of such proposed regulations, and until after the supervisors have considered the result of such referendum. The proposed regulations shall be embodied in a proposed ordinance. Copies of such proposed ordinance shall be available for the inspection of all eligible voters during the period between publication of such notice and the date of the referendum. The notices of the referendum shall recite the contents of such proposed ordinance, or shall state where copies of such proposed ordinance may be examined. The question shall be submitted by ballots, upon which the words "For approval of proposed ordinance number_____, prescribing land-use regulations for conservation of soil and prevention of erosion" and "Against approval of proposed ordinance number_____, prescribing land-use regulations for conservation of soil and prevention of erosion" shall appear, with a square before each proposition and a direction to insert an X mark in the square before one or the other of said propositions as the voter may favor or oppose approval of such proposed ordinance. The supervisors shall supervise such referendum, shall prescribe appropriate regulations, governing the conduct thereof, and shall publish the result thereof. All occupiers of lands within the district shall be eligible to vote in such referendum. Only such land occupiers shall be eligible to vote. No informalities in the conduct of such referendum or in any matters relating thereto shall invalidate said referendum or the result thereof if notice thereof shall have been given substantially as herein provided and said referendum shall have been fairly conducted.

The supervisors shall not have authority to enact such proposed ordinance into law unless at least two thirds of the votes cast in such referendum shall have been cast for approval of the said proposed ordinance. The approval of the proposed ordinance by a two thirds of the votes cast in such referendum shall not be deemed to require the supervisors to enact such proposed ordinance into law. Land-use regulations prescribed in ordinances adopted pursuant to the provisions of this section by the supervisors of any district shall have the force and effect of law in the said district and shall be binding and obligatory upon all occupiers of lands within such district.

Any occupier of land within such district may at any time file a petition with the supervisors asking that any or all of land-use regulations prescribed in any ordinance adopted by the supervisors under the provisions of this section shall be amended, supplemented, or repealed. Land-use regulations prescribed in any ordinance adopted pursuant to the provisions of this section shall not be amended, supplemented, or repealed except in accordance with the procedure prescribed in this section for adoption of land-use regulations. Referenda on

174

adoption, amendment, supplementation, or repeal of land-use regulations shall not be held more often than once in six months.

The regulations to be adopted by the supervisors under the provisions of this section may include:

(1)   Provisions requiring the carrying out of necessary engineering operations, including the construction of terraces, terrace outlets, check dams, dikes, ponds, ditches, and other necessary structures.

(2)   Provisions requiring observance of particular methods of cultivation including contour cultivating, contour furrowing, lister furrowing, sowing, planting, strip cropping, seeding, and planting of lands to water-conserving and erosion-preventing plants, trees and grasses, forestation, and reforestation.

(3)   Specifications of cropping programs and tillage practices to be observed.

(4)   Provisions requiring the retirement from cultivation of highly erosive areas or of areas on which erosion may not be adequately controlled if cultivation is carried on.

(5)   Provisions for such other means, measures, operations, and programs as may assist conservation of soil resources and prevent or control soil erosion in the district, having due regard to the legislative findings set forth in G.S. 139-2.

The regulations shall be uniform, throughout the territory comprised within the district except that the supervisors may classify the lands within the district with reference to such factors as soil type, degree of slope, degree of erosion threatened or existing, cropping and tillage practices in use, and other relevant factors, and may provide regulations varying with the type or class of land affected, but uniform as to all lands within each class or type. Copies of land-use regulations adopted under the provisions of this section shall be printed and made available to all occupiers of lands lying within the district. (1937, c. 393, s. 9.)

§ 139-10. Enforcement of land-use regulations.

The supervisors shall have authority to go upon any lands within the district to determine whether land-use regulations adopted under the provisions of G.S. 139-9 are being observed. The supervisors are further authorized to provide by ordinance that any land occupier who shall sustain damages from any violation of such regulations by any other land occupier may recover damages at law from such other land occupier for such violation. (1937, c. 393, s. 10.)

§ 139-11. Nonobservance of prescribed regulations; performance of work under the regulations by the supervisors.

Where the supervisors of any district shall find that any of the provisions of land-use regulations prescribed in an ordinance adopted in accordance with the provisions of G.S. 139-9 are not being observed on particular lands, and that such nonobservance tends to increase erosion on such lands and its interfering with the prevention of control of erosion on other lands within the district, the supervisors may present to the superior court for the county or counties within which the lands of the defendant lie a petition, duly verified, setting forth the adoption of the ordinance prescribing land-use regulations, the failure of the defendant land occupier to observe such regulations, and to perform particular work, operations, or avoidances as required thereby, and that such nonobservance tends to increase erosion on such lands and is interfering with the prevention or control of erosion on other lands within the district, and praying the court to require the defendant to perform the work, operations, or avoidances within a reasonable time and to order that if the defendant shall fail so to perform, the supervisors may go on the land, perform the work or other operations or otherwise bring the condition of such lands into conformity with the requirements of such regulations, and recover the cost and expenses thereof, with interest, from the occupier of such land. Upon the presentation of such petition, the court shall cause process to be issued against the defendant, and shall hear the case. If it appear to the court that testimony is necessary for the proper disposition of the matter, it may take evidence, or appoint a referee to take such evidence as it may direct and report the same to the court with his findings of fact and conclusions of law, which shall constitute a part of the proceedings upon which the determination of the court shall be made. The court may dismiss the petition, or it may require the defendant to perform the work, operations, or avoidances, and may provide that upon the failure of the defendant to initiate such performance within the time specified in the order of the court, and to prosecute the same to completion with reasonable diligence, the supervisors may enter upon the lands involved and perform the work or

176

operations or otherwise bring the condition of such lands into conformity with the requirements of the regulations and recover the costs and expenses thereof, with interest at the rate of five per centum (5%) per annum, from the occupier of such lands.

The court shall retain jurisdiction of the case until after the work has been completed. Upon completion of such work pursuant to such order of the court the supervisors may file a petition with the court, a copy of which shall be served upon the defendant in the case, stating the costs and expenses sustained by them in the performance of the work and praying judgment therefor with interest. The court shall have jurisdiction to enter judgment for the amount of such costs and expenses, with interest at the rate of five per centum (5%) per annum until paid, together with the costs of suit, including a reasonable attorney's fee to be fixed by the court. This judgment, when filed in accordance with the provisions of G.S. 1-234, shall constitute a lien upon such lands. (1937, c. 393, s. 11.)

§ 139-12. Cooperation between districts.

The supervisors of any two or more districts organized under the provisions of this Chapter may cooperate with one another in the exercise of any or all powers conferred in this Chapter. (1937, c. 393, s. 12.)

§ 139-13. Discontinuance of districts.

At any time after five years after the organization of a district under the provisions of this Chapter, any 25 occupiers of land lying within the boundaries of such districts may file a petition with the Soil and Water Conservation Commission praying that the operations of the district be terminated and the existence of the district discontinued. The Commission may conduct such public meetings and public hearings upon such petition as may be necessary to assist it in the consideration thereof. Within 60 days after such a petition has been received by the Commission it shall give due notice of the holding of a referendum, and shall supervise such referendum, and issue appropriate regulations governing the conduct thereof, the question to be submitted by ballots upon which the words "For terminating the existence of the _____ (name of the soil and water conservation district to be here inserted)" and "Against terminating the existence of the _____ (name of the soil and water

177

conservation district to be here inserted)" shall appear with a square before each proposition and a direction to insert an X mark in the square before one or the other of said propositions as the voter may favor or oppose discontinuance of such district. All occupiers of lands lying within the boundaries of the district shall be eligible to vote in such referendum. Only such land occupiers shall be eligible to vote. No informalities in the conduct of such referendum or in any matters relating thereto shall invalidate said referendum or the result thereof if notice thereof shall have been given substantially as herein provided and said referendum shall have been fairly conducted.

The Department of Agriculture and Consumer Services shall publish the result of such referendum and shall thereafter consider and determine whether the continued operation of the district within the defined boundaries is administratively practicable and feasible. If the Commission shall determine that the continued operation of such district is administratively practicable and feasible, it shall record such determination and deny the petition. If the Commission shall determine that the continued operation of such district is not administratively practicable and feasible, it shall record such determination and shall certify such determination to the supervisors of the district. In making such determination the Commission shall give due regard and weight to the attitudes of the occupiers of lands lying within the district, the number of land occupiers eligible to vote in such referendum who shall have voted, the proportion of the votes cast in such referendum in favor of the discontinuance of the district to the total number of votes cast, the approximate wealth and income of the land occupiers of the district, the probable expense of carrying on erosion control operations within such district, and such other economic and social factors as may be relevant to such determination, having due regard to the legislative findings set forth in G.S. 139-2: Provided, however, that the Commission shall not have authority to determine that the continued operation of the district is administratively practicable and feasible unless at least a majority of the votes cast in the referendum shall have been cast in favor of the continuance of such district.

Upon receipt from the Soil and Water Conservation Commission of a certification that the Commission has determined that the continued operation of the district is not administratively practicable and feasible, pursuant to the provisions of this section, the supervisors shall forthwith proceed to terminate the affairs of the district. The supervisors shall dispose of all property belonging to the district at public auction and shall pay over the proceeds of such sale to be covered into the State treasury. The supervisors shall thereupon file an application, duly verified, with the Secretary of State for the discontinuance of

178

such district, and shall transmit with such application the certificates of the Soil and Water Conservation Commission setting forth the determination of the Commission that the continued operation of such district is not administratively practicable and feasible. The application shall recite that the property of the district has been disposed of and the proceeds paid over as in this section provided, and shall set forth a full accounting of such properties and proceeds of the sale. The Secretary of State shall issue to the supervisors a certificate of dissolution and shall record such certificate in an appropriate book of record in his office.

Upon issuance of a certificate of dissolution under the provisions of this section, all ordinances and regulations theretofore adopted and in force within such districts shall be of no further force and effect. All contracts theretofore entered into, to which the district or supervisors are parties, shall remain in force and effect for the period provided in such contracts. The Soil and Water Conservation Commission shall be substituted for the district or supervisors as party to such contracts. The Commission shall be entitled to all benefits and subject to all liabilities under such contracts and shall have the same right and liability to perform, to require performance, to sue and be sued thereon, and to modify or terminate such contracts by mutual consent or otherwise as the supervisors of the district would have had. Such dissolution shall not affect the lien of any judgment entered under the provisions of G.S. 139-11, nor the pendency of any action instituted under the provisions of such section, and the Commission shall succeed to all the rights and obligations of the district or supervisors as to such liens and actions.

The Soil and Water Conservation Commission shall not entertain petitions for the discontinuance of any district nor conduct referenda upon such petitions, nor make determinations pursuant to such petitions, in accordance with the provisions of this Chapter, more often than once in five years. (1937, c. 393, s. 13; 1973, c. 1262, s. 38; 1977, c. 771, s. 4; 1989, c. 727, s. 218(94); 1997-443, s. 11A.119(a); 2011-145, s. 13.22A(o).)

§ 139-14. Dividing large districts.

Whenever the Soil and Water Conservation Commission shall receive a petition from any board of district supervisors signed by all supervisors of such district, the Commission shall have the authority to divide such district into two or more districts. The governing bodies of the resulting districts shall be composed of supervisors in the same manner and in the same number as is provided in G.S. 139-6 and 139-7. Upon the creating of new districts through dividing an existing district under the provisions of this section, the Commission shall appoint all district supervisors necessary to give such district its full quota of supervisors who shall serve until regular supervisors are elected or appointed, as the case may be, at the time of the next regular election of supervisors. The Commission shall assign a name to each district resulting from the division of the district under the provisions of this section and do all other things necessary to complete the organization of such new districts and place them on an operating basis. (1947, c. 131, s. 8; 1973, c. 1262, s. 38.)

§ 139-15. "County committeeman" construed to mean "county supervisor"; powers and duties.

Wherever the words "county committeeman" or "county committeemen" appear in this Chapter, the same shall be construed to mean "county supervisor" or "county supervisors"; and each such county committeeman or county supervisor shall receive the same compensation and have and exercise the same rights, powers, duties, responsibilities and voting privileges granted to or imposed upon district supervisors in respect to soil conservation activities under the provisions of this Chapter. (1949, c. 268, s. 2.)

Article 2.

Watershed Improvement Districts.

§§ 139-16 through 139-20: Repealed by Session Laws 1993, c. 391, ss. 2-6.

§ 139-20.1. Validation of creation of certain districts.

All actions had and taken prior to March 1, 1963, by supervisors of soil and water conservation districts, boards of county commissioners, boards of election, registrars, or other officials in the course of attempting to form and create watershed improvement districts, are hereby ratified, approved, validated and confirmed, as if accomplished in full and complete compliance with the law, and any watershed improvement district with respect to which formation may have been attempted and completed prior to March 1, 1963, is hereby declared to be lawfully formed, created, and in all respects constituted a legal and valid watershed improvement district. (1963, c. 918, s. 1.)

§§ 139-21 through 139-30: Repealed by Session Laws 1993, c. 391, ss. 7-16.

§ 139-31. Repealed by Session Laws 1963, c. 1228, s. 9.

§§ 139-32 through 139-36: Repealed by Session Laws 1993, c. 391, ss. 17-21.

§§ 139-37 through 139-37.1: Recodified as §§ 139-48, 139-49 by Session Laws 1993, c. 391, ss. 22, 23.

§ 139-38: Repealed by Session Laws 1993, c. 391, s. 24.

Article 3.

Watershed Improvement Programs; Expenditure by Counties.

§ 139-39. Alternative method of financing watershed improvement programs by special county tax.

The board of county commissioners in any county is authorized to call a special election to determine whether it be the will of the qualified voters of the county that they levy and cause to be collected annually, at the same time and in the same manner as the general county taxes are levied and collected, a special tax at a rate not to exceed twenty-five cents (25¢) on each one hundred dollars ($100.00) valuation of property in said county, to be known as a "Watershed Improvement Tax," the funds therefrom, if the levy be authorized by the voters of said county, to be used for the prevention of flood water and sediment damages, and for furthering the conservation, utilization and disposal of water and the development of water resources. Any special election shall be conducted in accordance with G.S. 163-287. (1959, c. 781, s. 10; 1967, c. 987, s. 8; 2013-381, s. 10.21.)

§ 139-40. Conduct of election.

(a)   There shall be no new registration of voters for such an election. Registration shall be open for registration of new voters in said county and registration of any and all legal residents of said county, who are or could legally be enfranchised as qualified voters for regular general elections, shall be carried out in accordance with the general election laws of the State of North Carolina as provided for local elections. Notice of such registration of new voters shall be published in a newspaper circulated in said county, once, not less than 55 days before and not more than 65 days before the election, stating the hours and days for registration. The special election, if called, shall be under the control and supervision of the county board of elections.

(b)   The form of the question shall be substantially the words "For Watershed Improvement Tax of Not More Than _____ Cents Per One Hundred Dollar ($100.00) Valuation," and "Against Watershed Improvement Tax of Not More Than _____ Cents Per One Hundred Dollar ($100.00) Valuation," which alternates shall appear separated from each other on one ballot containing opposite, and to the left of each alternate, squares of appropriate size in one of which squares the voter may make a mark "X" to designate the voter's choice for or against such tax, provided, the board of county commissioners may vary the aforesaid form of the question to be placed upon the ballot for the watershed improvement tax election in such manner as the board deems appropriate, and the board of elections shall cause to be placed upon the ballot such form of the question as may be requested by the board of county commissioners. The board of county commissioners shall designate the amount of the maximum annual rate of such tax to be levied, which amount may be less than but may not exceed twenty-five cents (25¢) on the one hundred dollar ($100.00) valuation of property in the county, and said amount shall be stated on the ballot in the question to be voted upon. Such ballot shall be printed on white paper and each polling place shall be supplied with a sufficient number of ballots not later than the day before the election. At such special election the election board shall cause to be placed at each voting precinct in said county a ballot box marked "Watershed Improvement Tax Election".

(c)   The duly appointed judges and other election officials who are named and fixed by the county board of elections shall count the ballots so cast in such election and the results of the election shall be officially canvassed, certified and announced by the proper officials of the board of elections, according to the manner of canvassing, certifying and announcing the elections held under the general election laws of the State as provided for local elections.

182

(d)   If a majority of those voting in such election favor the levying of such a tax, the board of commissioners of such county is authorized to levy a special tax at a rate not to exceed twenty-five cents (25¢) on each one hundred dollars ($100.00) of assessed value of real and personal property taxable in said county, not to exceed the maximum rate of tax approved by the voters in such election, and the General Assembly does hereby give its special approval for the levy of such special tax. (1959, c. 781, s. 10; 1961, c. 32; 1969, c. 711, s. 2; 1993 (Reg. Sess., 1994), c. 762, s. 10.)

§ 139-41. Powers of county commissioners.

(a)   If the majority of the qualified voters voting in such election favor the levying of such tax, then and in that event, the board of county commissioners shall have all powers of soil and water conservation districts as set forth in subdivisions (1), (2), (3), (4), (5), (6), (7), (8) and (10) of G.S. 139-8 (subject to the limitations set forth in subdivision (12) of such section) concerning flood prevention, development of water resources, floodwater and sediment damages, and conservation, utilization and disposal of water. It is the intention of the General Assembly that such powers shall normally be exercised within all or parts of one or more single watersheds, or of two or more watersheds tributary to one of the major drainage basins of the State, but exceptions to this policy may be permitted in appropriate cases; provided, however, it is not the intention of the General Assembly to authorize hereby the diversion of water from one stream or watershed to another.

(b)   The board of county commissioners may itself exercise such powers or, for that purpose, may create a watershed improvement commission to be composed of three members appointed by the board. The terms of office of the members of the commission shall be six years, with the exception of the first two years of existence of the commission, in which one member shall be appointed to serve for a period of two years, one for a period of four years, and one for a period of six years; thereafter all members shall be appointed for six years, and shall serve until their successors have been appointed and qualified. Vacancies in the membership of the commission occurring otherwise than by expiration of term shall be filled by appointment to the unexpired term by the board of county commissioners. The commission shall hold its first meeting within 30 days after its appointment as provided for in this Article, and the beginning date of all terms of office of commissioners shall be the date on which the commission holds its first meeting. The commission at its first meeting shall select a chair, vice-chair, and secretary-treasurer to serve two-year terms. All acts done by the commission shall be entered in a book of minutes to be kept by the secretary-treasurer. A majority of the membership of the commission shall constitute a quorum. The commission shall meet in regular session at least quarterly and may meet specially upon the call of the chair or any members, and upon at least three-day notice of the time, place, and purpose of the meeting. The commission shall provide the board of county commissioners 30 days prior to July 1 a proposed budget for the fiscal year commencing on July 1 and shall provide the board of county commissioners an audit by a certified public accountant within 60 days after the expiration of the fiscal year ending on June 30.

(c)   The board of county commissioners may create a single watershed improvement commission for the entire county or may create separate commissions for individual projects or watersheds.

(d)   The board of county commissioners, as an alternative to itself exercising the powers set forth in subsection (a) of this section or to creating a watershed improvement commission for that purpose, may by resolution designate the soil and water conservation district having jurisdiction in the county to exercise authority for the board of county commissioners in carrying out the county watershed improvement program. The soil and water conservation district shall provide the board of county commissioners 30 days prior to July 1 a proposed budget for the fiscal year commencing on July 1 and shall provide the board of county commissioners an audit by a certified public accountant within 60 days after the expiration of the fiscal year ending on June 30.

(e)   Repealed by Session Laws 1981, c. 326, s. 5.

(f)   Any industry or private water user, the State of North Carolina, the United States or any of its agencies, any municipality, any other county, or any other political subdivision may participate in county watershed improvement programs hereunder in the same manner and to the same extent as provided by G.S. 139-37 with respect to participation in watershed improvement district programs.

(g)   The board of county commissioners may provide for county watershed improvement programs and any or all other related activities (such as water supply systems, sewerage systems, water resources programs, beach erosion control programs, and conservation programs) to be coordinated, to be jointly undertaken by two or more local agencies, or to be assigned to a single county agency designated by such name and organized in such manner as the board deems appropriate.

(h)   A Watershed Improvement Commission created pursuant to subsection (b) of this section or a soil and water conservation district designated pursuant to subsection (d) of this section may employ such officers, agents, consultants, and other employees as they may require; shall determine their qualifications, duties, and compensation; shall provide for the execution of surety bonds for the secretary-treasurer and such other officers, agents, and employees as shall be entrusted with funds or property, and shall provide for making and publication of an annual audit of the accounts of receipts and disbursements of the watershed improvement program.

(i)   District supervisors and watershed improvement commissioners shall receive a per diem allowance of seven dollars ($7.00) and necessary expenses while engaged in the discharge of official duties pursuant to subsections (b) and (d) of this section. Claims for per diem and expenses for any duty except attendance upon a meeting shall be paid only after approval of the commission or the Board of Supervisors respectively. (1959, c. 781, s. 10; 1967, c. 987, s. 10; 1969, c. 711, s. 3; 1971, c. 1138, s. 2; 1973, c. 1262, s. 38; 1981, c. 326, s. 5; 1993, c. 391, s. 25.)

§ 139-41.1. Powers of counties that are not authorized to levy watershed improvement taxes.

A county may exercise any of the powers set out in this Article without having been authorized to levy a watershed improvement tax pursuant to the procedures of G.S. 139-39 and 139-40 or otherwise. (1981, c. 251, s. 1.)

§ 139-41.2. Review of watershed work plans.

(a)   Watershed work plans developed under Public Law 566 (83rd Congress) as amended, and all other work plans developed pursuant to this Chapter, shall be submitted to the Soil and Water Conservation Commission for review and approval or disapproval. No work of improvement may be constructed or established without the approval of work plans by the Soil and Water Conservation Commission pursuant to this section.

185

(b)   The Soil and Water Conservation Commission shall approve a watershed work plan if, in its judgment, it:

(1)   Provides for proper and safe construction of proposed works of improvement;

(2)   Shows that the construction and operation of the proposed works of improvement (in conjunction with other such works and related structures of the district and the watershed) will not appreciably diminish the flow of useful water that would otherwise be available to existing downstream water users during critical periods;

(3)   Determines whether a program of floodplain management in connection with such proposed works is in the public interest, and the Soil and Water Conservation Commission may withhold approval until satisfactory floodplain management measures are incorporated; and

(4)   Is otherwise in compliance with law.

(c)   Amendments to the work plan involving major changes shall be approved by the Soil and Water Conservation Commission. Determinations by the Soil and Water Conservation Commission that an amendment involve major changes shall be conclusive for purposes of this section. No work of improvement may be constructed or established without the approval of work plans by the Soil and Water Conservation Commission pursuant to this subsection. The construction or establishment of any such work of improvement without such approval, or without conforming to a work plan approved by the Soil and Water Conservation Commission, may be enjoined. The Soil and Water Conservation Commission may institute an action for such injunctive relief in the superior court of any county wherein such construction or establishment takes place.

(d)   In conjunction with any work plans submitted to the Soil and Water Conservation Commission under subsection (c) of this section, a county shall submit in such form as the Soil and Water Conservation Commission may prescribe a plan of its proposed method of operations for works of improvement covered by the work plans and for related structures. With the approval of the Soil and Water Conservation Commission, the county may amend its initial plan of operations from time to time. Soil and Water Conservation Commission approval of the initial plan of operations shall not be required.

(e)   If the Soil and Water Conservation Commission has reason to believe that a county is not operating any work of improvement or properly related structure in accordance with its plan of operations as amended, the Soil and Water Conservation Commission on its own motion or upon complaint may order a hearing to be held thereon upon not less than 30 days' written notification to the county and complainant, if any, by personal service or registered mail. Notice of such hearing shall be published at least once a week for two successive weeks. In connection with any such hearing the Soil and Water Conservation Commission shall be empowered to administer oaths; to take testimony; and, in the same manner as the superior court, to order the taking of depositions, issue subpoenas, and to compel the attendance of witnesses and production of documents. If the Soil and Water Conservation Commission determines from evidence of record that the county is not operating any work of improvement or related structure in accordance with its plan of operations, as amended, the Soil and Water Conservation Commission may issue an order directing the county to comply therewith or to take other appropriate corrective action. Upon failure by a county to comply with any such order, the Soil and Water Conservation Commission may institute an action for injunctive relief in the superior court of any county wherein such noncompliance occurs. (1981, c. 326, s. 6; 2007-495, s. 16.)

§ 139-41.3. Liability of owners of land associated with watershed improvement projects.

(a)   Purpose. - The purpose of this section is to encourage owners of land to make land and water areas available to the public at no cost for educational and recreational purposes by limiting the liability of the owner to persons entering the land for those purposes. The further purpose of this section is to establish a statutory rule of landowner liability law to govern the liability of a landowner whose land is associated with a watershed improvement project as defined by this Chapter to persons entering the land for educational and recreational purposes without charge. This statutory rule modifies the common law of North Carolina concerning landowner liability.

(b)   Definitions. - The following definitions apply in this section, unless otherwise specified:

(1)   Charge. - A price or fee asked for services, entertainment, recreation performed, or products offered for sale on land or in return for an invitation or permission to enter upon land, except as otherwise excluded in this section.

(2)   Educational purpose. - Any activity undertaken as part of a formal or informal educational program, and viewing historical, natural, archaeological, or scientific sites.

(3)   Land. - Real property, land, and water. The term does not include a dwelling or the property immediately adjacent to and surrounding the dwelling that is generally used for activities associated with occupancy of the dwelling as a living space.

(4)   Land associated with watershed improvement projects. - The entire parcel or set of parcels on which any part of a watershed improvement project is located, including any fee easement, leasehold interest or legal possession.

(5)   Legal entity. - The term includes (in addition to a private entity) a county, city, special district, public authority, or other unit or agency of government.

(6)   Owner. - Any individual or legal entity that has any fee, easement, leasehold interest, or legal possession, and any employee or agent of the individual or legal entity.

(7)   Recreational purpose. - Any activity undertaken for recreation, exercise, education, relaxation, refreshment, diversion, or pleasure.

(c)   Exclusion. - For purposes of this Chapter, the term "charge" does not include any of the following:

(1)   Any contribution in-kind, services, or cash contributed by a person, legal entity, nonprofit organization, or governmental entity other than the owner, whether or not sanctioned or solicited by the owner, the purpose of which is to: (i) remedy damage to land caused by educational or recreational use; or (ii) provide warning of hazards on, or remove hazards from, land used for educational or recreational purposes.

(2)   Unless otherwise agreed in writing or otherwise provided by the State or federal tax codes, any property tax abatement or relief received by the owner from the State or local taxing authority in exchange for the owner's agreement to open the land for educational or recreational purposes.

188

(3)   Any volunteer service involving trash pickup, stream cleanup, or stream bank restoration.

(d)   Limitation of Liability. - Except as specifically recognized by or provided for in this section, an owner of land associated with a watershed improvement project, as defined by this Chapter, who either directly or indirectly invites or permits without charge any person to use the land for educational or recreational purposes owes the person the same duty of care that he or she owes a trespasser, except that nothing in this Chapter shall be construed to limit or nullify the doctrine of attractive nuisance and the owner shall inform direct invitees of artificial or unusual hazards of which the owner has actual knowledge.

This section does not apply to an owner who invites or permits any person to use land for a purpose for which the land is regularly used and for which a price or fee is usually charged even if it is not charged in that instance, or to an owner whose purpose in extending an invitation or granting permission is to promote a commercial enterprise. (2001-272, s. 1.)

§ 139-42. Article intended as supplementary.

This Article is intended to provide an alternative method of financing and operating watershed improvement programs, supplementary to any other method authorized by law. (1959, c. 781, s. 10; 1993, c. 391, s. 26.)

§ 139-43: Repealed by Session Laws 1993, c. 391, s. 27.

§ 139-44. Power of eminent domain conferred on counties.

(a)   A county shall have the power to acquire by condemnation any interest in land needed in carrying out the purposes of this act, except interests in land within the boundaries of any project licensed by the Federal Power Commission or interests in land owned or held for use by a public utility as defined in G.S. 62-3. This power may be exercised only after:

(1)   The county makes application to the Soil and Water Conservation Commission, identifying the land sought to be condemned and stating the purposes for which said land is needed; and

(2)   The Soil and Water Conservation Commission finds that the land is sought to be acquired for a proper county purpose. The findings of the Soil and Water Conservation Commission shall be conclusive in the absence of fraud, notwithstanding any other provision of law.

(b)   The Soil and Water Conservation Commission shall certify copies of its findings to the applicant county, the Environmental Management Commission and the clerk of the superior court of the county or counties wherein any part of the project lies for recordation in the special proceedings thereof.

(c)   For purposes of this section:

(1)   The term "interest in land" means any land, right-of-way, right of access, privilege, easement, or other interest in or relating to land. Said "interest in land" does not include an interest in land which is held or used in whole or in part for a public water supply, unless such "interest in land" is not necessary or essential for such uses or purposes.

(2)   A "description" of land shall be sufficient if the boundaries of the land are described in such a way as to convey an intelligent understanding of the location of the land. In the discretion of the applicant county, boundaries may be described by any of the following methods or any combination thereof: by reference to a map; by metes and bounds; by general description referring to natural boundaries, or to boundaries of existing political subdivisions or municipalities, or to boundaries of particular tracts or parcels of land.

(3)   "Commission" means the Soil and Water Conservation Commission.

(d)   The procedure in all condemnation proceedings pursuant to this section shall conform as nearly as possible to the procedure provided in Chapter 40A and all acts amendatory thereof.

(e)   Interests in land acquired pursuant to this section may be used in such manner and for such purposes as the board of county commissioners deem best. If, in the opinion of the board, such lands should be sold, leased or rented, the board may do so, subject to the approval of the Soil and Water Conservation Commission.

(f)   All provisions of local acts inconsistent herewith limiting condemnation powers of counties for county watershed improvement programs are hereby repealed. (1967, c. 987, s. 5; 1973, c. 1262, s. 38; 1981, c. 326, s. 4; c. 919, s. 19; 1993, c. 391, ss. 28, 29.)

§ 139-45. Extraterritorial powers of counties.

A county which has been authorized to levy a watershed improvement tax, whether pursuant to Article 3 of General Statutes 139 or by special act or otherwise, may take any authorized watershed action and may expend funds for any authorized watershed purpose (including acquisition of real and personal property, easements, options, or other interests in real property) outside as well as inside the boundaries of the county, if the board of county commissioners finds that substantial flood prevention, drainage or water supply benefits will accrue to property located within the boundaries of the county as a result of such action or expenditure. The board of county commissioners may delegate to a watershed improvement commission the function of making such findings, either generally or in a particular case. (1967, c. 987, s. 7.)

§ 139-46. Recreational and related aspects of watershed improvement programs.

(a)   Local watershed sponsors may install and maintain recreational facilities and services in connection with watershed improvement works or projects, and may provide areas (including structures) for the conservation and replacement of fish and wildlife habitat. For any of these purposes said sponsors may appropriate and expend funds, may levy taxes and assessments, and may issue bonds and notes, to the same extent as in the case of other authorized watershed activities. Such recreational facilities and services may include but are not limited to any or all of the water-related recreational facilities provided for in subsection (b) of this section, and parking areas, ingress and egress roads, hiking or nature trails, picnic areas and campsites. No application for watershed planning under Public Law 566 (83rd Congress, United States), as amended, may be approved by the Soil and Water Conservation Commission until after receipt and consideration of recommendations from the appropriate fish and wildlife agency concerning replacement of fish and wildlife habitat in mitigation of anticipated damages: Provided that this requirement for consideration of fish

191

and wildlife recommendations shall not apply if such recommendations are not received by the Soil and Water Conservation Commission within 30 days after the Soil and Water Conservation Commission requests such recommendations. Within the meaning of this provision the "appropriate fish and wildlife agency" means the North Carolina Wildlife Resources Commission as to matters within its jurisdiction, and the North Carolina Department of Environment and Natural Resources as to matters within its jurisdiction, or both such agencies as to matters within their concurrent jurisdiction.

(b)   It is hereby declared that the provisions of this Chapter authorizing works of improvement, structures, plans, surveys and investigations for the development of water resources were intended to include water-related recreational facilities, including but not limited to boat launching areas and facilities, bathhouses, campsites and picnic areas adjacent to the water, and other basic facilities for water recreational areas. All expenditures heretofore incurred by any local watershed sponsor for such water-related recreational facilities are hereby validated and confirmed. The proceeds of any tax heretofore approved by the voters of a county for a county watershed improvement program, or authorized by special or local act for a county watershed improvement program, may be expended for such water-related recreational facilities, if the board of county commissioners after a public hearing determines that the proceeds should be so expended. Notice of such hearing shall be published at least once a week for two consecutive weeks in at least one newspaper of general circulation published in the county, in lieu thereof, in a newspaper of general circulation in the county. No action based on the alleged invalidity of the expenditures herein confirmed or of the use of tax proceeds herein authorized shall lie after January 1, 1968, to enjoin or contest any such expenditure or any such use of tax proceeds.

(c)   Within the meaning of this section "local watershed sponsors" include soil and water conservation districts, drainage districts, municipalities, and counties undertaking county watershed programs under Article 3 of this Chapter or any local act granting similar powers. (1967, c. 987, s. 9; 1973, c. 1262, ss. 38, 86; 1977, c. 771, s. 4; 1989, c. 727, s. 218(95); 1993, c. 391, s. 30; 1997-443, s. 11A.119(a).)

§ 139-47: Repealed by Session Laws 1993, c. 391, s. 31.

192

§ 139-48. Participation by cities, counties, industries and others.

(a)   Any industry, or private water user, the State of North Carolina, the United States or any of its agencies, any county, municipality or any other political subdivision may participate in watershed improvement works or projects upon mutually agreeable terms relating to such matters as the construction, financing, maintenance and operation thereof.

(b)   Any county or municipality may contribute funds toward the construction, maintenance and operation of watershed improvement works or projects, to the extent that such works or projects:

(1)   Provide a source (respectively) of county or municipal water supply; or protect an existing source of such supply, enhance its quality or increase its dependable capacity or quantity; or

(2)   Protect against or alleviate the effects of flood-water or sediment damages affecting, or provide drainage benefits for, (respectively) county or municipally owned property or the property (respectively) of county or municipal inhabitants located outside the boundaries of such works or projects but within the respective boundaries of such county or municipality.

Each county and city may fund appropriations for the purposes of this section by levy of property taxes pursuant to G.S. 153A-149 and G.S. 160A-209 and by the allocation of other revenues whose use is not otherwise restricted by law. (1959, c. 781, s. 8; 1973, c. 803, s. 33; 1993, c. 391, ss. 22, 32.)

§ 139-49. Borrowing by local units for anticipated water supplies.

(a)   Any local unit may issue bonds or other obligations in the manner provided by this section (and may appropriate and expend funds derived therefrom) for the purpose of financing all or any part of the cost of providing storage capacity for anticipated future or present water supply needs, in conjunction with any watershed improvement work or project.

(b)   Any two or more local units, each situated in whole or in part in the basin of the same river in which a watershed improvement work or project is located, may issue bonds or other obligations for the purpose stated in subsection (a) of this section in such amounts as constitute their proportionate parts, respectively, of the estimated cost of such a work or project. The governing bodies of said local units shall jointly determine and agree upon the proportionate part of the estimated cost which each local unit is to bear, taking into consideration the taxable resources of each local unit and such other economic and beneficial factors as deemed pertinent and advisable, and such determination shall be recorded in the minutes of each such body.

(c)   Such bonds or other obligations of counties shall be issued pursuant to the Local Government Finance Act, Chapter 159 of the General Statutes: Provided, the amount thereof shall constitute a deduction from the gross debt under G.S. 159-55(a)(2): Provided, further, the provisions of G.S. 159-65(2) shall not apply to such bonds.

(d)   Such bonds or other obligations of municipalities shall be issued pursuant to the Local Government Finance Act, Chapter 159 of the General Statutes, and the amount thereof shall constitute a deduction from the gross debt under G.S. 159-55(a)(2): Provided, such bonds may not be consolidated with bonds authorized by another ordinance as provided in G.S. 159-65(2).

(e)   Notwithstanding any other provisions of law, the Local Government Commission may sell any bonds or other obligations issued pursuant to this section to the United States of America, or any agency thereof, at private sale and without advertisement. The first installment of principal of bonds or other obligations issued under this section may be made payable not more than 10 years after the date of the bonds or obligations. Accrual of interest may be deferred not more than 10 years. Any such bonds or other obligations may contain appropriate provisions which will authorize the initiation of payments of interest and installments of principal on the bonds on a date not later than 10 years from the date of such bonds or obligations, or on the date when the local unit shall begin to use such local water supplies, whichever date shall occur first. The date on which such use of local water supplies begins shall be determined by the governing body of the local unit issuing such bonds or other obligations, which determination shall be binding and conclusive.

(f)   If the bonds or other obligations of one or more local units which have agreed upon their proportionate part of the estimated cost, as provided for in subsection (b) of this section, are required by the laws or the Constitution to be submitted to the voters of such local unit at an election and a majority of said voters voting in said election vote against the issuance of such bonds, the bonds or other obligations of any other local unit which have been duly authorized may be issued in whole or in part only when a sufficient number of

194

local units have agreed upon their proportionate part as provided in subsection (b) of this section and have duly authorized their bonds or obligations so that the full amount of such estimated cost may be paid.

(g)   As used in this section the following terms have the following meanings:

"Local unit" means any county or municipality.

"Local water supplies" include any municipal or county water supplies, whether or not the purposes served by a particular storage facility financed under this section initially include service to domestic or any other water supply customers.

"Costs" include the cost of water storage capacity in a structure or facility (or other equivalent costs for water supply purposes) and the cost of facilities for release or withdrawal of water stored for water supply purposes, as well as other installation costs of a structure or facility including costs of real and personal property, easements, options, or other interests in real property, and water rights, engineering and inspection fees, contract administration costs, and costs of conveyance facilities for local water supplies. (1967, c. 987, s. 4; 1993, c. 391, ss. 23, 33(a), (b).)

§ 139-50. Reserved for future codification purposes.

§ 139-51. Reserved for future codification purposes.

§ 139-52. Reserved for future codification purposes.

Article 4.

Grants for Small Watershed Projects.

§ 139-53. State Soil and Water Conservation Commission authorized to accept applications.

The State Soil and Water Conservation Commission is authorized to accept applications for grants for nonfederal costs relating to small watershed projects authorized under Public Law 566 (83rd Congress as amended) from local sponsors of such projects properly organized under the provisions of either Chapter 156 of the General Statutes of North Carolina or Chapter 139 of the

General Statutes of North Carolina, or from county service districts authorized by G.S. 153A-301, or from municipal service districts authorized by G.S. 160A-536. Applications shall be made on forms prescribed by the Commission. (1977, 2nd Sess., c. 1206; 1981, c. 326, s. 9.)

§ 139-54. Purposes for which grants may be requested.

Applications for grants may be made for the nonfederal share of small watershed projects for the following purposes in amounts not to exceed the percentage of the nonfederal costs indicated:

(1)   Land rights acquisition for impounding or retarding water - fifty percent (50%).

(2)   Engineering fees - fifty percent (50%).

(3)   Anticipated future and present water supply needs in conjunction with watershed improvement works or projects as described in G.S. 139-37.1 - fifty percent (50%).

(4)   Installation of recreational facilities and services (to include land acquisition) as described in G.S. 139-46 - fifty percent (50%).

(5)   Construction costs for water management (drainage or irrigation) purposes, including utility and road relocations not funded by the State Department of Transportation - sixty-six and two-thirds percent (66 2/3%).

(6)   Conservation and replacement of fish and wildlife habitat as described in G.S. 139-46 - seventy-five percent (75%).

(7)   Rehabilitation or improvement of water resources structural measures in accordance with criteria established by the Natural Resources Conservation Service of the United States Department of Agriculture pursuant to the Watershed Protection and Flood Prevention Act of 1954, as amended by the Small Watershed Rehabilitation Amendments of 2000 (Pub. L. No. 106-472, 114 Stat. 2007), codified at 16 U.S.C. § 1001, et. seq.; the Dam Safety Law of 1967, G.S. 143-215.23, et. seq.; and rules adopted pursuant thereto - fifty percent (50%). (1977, 2nd Sess., c. 1206; 1979, c. 1046, s. 2; 2002-176, s. 3.)

§ 139-55. Review of applications.

(a)   The State Soil and Water Conservation Commission shall receive and review applications for grants for small watershed projects authorized under Public Law 566 (83rd Congress, as amended) and approve, approve in part, or disapprove all such applications.

(b)   In reviewing each application, the State Soil and Water Conservation Commission shall consider:

(1)   The financial resources of the local sponsoring organization;

(2)   Nonstructural measures such as sedimentation control ordinances and floodplain zoning ordinances enacted and enforced by local governments to alleviate flooding;

(3)   Regional benefits of projects to an area greater than the area under jurisdiction of the local sponsoring organization;

(4)   Any direct benefit to State-owned lands and properties. (1977, 2nd Sess., c. 1206; 2002-165, s. 2.17; 2007-495, s. 17.)

§ 139-56. Recommendation of priorities and disbursal of grant funds.

Whenever two or more applications for grants are approved in whole or in part, the State Soil and Water Conservation Commission shall establish priorities among the several applications for disbursal of grant funds. To the extent that funds are available, the State Soil and Water Conservation Commission may authorize the disbursal of grant funds to the applicants consistent with the established priorities. The State Soil and Water Conservation Commission shall promulgate regulations to provide for an audit of grant funds to assure that they are spent for the purposes delineated in the application. Established priorities may be reviewed from time to time and revised if circumstances warrant such revision. (1977, 2nd Sess., c. 1206.)

§ 139-57. Availability of funds.

All grants shall be contingent upon the availability of funds for disbursement to applicants. At the end of each fiscal year the State Soil and Water Conservation Commission shall notify all applicants whose applications have been approved and to whom grant funds have not been disbursed of the status of their application. At the time of notification the State Soil and Water Conservation Commission shall notify the applicants of the availability of funds for grants in the upcoming fiscal year and at the same time shall notify the applicants of their position on any priority list that may have been established for the disbursal of grant funds for small watershed projects. (1977, 2nd Sess., c. 1206.)

§ 139-58: Reserved for future codification purposes.

§ 139-59: Reserved for future codification purposes.

Article 5.

Agricultural Water Resources Assistance Program.

§ 139-60. Agricultural Water Resources Assistance Program.

(a)   Program Established. - The Agricultural Water Resources Assistance Program is established. The purpose of the Program shall be to assist farmers and landowners in doing any one or more of the following:

(1)   Identify opportunities to increase water use efficiency, availability, and storage.

(2)   Implement best management practices to conserve and protect water resources.

(3)   Increase water use efficiency.

(4)   Increase water storage and availability for agricultural purposes.

198

(b)   Program Administration. - The Agricultural Water Resources Assistance Program shall be implemented by the Soil and Water Conservation Commission through the soil and water conservation districts in the same manner as the Agriculture Cost Share Program for Nonpoint Source Pollution Control under Article 72 of Chapter 106 of the General Statutes. The Soil and Water Conservation Commission shall supervise and administer this Program as provided in this section and as provided in Article 72 of Chapter 106 of the General Statutes for the Agriculture Cost Share Program for Nonpoint Source Pollution Control. At least once each calendar year, the Director of the Division of Soil and Water Conservation of the Department of Agriculture and Consumer Services and the Commissioner of Agriculture shall meet with stakeholders for the purpose of advising the Soil and Water Conservation Commission on the development and administration of the Program, including the development of annual goals for the Program.

(c)   Program Functions. - Under the Agricultural Water Resources Assistance Program, the Soil and Water Conservation Commission shall do the following:

(1)   Within funds available for this Program, provide cost-share funds subject to all of the following limitations and requirements:

a.   Except as provided in G.S. 106-850(b)(9), State funding shall be limited to:

1.   Seventy-five percent (75%) of the average cost for each project, with the assisted person providing twenty-five percent (25%) of the project cost, which may include in-kind support of the project.

2.   A maximum of seventy-five thousand dollars ($75,000) per year to each applicant.

b.   Applicants shall be limited to farmers who have an adjusted gross income in each of the previous two years that is at or below two hundred fifty thousand dollars ($250,000), unless at least seventy-five percent (75%) of this adjusted gross income is derived directly from farming, ranching, or forestry operations.

c.   The requirements and limitations under subdivisions (1), (2), (5), (7), and (8) of subsection (b) of G.S. 106-850 do not apply. All other limitations and requirements set out in Article 72 of Chapter 106 of the General Statutes, as modified by this section, apply.

(2)   Approve best management practices eligible for cost-share funds under this Program.

(3)   Establish criteria to allocate funds to local soil and water conservation districts.

(4)   Develop a process for soliciting and reviewing applications and for selecting farmers to participate in the Program.

(5)   Investigate and pursue other funding sources to supplement State funds, including federal, local, and private funding sources.

(6)   Provide technical assistance to participating persons to assist with the projects that are eligible for cost-share funds under subsection (a) of this section and to facilitate the timely transfer of technology among participating persons.

(7)   Adopt temporary and permanent rules as necessary to implement this Program.

(c1)   To be eligible for assistance under this program, each applicant must establish that he or she is engaged in farming by providing to the Soil and Water Conservation Commission with his or her application:

(1)   A copy of the farm owner's or operator's federal tax Schedule F (Form 1040) or an equivalent form for the most recent tax year showing the owner's or operator's profit or loss from farming.

(2)   A copy of the farm's agricultural exemption certificate issued to the farm owner or operator by the Department of Revenue.

(3)   For forestland actively engaged in the commercial growing of trees under a sound management program as defined in G.S. 105-277.2(6), a copy of the sound forest management plan described in G.S. 105-277.3(g).

(c2)   In extraordinary circumstances, the Commission may permit an applicant to establish that he or she is engaged in farming with an alternate form of documentation if the farm has a conservation plan that meets the statutory purposes of the program.

(d)   Report. - No later than January 31 of each year, the Division of Soil and Water Conservation of the Department of Agriculture and Consumer Services shall prepare a comprehensive report on the implementation of subsections (a) through (c) of this section. The report shall be submitted to the Environmental Review Commission as a part of the report required by G.S. 106-850(e). (2011-145, ss. 13.23(a), 13.23A(b); 2011-391, s. 32; 2012-142, s. 11.2A(b).)

Chapter 140.

State Art Museum; Symphony and Art Societies.

Article 1.

North Carolina Museum of Art.

§§ 140-1 through 140-5.1. Recodified as §§ 140-5.12 to 140-5.17.

Article 1A.

Art Museum Building Commission.

§ 140-5.2. Repealed by Session Laws 1973, c. 476, s. 43.

§§ 140-5.3 through 140-5.6. Repealed by Session Laws 1985 (Reg. Sess., 1986), c. 1028, s. 16.

§§ 140-5.7 through 140-5.11. Reserved for future codification purposes.

Article 1B.

North Carolina Museum of Art.

§ 140-5.12. Agency of State; functions.

The North Carolina Museum of Art is an agency of the State of North Carolina within the Department of Cultural Resources. The functions of the North Carolina Museum of Art shall be to acquire, preserve, and exhibit works of art for the education and enjoyment of the people of the State, and to conduct programs of education, research, and publication designed to encourage an interest in and an appreciation of art on the part of the people of the State. (1961, c. 731; 1979, 2nd Sess., c. 1306, s. 1.)

§ 140-5.13. Board of Trustees - establishment; members; selection; quorum; compensation; officers; meetings.

(a)   It is the duty of the Department of Cultural Resources to develop policy and to establish and enforce standards for resources, services, and programs involving the arts and the cultural aspects of the lives of the citizens of North Carolina. To attain these objectives, there is hereby established within the Department of Cultural Resources the Board of Trustees of the North Carolina Museum of Art.

(b)   The Board of Trustees of the North Carolina Museum of Art shall consist of 25 members, chosen as follows:

(1)   The Governor shall appoint 13 members, one from each congressional district in the State in accordance with G.S. 147-12(3b);

(2)   Repealed by Session Laws 2012-120, s. 1(e), effective October 1, 2012.

(3)   The North Carolina Museum of Art Foundation, Incorporated, shall elect four members;

(4)   The Board of Trustees of the North Carolina Museum of Art shall elect four members;

(5)   The General Assembly shall appoint four members, two upon the recommendation of the Speaker of the House of Representatives, and two upon the recommendation of the President Pro Tempore of the Senate in accordance with G.S. 120-121;

(6)   Repealed by Session Laws 1981 (Regular Session, 1982), c. 1191, s. 49.

All regular appointments or elections except those by the General Assembly shall be for terms of six years, except that each member shall serve until the member's successor is chosen and qualifies. No person may be appointed or elected to more than two consecutive terms of six years. All regular appointments by the General Assembly shall be for the then current legislative term, and no appointee of the General Assembly may be appointed to more than two consecutive terms of two years.

(c)   Vacancies in appointments made by the General Assembly shall be filled in accordance with G.S. 120-122. All other vacancies occurring in the regular membership of the Board of Trustees prior to the expiration of a term shall be filled by the same authority and in the same manner as the vacating member was chosen, and the successor member so chosen shall serve for the remainder of the unexpired term of the vacating member.

(d)   All initial appointments and elections to the Board of Trustees shall be made on July 1, 1980, or as soon as feasible thereafter except as provided in this subsection, and the terms of all except the legislative appointees shall expire on June 30, 1983, or June 30, 1986, as the case may be. In order to establish regularly overlapping terms, initial appointments and elections to the Board of Trustees shall be made as follows:

(1)   Four members at large shall be appointed by the Governor for initial terms of three years and four members at large shall be appointed by the Governor for initial terms of six years.

(2)   One member shall be elected by the North Carolina State Art Society, Incorporated, for an initial term of three years and two members shall be elected by that Society for initial terms of six years.

(3)   One member shall be elected by the North Carolina Museum of Art Foundation, Incorporated, for an initial term of three years and two members shall be elected by that Foundation for initial terms of six years.

(4)   One member shall be elected by the Art Commission prior to July 1, 1980, for an initial term of three years and two members shall be elected by that Commission for initial terms of six years. Upon the expiration of the terms of

203

those three members, their successors shall be elected by the Board of Trustees of the North Carolina Museum of Art.

(5)   Three members shall be elected by the State Art Museum Building Commission to serve until the termination of that Commission or until June 30, 1983, whichever shall first occur. Upon the termination of the terms of those three members, should such termination occur prior to June 30, 1983, their successors shall be elected as follows: one by the North Carolina State Art Society, Incorporated, one by the North Carolina Museum of Art Foundation, Incorporated, and one by the Board of Trustees of the North Carolina Museum of Art; the terms of the successor members so elected shall expire on June 30, 1983. On July 1, 1983, or as soon as feasible thereafter, the successors of these three members shall be elected for terms of six years, as follows: one by the North Carolina State Art Society, Incorporated, one by the North Carolina Museum of Art Foundation, Incorporated, and one by the Board of Trustees of the North Carolina Museum of Art.

(6)   The initial appointments by the General Assembly shall serve until June 30, 1983. Subsequent appointments shall be for two-year terms commencing July 1, 1983, and biennially thereafter.

(7)   Repealed by Session Laws 1981 (Regular Session, 1982), c. 1191, s. 51.

Every vacancy occurring in the initial membership of the Board of Trustees prior to the expiration of a term of office shall be filled by the same authority and in the same manner as the vacating member was chosen and the successor member so appointed shall serve for the remainder of the unexpired term of the vacating member.

(e)   Any member of the Board of Trustees may be removed from office by the authority that appointed or elected that member for misfeasance, malfeasance, or nonfeasance in office. In the case of an appointment made by the Governor, removal shall be made in accordance with the provisions of G.S. 143B-13 of the Executive Organization Act of 1973.

(f)   A public officer who is appointed or elected to serve on the Board of Trustees shall be deemed to serve thereon as a trustee ex officio and his duties as a trustee shall be deemed additional duties of his primary public office.

(g)   The Board of Trustees shall have a chairman, a vice-chairman, and such other officers as the Board deems necessary. The chairman shall be designated by the Governor from among the members of the Board. The vice-chairman shall be elected by and from among the members of the Board. The chairman and vice-chairman shall be chosen for terms of two years or for so long as they are members of the Board, whichever is the shorter period. The Director of the North Carolina Museum of Art shall serve as Secretary to the Board of Trustees and shall attend all meetings.

(h)   The Board of Trustees shall meet at least once in each quarter. The Board may hold special meetings at any time and place within the State at the call of the chairman. The chairman may call a special meeting at his discretion, and he shall call a special meeting upon the written request of a majority of the authorized membership of the Board of Trustees.

(i)   A majority of the authorized membership of the Board of Trustees shall constitute a quorum for the transaction of business.

(j)   Members of the Board of Trustees who are officers or employees of State agencies or institutions shall receive from funds available to the Department of Cultural Resources subsistence and travel allowances at the rates authorized by G.S. 138-6. All other members of the Board of Trustees shall receive from funds available to the Department of Cultural Resources per diem and travel and subsistence allowances at the rates authorized by G.S. 138-5.

(k)   All clerical and administrative services required by the Board of Trustees shall be supplied by the office of the Director of the North Carolina Museum of Art. (1979, 2nd Sess., c. 1306, s. 1; 1981 (Reg. Sess., 1982), c. 1191, ss. 49-52; 1987, c. 842, ss. 1, 2; 1991, c. 756, s. 35; 1995, c. 490, s. 8; 2001-486, s. 2.10; 2006-66, s. 22.22(b); 2006-221, s. 23; 2008-194, s. 6(d); 2012-120, ss. 1(e), 2(b); 2013-410, s. 16.)

§ 140-5.14. Board of Trustees - powers and duties.

The Board of Trustees shall be the governing body of the North Carolina Museum of Art and shall have the following powers and duties:

(1)   To adopt bylaws for its own government;

(2)   To adopt policies, rules, and regulations for the conduct of the North Carolina Museum of Art;

(3)   To prescribe the powers and duties of the Director of the North Carolina Museum of Art, consistent with the provisions of this Article;

(4)   To establish such advisory boards and committees as it may deem advisable;

(5)   To advise the Secretary of Cultural Resources with respect to inspecting, appraising, obtaining attributions and evaluations of, transporting, exhibiting, lending, storing, and receiving upon consignment or upon loan of statuary, paintings, and other works of art of any and every kind and description that are worthy of acquisition, preservation, and exhibition by the North Carolina Museum of Art;

(6)   To advise the Secretary of Cultural Resources on the care, custody, storage, and preservation of all works of art acquired or received upon consignment or loan by the North Carolina Museum of Art;

(7)   After consultation with the Secretary of Cultural Resources, on behalf of and in the name of the North Carolina Museum of Art, to acquire by purchase, gift, or will, absolutely or in trust, from individuals, corporations, the federal government, or from any other source, money, works of art, or other property which may be retained, sold, or otherwise used to promote the purposes of the North Carolina Museum of Art as provided in G.S. 140-5.12. The net proceeds of the sale of all property acquired under the provisions of this paragraph shall be deposited in the State Treasury to the credit of the "The North Carolina Museum of Art Special Fund";

(8)   After consultation with the Secretary of Cultural Resources, to exchange works of art owned by the North Carolina Museum of Art for other works of art which, in the opinion of the Board, would improve the quality, value, or representative character of the art collection of the Museum;

(9)   After consultation with the Secretary of Cultural Resources, to sell any work of art owned by the North Carolina Museum of Art if the Board finds that it is in the best interest of the Museum to do so, unless such sale would be contrary to the terms of acquisition. The net proceeds of each such sale, after deduction of the expenses attributable to that sale, shall be deposited in the State treasury to the credit of "The North Carolina Museum of Art Special Fund,"

and shall be used only for the purchase of other works of art. No work of art owned by the North Carolina Museum of Art may be pledged or mortgaged;

(10) To make a biennial report to the Governor and the General Assembly on the activities of the Board of Trustees and of the North Carolina Museum of Art;

(11) To adopt, amend, and rescind rules and regulations consistent with the provisions of this Article. All rules and regulations heretofore adopted by the Art Commission shall remain in full force and effect unless and until repealed or superseded by action of the Board. All rules and regulations adopted by the Board shall be enforced by the Department of Cultural Resources;

(12) To determine the sites for expansion of the North Carolina Museum of Art with the approval of the Governor and Council of State;

(13) To provide auxiliary services at the North Carolina Museum of Art. Such services may include the sale of books, periodicals, art works, art supplies and providing facilities for the operation of food and beverage services. The operation of food and beverage services shall be by contract with private enterprises, and subject to the provisions of Article 3 of Chapter 111. (1979, 2nd Sess., c. 1306, s. 1; 1981, c. 301; 2011-266, s. 1.11(b).)

§ 140-5.15. Director of Museum of Art; appointment; dismissal; powers and duties; staff.

(a) The Director's Committee shall elect and supervise the Director of the North Carolina Museum of Art and may dismiss the Director. The Director's Committee shall evaluate the performance of the Director and shall determine the Director's compensation within the limitations of available funding.

(b) Repealed by Session Laws 2012-120, s. 2(a), effective June 28, 2012.

(b1) The Director's Committee shall consist of five members chosen as follows:

(1) The Secretary of Cultural Resources, who shall serve as the chairman of the Committee.

(2) The Chair of the Board of Trustees of the North Carolina Museum of Art.

(3)   One member designated by the Board of Trustees of the North Carolina Museum of Art.

(4)   The President of the Board of Directors of the North Carolina Museum of Art Foundation, Inc., or the President's designee.

(5)   One member designated by the Board of the North Carolina Museum of Art Foundation, Inc.

(b2)   The members of the Director's Committee selected under subdivisions (b1)(3) and (b1)(5) of this section shall serve terms of four years and may not serve more than two consecutive terms of four years. Four members of the Committee shall constitute a quorum for the transaction of business.

(c)   The State-funded portion of the salary of the Director shall be fixed by the Governor.

(d)   The Director shall have the following powers and duties:

(1)   Under the supervision of the Director's Committee, to direct and administer the North Carolina Museum of Art in accordance with the policies, rules, and regulations adopted by the Board of Trustees;

(2)   To employ such persons as are necessary to perform the functions of the North Carolina Museum of Art and are provided for in the budget of the Museum and to promote, demote, and dismiss such persons in accordance with State personnel policies, rules, and regulations. This paragraph shall not apply to associate directors and curators;

(3)   To serve as director of collections of the North Carolina Museum of Art;

(4)   To serve as Secretary to the Board of Trustees.

(e)   The Director, associate directors, and curators shall be exempt from the provisions of the North Carolina Human Resources Act. The Board of Trustees shall adopt, subject to the approval of the Secretary of Cultural Resources, rules and regulations governing the employment, promotion, demotion, and dismissal of associate directors and curators. (1961, c. 731; 1973, c. 476, s. 38; 1979, 2nd Sess., c. 1306, s. 1; 1985, c. 122, s. 6; c. 479, s. 218; 1987, c. 827, s. 81; 2006-66, s. 22.22(g); 2006-221, s. 23; 2012-120, s. 2(a); 2012-142, s. 25.1(d); 2013-382, s. 9.1(c).)

§ 140-5.16. Gifts; special fund; exemption from taxation.

(a)   All gifts of money to the North Carolina Museum of Art and all interest earned thereon shall be paid into the State treasury and maintained as a fund to be designated "The North Carolina Museum of Art Special Fund."

(b)   All gifts made to the North Carolina Museum of Art shall be exempt from every form of taxation including, but not by way of limitation, ad valorem, intangible, gift, inheritance, and income taxation. (1961, c. 731; 1979, 2nd Sess., c. 1306, s. 1.)

§ 140-5.17: Repealed by Session Laws 2007-484, s. 19, effective August 30, 2007.

Article 2.

North Carolina Symphony Society.

§ 140-6. Repealed by Session Laws 1973, c. 476, s. 89.

§ 140-7. Adoption of bylaws; amendments.

The said board of trustees, when organized under the terms of this Article, shall have authority to adopt bylaws for the Society and said bylaws shall thereafter be subject to change only by a three-fifths vote of a quorum of said board of trustees. (1943, c. 755, s. 3; 1947, c. 1049, s. 2.)

§ 140-8. Audit.

The operations of the North Carolina Symphony Society, Inc., shall be subject to the oversight of the State Auditor pursuant to Article 5A of Chapter 147 of the General Statutes. (1943, c. 755, s. 4; 1983, c. 913, s. 28.)

§ 140-9. Allocations from Contingency and Emergency Fund; expenditures.

The Governor and Council of State are hereby authorized to allot such sums as they may deem appropriate, from the Contingency and Emergency Fund, to the North Carolina Symphony Society, to aid in carrying on the activities of the said Society. All expenditures made by said Society shall be subject to the provisions of the State Budget Act, Chapter 143C of the General Statutes. (1943, c. 755, s. 5; 1955, c. 1309; 2006-203, s. 80.)

§ 140-10. Counties and municipalities authorized to make contributions.

The governing body of any county or incorporated municipality is hereby authorized and empowered to appropriate and make voluntary contributions out of nontax funds to the North Carolina Symphony Society. (1953, c. 1212.)

§ 140-10.1: Repealed by Session Laws 2013-316, s. 5, effective January 1, 2014.

Article 3.

North Carolina State Art Society.

§ 140-11. Repealed by Session Laws 1973, c. 476, s. 81.

§ 140-12: Repealed by Session Laws 2012-120, s. 1(c), effective October 1, 2012.

§ 140-13: Repealed by Session Laws 2012-120, s. 1(c), effective October 1, 2012.

§ 140-14: Repealed by Session Laws 2012-120, s. 1(c), effective October 1, 2012.

§ 140-15: Repealed by Session Laws 1999-337, s. 35(b).

Chapter 140A.

State Awards System.

§ 140A-1. Annual awards established; form and design.

The State of North Carolina hereby establishes annual awards, not to exceed six in number, each bearing the name of the recipient, with an appropriate inscription reciting the reason for the award, which form and design shall be approved by the Governor and Council of State. (1961, c. 1143, s. 1.)

§ 140A-2. Fields of recognition; periods covered.

These recognitions shall be known as the North Carolina Awards for Literature, Science, the Fine Arts and Public Service, and shall be conferred upon citizens of North Carolina for the most notable attainments in these respective fields during the current year, terminating four months before the date of award, though such distinctions can be exceptionally conferred, with the approval of the Governor and the Council of State, for eminence achieved during years prior to the award. (1961, c. 1143, s. 2.)

§ 140A-3. Annual awards to natives living outside State.

Awards may be made annually to native-born North Carolinians, living outside of North Carolina, for preeminent accomplishment in not more than two of the above fields of creative endeavor. (1961, c. 1143, s. 3; 1991, c. 131, s. 1.)

§ 140A-4. Repealed by Session Laws 1973, c. 476, s. 73.

§ 140A-5. Selection of recipients for awards.

The recipients of the awards shall be chosen by a committee named by the North Carolina Awards Committee, for each category of achievement, but no award shall be made in any field unless the committee of awards deems the recognized accomplishment to be outstanding in merit, value, and distinction. (1961, c. 1143, s. 5; 1973, c. 476, s. 73.)

§ 140A-6. Administration expense.

The expense of administering this Chapter shall be paid out of the Contingency and Emergency Fund subject to the approval of the Governor and Council of State. (1961, c. 1143, s. 6.)

Chapter 141.

State Boundaries.

§ 141-1. Governor to cause boundaries to be established and protected.

The Governor of North Carolina is hereby authorized to appoint two competent commissioners and a surveyor and a sufficient number of chainbearers, on the part of the State of North Carolina, to act with the commissioners or surveyors appointed or to be appointed by any of the contiguous states of Virginia, Tennessee, South Carolina, and Georgia, to return and remark, by some permanent monuments at convenient intervals, not greater than five miles, the boundary lines between this State and any of the said states.

The Governor is also authorized, whenever in his judgment it shall be deemed necessary to protect or establish the boundary lines between this State and any other state, to institute and prosecute in the name of the State of North Carolina any and all such actions, suits, or proceedings at law or in equity, and to direct the Attorney General or such other person as he may designate to conduct and prosecute such actions, suits, or proceedings. (1881, c. 347, s. 1; Code, s. 2289; 1889, c. 475, s. 1; Rev., s. 5315; 1909, c. 51, s. 1; C.S., s. 7396.)

§ 141-2. Payment of expenses of establishing boundaries.

When the line has been rerun and remarked as above provided between this State and any of the contiguous states, or such portion of said lines as shall be mutually agreed by the commissioners, the Governor is authorized to issue his warrant upon the State Treasurer for such portion of the expenses as shall fall to the share of this State. (1881, c. 347, s. 2; Code, s. 2290; 1889, c. 475, s. 2; Rev., s. 5316; C.S., s. 7397.)

§ 141-3. Appointment of arbitrators.

If any disagreement shall arise between the commissioners, the Governor of this State is hereby authorized to appoint arbitrators to act with similar officers to be appointed by the other states in the settlement of the exact boundary. (1881, c. 347, s. 3; Code, s. 2291; 1889, c. 475, s. 3; Rev., s. 5317; C.S., s. 7398.)

§ 141-4. Disagreement of arbitrators reported to General Assembly.

In case of any serious disagreement and inability on the part of the said arbitrators to agree upon said boundary, such fact shall be reported by the Governor to the next General Assembly for their action. (1881, c. 347, s. 4; Code, s. 2292; 1889, c. 475, s. 4; Rev., s. 5318; C.S., s. 7399.)

§ 141-5. Approval of survey.

When the commissioners shall have completed the survey, or so much as shall be necessary, they shall report the same to the Governor, who shall lay the same before the Council of State; and when the Governor and the Council of State shall have approved the same the Governor shall issue his proclamation, declaring said lines to be the true boundary line or lines, and the same shall be the true boundary line or lines between this and the states above referred to. (1881, c. 347, s. 5; Code, s. 2293; 1889, c. 475, s. 5; Rev., s. 5319; C.S., s. 7400.)

§ 141-6. Eastern boundary of State; jurisdiction over territory within littoral waters and lands under same.

(a)   The Constitution of the State of North Carolina, adopted in 1868, having provided in Article I, Sec. 34, that the "limits and boundaries of the State shall be and remain as they now are," and the eastern limit and boundary of the State of North Carolina on the Atlantic seaboard having always been, since the Treaty of Peace with Great Britain in 1783 and the Declaration of Independence of July 4, 1776, one marine league eastward from the Atlantic seashore, measured from the extreme low-water mark, the eastern boundary of the State of North Carolina is hereby declared to be fixed as it has always been at one marine league eastward from the seashore of the Atlantic Ocean bordering the State of North Carolina, measured from the extreme low-water mark of the Atlantic Ocean seashore aforesaid.

(b)   The State of North Carolina shall continue as it always has to exercise jurisdiction over the territory within the littoral waters and ownership of the lands under the same within the boundaries of the State, subject only to the jurisdiction of the federal government over navigation within such territorial waters.

(c)   The Governor and the Attorney General are hereby directed to take all such action as may be found appropriate to defend the jurisdiction of the State over its littoral waters and the ownership of the lands beneath the same. (1947, c. 1031, ss. 1-3; 1969, c. 541, s. 1.)

§ 141-7. Repealed by Session Laws 1977, c. 342.

§ 141-7.1. Southern lateral seaward boundary.

The lateral seaward boundary between North Carolina and South Carolina from the low-water mark of the Atlantic Ocean shall be and is hereby designated as a continuation of the North Carolina-South Carolina boundary line as described by monuments located at Latitude 33° 51' 50.7214" North, Longitude 78° 33' 22.9448" West, at Latitude 33° 51' 36.4626" North, Longitude 78° 33' 06.1937" West, and at Latitude 33° 51' 07.8792" North, Longitude 78° 32' 32.6210" West, in a straight line projection of said line to the seaward limits of the States' territorial jurisdiction, such line to be extended on the same bearing insofar as a need for further delimitation may arise. (1979, c. 894; 1981, c. 744.)

§ 141-8. Northern lateral seaward boundary.

The lateral seaward boundary between North Carolina and Virginia eastward from the low-water mark of the Atlantic Ocean shall be and is hereby designated as a line beginning at the intersection of the low-water mark of the Atlantic Ocean and the existing North Carolina-Virginia boundary line; thence due east on a true 90 degree bearing to the seaward jurisdictional limit of North Carolina; such boundary line to be extended on the true 90 degree bearing as far as a need for further delineation may arise. (1969, c. 841; 1971, c. 452, s. 1.)

Chapter 142.

State Debt.

Article 1.

General Provisions.

§ 142-1. How bonds executed; interest coupons attached; where payable; not to be sold at less than par.

All bonds or certificates of debt of the State shall be signed by the Governor, and countersigned by the State Treasurer, and sealed with the great seal of the State, and shall be made payable to bearer unless registered as hereinafter provided. The principal shall be made payable by the State at a day named in the bonds or certificates. Interest coupons shall be attached to the bonds or certificates unless they be bonds or certificates registered as to both principal and interest, and the bonds, certificates and coupons shall be made payable at such banks or trust companies within or without the State as shall be designated by the State Treasurer, or at the office of the State Treasurer in Raleigh. Any bank or trust company serving as a paying agent may be paid such reasonable fees and charges for such services as shall be agreed upon by and between such bank or trust company and the State Treasurer. No original bond or certificate of debt of the State shall be sold for a sum less than the par value thereof, nor shall any such bond or certificate, issued in lieu of a transferred bond or certificate, be payable elsewhere than may be the original, except by the consent of the holder it may be made payable at the State treasury. (1848, c. 89, s. 22; 1852, c. 9; c. 10, s. 10; R.C., c. 90, s. 3; Code, s. 3563; Rev., s. 5020; C.S., s. 7401; Ex. Sess. 1921, c. 66, ss. 1, 2; 1977, c. 405.)

§ 142-2. Title of act and year of enactment recited in bonds.

In every bond or certificate of debt issued by the State, and in the body thereof, shall be set forth the title of the act, with the year of its enactment, under the authority of which the same may be issued; or reference shall be made thereto by the number of the Chapter, and the year of the legislative session. (1850, c. 90, s. 6; R.C., c. 90, s. 6; Code, s. 3566; Rev., s. 5023; C.S., s. 7402.)

§ 142-3. Record of bonds kept by State Treasurer.

The State Treasurer shall enter in a book to be kept for that purpose a memorandum of every bond or certificate of debt of the State, issued or to be issued under any act whatever, together with the numbers, dates of issue, when and where payable, at what premium, and to whom the same may have been sold or issued. (1852, c. 10, s. 2; R.C., c. 90, s. 4; Code, s. 3564; Rev., s. 5021; C.S., s. 7403.)

§ 142-4. Books for registration and transfer.

The State Treasurer shall keep in his office a register or registers for the registration and transfer of all bonds and certificates of the State heretofore or hereafter issued, in which he may register any bond or certificate at the time of its issue or at the request of the holder. When any bond or certificate shall have been registered as hereinafter provided, the State Treasurer shall enter in a manner to be of easy and ready reference, a description of said bond, or certificates giving the number, series, date of issue, denomination, by whom signed, and such other data as may be necessary for the ready identification thereof, together with the name of the person in whose name the same is then to be registered and whether in his individual capacity or in a fiduciary relation, and if the latter, for whose benefit the same is to be registered. (1848, c. 37, s. 5; 1850, c. 58, s. 4; 1852, c. 11; R.C., c. 90, s. 2; Code, s. 3562; Rev., s. 5019; C.S., s. 7404; Ex. Sess. 1921, c. 66, s. 3.)

§ 142-5. Registration as to principal.

Upon the presentation at the office of the State Treasurer of any bond or certificate that has heretofore been or may hereafter be issued by the State, or upon the first issuance of any bond or certificate, the same may be registered as to principal in the name of the holder upon such register, such registration to be noted on the reverse of the bond or certificate by the State Treasurer. The principal of any bond or certificate so registered shall be payable only to the registered payee or his legal representative, and such bond or certificate shall be transferable to another holder or back to bearer only upon presentation of the State Treasurer with a written assignment acknowledged or approved in a form satisfactory to the Treasurer. The name of the registered assignee shall be written in said register and upon any bond or certificate so transferred. A bond or certificate so transferred to bearer shall be subject to future registration and transfer as before. (1883, c. 25; Code, s. 3568; 1887, c. 287; Rev., s. 5025; C.S., s. 7405; Ex. Sess. 1921, c. 66, s. 4.)

§ 142-6. Registration as to principal and interest.

(a)   If, upon the registration of any such bond or certificate dated prior to January 1, 1965, or at any time after such registration, the coupons thereto attached, evidencing all interest to be paid thereon to the date of maturity, shall be surrendered, such coupons shall be canceled by the Treasurer, and he shall sign a statement endorsed upon such bond or certificate of the cancellation of all unmatured coupons and of the fact that such bond or certificate has been converted into a fully registered bond or certificate, and shall make like entry in the said register. Thereafter the interest evidenced by such canceled coupons shall be paid at the time provided therein, to the registered owner or his legal representatives, in New York exchange, mailed to his address, unless he shall have requested the State Treasurer to pay such interest in funds current at the State capital, which request shall be entered in the said register.

(b)   If, upon the registration of any such bond or certificate dated on or after January 1, 1965, or at any time after such registration, the coupons thereto attached, evidencing all interest to be paid thereon to the date of maturity, shall be surrendered, such coupons shall be detached and retained in the custody of the State Treasurer, and the State Treasurer shall endorse upon such bond or certificate the fact that such bond or certificate has been converted into a fully registered bond or certificate, and shall make like entry in said register. Thereafter the interest evidenced by such detached coupons shall be paid at the times provided therein to the registered owner or his legal representatives, in

New York exchange, mailed to his address, unless he shall have requested the State Treasurer to pay such interest in funds current at the State capital, which request shall be entered in said register. Any such bond or certificate, if converted into a bond or certificate registered as to both principal and interest, may be reconverted at the expense of the registered owner into a coupon bond or certificate upon presentation thereof to the State Treasurer, accompanied by an instrument duly executed by the registered owner or his legal representatives in such form as shall be satisfactory to the State Treasurer; upon any such reconversion the State Treasurer shall reattach thereto the coupons representing the interest to become due thereafter on such bond or certificate to the date of maturity and shall make notation upon such bond or certificate whether such bond or certificate is registered as to principal alone or is payable to bearer, and shall make like entry in said register and he shall cancel any detached coupons retained by him representing interest that has been paid. (1856, c. 16; 1883, c. 25, s. 2; Code, s. 3569; 1887, c. 287, s. 2; Rev., s. 5026; C.S., s. 7406; Ex. Sess. 1921, c. 66, s. 5; 1965, c. 181, s. 1.)

§ 142-7. No charge for registration.

There shall be no charge for the registration of any bond or certificate whether registered at the time of issuance thereof or subsequently registered, and no charge for the transfer of registered bonds and certificates shall be made. (1887, c. 287, ss. 4, 5; Rev., s. 5027; C.S., s. 7407; Ex. Sess. 1921, c. 66, s. 6; 1925, c. 49.)

§ 142-8. Application of §§ 142-1 to 142-9.

General Statutes 142-1 to 142-9, both inclusive, as amended, shall be applicable to all bonds or certificates of the State heretofore issued and now outstanding, and to all bonds or certificates of the State that may hereafter be issued in accordance with any law now in force or hereafter to be enacted. However, any provisions of G.S. 142-1 to G.S. 142-9 in conflict with the "Registered Public Obligations Act", Chapter 159E of the General Statutes, shall not apply. (Code, s. 3570; 1887, c. 287, s. 3; Rev., s. 5028; C.S., s. 7408; Ex. Sess. 1921, c. 66, s. 7; 1965, c. 181, s. 2; 1983, c. 322, s. 2.)

§ 142-9. Duties performed by other officers.

If the Council of State shall at any time find that either the Governor or the State Treasurer is unable by reason of absence, disability, or otherwise, to sign any bonds or certificates, the Lieutenant-Governor may sign the same in lieu of the Governor, and they may be signed in lieu of the Treasurer by any member of the Council of State designated by it. (1864-5, c. 24; Code, s. 3567; Rev., s. 5024; C.S., s. 7409; Ex. Sess. 1921, c. 66, s. 8.)

§ 142-10. Chief clerk may issue when Treasurer unable to act.

Whenever it shall appear by formal finding of the Governor and Council of State, within seven days before any bonds or notes of the State or any interest thereon shall fall due, that it is advisable to issue notice of the State to provide for the renewal or payment of such bonds, notes or interest and that the State Treasurer is unable for any reason to negotiate or to issue such notes, it shall be the duty of the chief clerk of the State treasury, if the issuance of such notice shall have been authorized by law, upon certification to him of such finding, and in the name of the State Treasurer, to make all necessary negotiations and to sign and deliver such notes for value and to attach thereto the seal of the State Treasurer. (1927, c. 12.)

§ 142-11. When bonds deemed duly executed.

State bonds duly authorized by law and approved by the Governor and Council of State shall be regarded as duly executed by proper officers if signed and sealed while in office by the officer or officers then authorized to sign and seal the same, notwithstanding one or more of such officers shall not be in office at the time of actual delivery of such bonds. (1925, c. 2.)

§ 142-12. State bonds exempt from taxation.

Bonds and other evidences of indebtedness issued by the State are exempt from State taxation to the extent provided in the act authorizing their issuance. If the act authorizing the issuance of the instruments does not address exemption from taxation, then they are exempt from taxation by the State or any of its subdivisions, except for inheritance or gift taxes, income taxes on the gain from the transfer of the instruments, and franchise taxes. Unless the act authorizing the issuance of the instruments provides otherwise, the interest on the instruments is not subject to taxation as income. (1852, c. 10, s. 4; R.C., c. 90, s. 5; Code, s. 3565; Rev., s. 5022; C.S., s. 7410; 1995, c. 46, s. 14.)

§ 142-12.1. Effect of federal taxation of interest income on state or local bonds on issuance thereof; continuation of state tax exemptions.

(a)   It is hereby found, determined and declared that:

(1)   From time to time bills have been introduced in the United States Congress providing that the interest on all or certain state and municipal bonds or debt obligations, whether issued by or on behalf of states or local governmental units, be subject to federal income taxation; and

(2)   The Tax Reform Act of 1986 requires, in certain circumstances, the inclusion in the gross income of the recipient thereof of interest on bonds or obligations issued by or on behalf of certain state or local governmental units for purposes of federal income tax which heretofore would have been exempt from federal income taxation.

(b)   Nothing in any act, general, special or private, shall be deemed to limit or restrict the right of the State or any agency or instrumentality thereof, or The University of North Carolina or any agency or instrumentality thereof, or any county, city, town, special district, authority or other political subdivision or local governmental unit or any agency or instrumentality thereof, to issue, or have issued on its behalf, bonds or obligations the interest income on which is or may be subject to federal income taxation.

(c)   The interest on any of these bonds or obligations shall maintain its existing exemption from State income taxation, or other taxation, if any, notwithstanding that the interest may be or become subject to federal income taxation as a result of legislative action by the federal government.

(d)   If the provisions of this section are inconsistent with the provisions of any other laws, the provisions of this section shall be controlling. (1987, c. 587, ss. 1-4; 1995, c. 41, s. 10.)

220

§ 142-13. Destruction of canceled bonds, notes and coupons.

All canceled bonds, notes and interest coupons of the State may be destroyed in one of the following ways, in the discretion of the Treasurer:

(1)   Method 1. The Treasurer shall make an entry in a substantially bound book kept by him for the purpose of recording the destruction of bonds, notes and coupons, showing

a.   With respect to bonds and notes, the designation, the date of issue, serial numbers (if any), denomination, maturity date, and total principal amount.

b.   With respect to coupons, the designation and date of the bonds to which the coupons appertain, the maturity date of the coupons and, as to each maturity date, the denomination, quantity and total amount of coupons.

        After this entry has been made, the paid bonds, notes or coupons shall be destroyed, by either burning or shredding, in the presence of the Council of State. Each member of the Council of State in attendance shall certify under his hand in the book kept by the Treasurer that he saw the bonds, notes or coupons destroyed. Canceled bonds, notes or coupons shall not be destroyed until after one year from the date of payment.

(2)   Method 2. The Treasurer may contract with the bank or trust company acting as paying agent for a bond issue for the destruction of bonds and interest coupons which have been canceled by the paying agent. The contract shall require that the paying agent give the Treasurer a written certificate of each destruction containing the same information required by Method 1 to be entered in the record of destroyed bonds and coupons. The certificates shall be filed among the permanent records of the Treasurer. Canceled bonds or coupons shall not be destroyed until one year from the date of payment.

The provisions of G.S. 121-5 and 132-3 shall not apply to any such paid bonds, notes or coupons.

Notwithstanding the foregoing, in lieu of destroying all canceled bonds, notes and interest coupons, the Treasurer is authorized, with the approval of the Council of State, to distribute the bonds, notes, and coupons to the public schools of North Carolina and to the Department of Cultural Resources to be used for educational and historical purposes. The Department of Public Instruction and the Department of Cultural Resources may cooperate and assist

221

in implementing such purposes. (1879, c. 98, s. 8; Code, s. 3578; Rev., s. 5035; C.S., s. 7415; 1941, c. 28; 1975, c. 527; 1987, c. 522, s. 1.)

§ 142-14. Issuance of temporary bonds.

Whenever the State Treasurer shall be authorized by law to issue bonds or notes of the State, and all acts, conditions and things required by law to happen, exist and be performed, before the delivery thereof for value, shall have happened, shall exist and shall have been performed, except the printing, lithographing or engraving of the definitive bonds or notes authorized and the execution thereof, the State Treasurer is authorized, by and with the consent of the Governor and Council of State, to issue and deliver for value temporary bonds or notes, with or without coupons, which may be printed or lithographed in any denomination or denominations which may be a multiple of one thousand dollars ($1,000), and shall be signed and sealed as shall be provided for the signing and sealing of such definitive bonds or notes, and shall be substantially of the tenor of such definitive bonds or notes except as herein otherwise provided and except that such temporary bonds or notes shall contain such provisions as the Treasurer may elect as to the conditions of payment of the semiannual interest thereon. Every such temporary bond or note shall bear upon its face the words "Temporary Bond (or Note) Exchangeable for Definitive Bond." Upon the completion and execution of the definitive bonds or notes, such temporary bonds or notes shall be exchangeable without charge therefor to the holder of such temporary bonds or notes for definitive bonds or notes of an equal amount of principal. Such exchange shall be made by the Treasurer or by a bank or trust company in North Carolina or elsewhere appointed by him as agent which shall have a capital and surplus of not less than the amount of the definitive bonds or notes to be so exchanged, and in making such exchange the Treasurer shall detach from the definitive bonds or notes all coupons which represent interest theretofore paid upon the temporary bonds or notes to be exchanged therefor, and shall cancel all such coupons; and upon such exchange such temporary bonds or notes and the coupons attached thereto, if any, shall be forthwith canceled by the Treasurer of such agent. Until so exchanged, temporary bonds and notes issued under the authority hereof shall in all respects be entitled to all the rights and privileges of the definitive securities. (1925, c. 43.)

§ 142-15. Reimbursement of Treasurer for interest.

Whenever it shall become necessary for the State Treasurer to borrow money to provide the maintenance fund for any State institution, the said Treasurer is authorized to deduct from the sum appropriated for maintenance of said institution the amount of interest the Treasurer shall have to pay for the use of said fund. This section shall apply to all future laws creating a maintenance fund for any State institution, unless said laws shall specifically state otherwise. (1923, c. 210; C.S., s. 7466(a).)

§ 142-15.1. Lost, stolen, defaced, or destroyed State bonds.

(a)   If lost, stolen, or completely destroyed, any State bond, note, or coupon may be reissued in the same form and tenor upon the owner's furnishing to the satisfaction of the State Treasurer:

(1)   Proof of ownership,

(2)   Proof of loss or destruction,

(3)   A surety bond in twice the face amount of bond or note and coupon, and

(4)   Payment of the cost of preparing and issuing the new bond, note, or coupon.

(b)   If defaced or partially destroyed, any State bond, note, or coupon may be reissued in the same form and tenor to the bearer or registered holder, at his expense, upon surrender of the defaced or partially destroyed bond, note, or coupon and on such other conditions as the State Treasurer may prescribe. The State Treasurer may also provide for authentication of defaced or partially destroyed bonds, notes, or coupons instead of reissuing them.

(c)   Each new State bond, note, or coupon issued under this section shall be signed by the State Treasurer and shall contain a recital to the effect that it is issued in exchange for or replacement of a certain bond, note, or coupon (describing it sufficiently to identify it) and is to be deemed a part of the same issue as the original bond, note, or coupon.

(d)   Before taking action under this section to replace, exchange, or authenticate a State bond, note, or coupon, the State Treasurer shall obtain the advice and consent of the Council of State. (1971, c. 780, s. 36.)

§ 142-15.3. Capital appreciation bonds.

(a)   Cross-Reference. - The provisions of G.S. 159-99 govern capital appreciation bonds.

(b)   Authorization. - The State is authorized to issue capital appreciation bonds pursuant to the provisions of The State and Local Government Revenue Bond Act. The State is authorized to issue capital appreciation bonds pursuant to the provisions of applicable law and pursuant to the provisions of any law enacted in the future. (1987-650, ss. 2, 4 and 5; 2004-170, s. 41(a), (b).)

Article 2.

Borrowing Money in Emergencies and in Anticipation of Collection of Taxes.

§ 142-16. Governor and Council of State may borrow on note.

The Governor and Council of State may authorize and empower the State Treasurer in the intervals between sessions of the General Assembly, to borrow money on short term notes to meet any emergency arising from the destruction of the State's property, whether used by department or institution, or from some unforeseen calamity not amounting to its destruction. (1927, c. 49, s. 1.)

§ 142-17. Recital of facts entered on minutes; directions to Treasurer; limit of amount.

The Council of State, when such emergency arises during such interval, shall recite upon its minutes the facts out of which it does arise, and thereupon direct the State Treasurer to borrow from time to time money needed to meet such emergency or calamity, not exceeding, however in the whole, five hundred thousand dollars ($500,000) in the aggregate in the period between the adjournment of the present session of the General Assembly and the convening of the General Assembly in regular session in 1929 and not exceeding five hundred thousand dollars ($500,000) in the aggregate in any succeeding interval between regular sessions of the General Assembly, and to execute in behalf of the State of North Carolina notes for said money so borrowed to run not exceeding two years, and to bear interest not exceeding five percent (5%) per annum, payable semiannually. Said notes shall be in such forms as the State Treasurer may determine, and the obligations for the interest thereupon after maturity shall be receivable in payment of taxes, debts, dues, licenses, fines and demands due the State of any kind whatsoever. The said notes shall be exempt from all State, county and municipal taxation or assessment, direct or indirect, general or special, whether imposed for the purpose of general revenue or otherwise, and the interest thereon shall not be subject to taxation as for income, nor shall said notes be subject to taxation when constituting a part of the surplus of any bank, trust company, or other corporation. (1927, c. 49, s. 2.)

§ 142-18. Report to General Assembly.

At each, the next regular or extra session of the General Assembly, the Governor and Council of State shall report to it the proceedings of the Governor and Council of State in borrowing money under this Article, setting out fully the facts upon which they held that the emergency existed which authorized such borrowing. (1927, c. 49, s. 3.)

§ 142-19. Power given to Director of Budget to authorize State Treasurer to borrow money.

The Director of the Budget by and with the consent of the Governor and Council of State shall have authority to authorize and direct the State Treasurer to borrow, in the name of the State and pledge the credit of the State for the payment thereof, in anticipation of the collection of taxes, such sums as may be necessary to make the payment on appropriations to the various institutions, departments and agencies of the State as even as possible so as to preserve the best interest of the State in the conduct of the various institutions, departments and agencies of the State during each fiscal year. (1927, c. 195.)

Article 3.

Refunding Bonds.

§§ 142-20 through 142-29. Repealed by Session Laws 1985 (Reg. Sess., 1986), c. 823, s. 1.

Article 3A.

Refunding Bonds.

§ 142-29.1. Title of Article.

This Article may be known and cited as the "State Refunding Bond Act." (1935, c. 445, s. 1; 1985 (Reg. Sess., 1986), c. 823, s. 1.)

§ 142-29.2. Definitions.

The words and phrases defined in this section shall have the meanings indicated when used in this Article, unless the context clearly requires another meaning:

(1)   "Authorized investments" means

a.   Direct obligations of the United States government,

b.   Obligations the principal of and the interest on which are guaranteed by the United States government,

c.   Evidences of ownership of proportionate interests in future interest and principal payments on specified obligations described in a. and b. above, which obligations are held by a bank or trust company organized and existing under the laws of the United States of America or any state thereof in the capacity of custodian,

d.   Obligations of state or local government municipal bond issuers, provision for the payment of the principal of and interest on which shall have been made by deposit with a trustee or escrow agent of obligations described in a., b. or c. above, the maturing principal of and interest on which, when due and payable, shall provide sufficient money with any other money held in trust for such purpose to pay the principal of, premium, if any, and interest on such obligations of state or local government municipal bond issuers, and which are rated in the highest rating by Standard & Poor's Corporation and Moody's Investors Service, Inc.,

e.   Obligations of state or local government municipal bond issuers, the principal of and interest on which, when due and payable, have been insured by a bond insurance company which is rated in the highest rating category by Standard & Poor's Corporation and Moody's Investors Service, Inc.,

f.   Full faith and credit obligations of state or local government bond issuers which are rated in the highest rating category by Standard & Poor's Corporation and Moody's Investors Service, Inc., and

g.   Any obligations or investments in which the State Treasurer is authorized, at the time of such investment, to invest funds of the State.

(2)   "Bond documentation" means any resolution, order, trust agreement, trust indenture or other document authorizing the issuance of and securing any outstanding obligations.

(3)   "Bonds" means any bonds issued under the provisions of this Article.

(4)   "Credit facility" means an agreement entered into by the State Treasurer on behalf of the State with a bank, savings and loan association or other banking institution, an insurance company, reinsurance company, surety company or other insurance institution, a corporation, investment banking firm or other investment institution, or any financial institution providing for prompt payment of all or any part of the principal (whether at maturity, presentment for purchase, redemption or acceleration), redemption premium, if any, and interest on any refunding obligations payable on demand or tender by the owner issued in accordance with this Article, in consideration of the State agreeing to repay the provider of such credit facility in accordance with terms and provisions of such agreement, provided, that any such agreement shall provide that the obligation of the State thereunder shall have only such sources of payment as are permitted for the payment of refunding obligations issued under this Article.

227

(5)   "Notes" means any bond anticipation notes or notes issued under the provisions of this Article.

(6)   "Outstanding obligations" means any outstanding bonds, bond anticipation notes or notes of the State, whether now outstanding or hereafter issued, the payment of the principal of and the interest on which are secured by a pledge of the full faith, credit and taxing power of the State and which may also be secured, as and to the extent provided in applicable bond documentation, by additional security.

(7)   "Par formula" shall mean any provision or formula adopted by the State to provide for the adjustment, from time to time, of the interest rate or rates borne by any refunding obligations so that the purchase price of such refunding obligations in the open market would be as close to par as possible.

(8)   "Refunding obligations" means any notes or bonds issued under the provisions of this Article. (1935, c. 445, s. 2; 1985 (Reg. Sess., 1986), c. 823, s. 1.)

§ 142-29.3. Purpose.

The purpose of this Article is to provide statutory procedures or to supplement existing procedures for the issuance of refunding obligations. (1935, c. 445, s. 3; 1985 (Reg. Sess., 1986), c. 823, s. 1.)

§ 142-29.4. Powers.

In addition to the powers it may now or hereafter have, the State shall have the following powers, subject to the provisions of this Article and applicable bond documentation:

(1)   to borrow money and issue one or more series of refunding obligations for the purpose of refunding all or any part of any series or combination of series of outstanding obligations including, without limitation, the payment of any redemption premium thereon and any interest accrued or to accrue to the date of redemption or maturity or maturities of such outstanding obligations;

228

(2)   to apply the proceeds of refunding obligations

a.   to the payment and retirement of outstanding obligations by direct application to such payment and retirement,

b.   to the payment and retirement of outstanding obligations, whether by redemption or in accordance with their terms, by the deposit in trust of such proceeds,

c.   to the payment of any expenses incurred in connection with such refunding, including the expense of any credit facility employed in connection with such refunding obligations, including, without limitation, bond insurance policies, letters of credit and lines of credit, and

d.   for such other uses not inconsistent with any such refunding,

(3)   to issue refunding obligations in combination with any other bonds, bond anticipation notes, notes or financial obligations issued by the State;

(4)   to issue refunding obligations bearing interest at rates lower, the same as or higher than and having maturities shorter, the same as or longer than the outstanding obligations being refunded;

(5)   to issue one series of refunding obligations to refund one or more series of outstanding obligations;

(6)   to issue refunding obligations in exchange for outstanding obligations;

(7)   to apply to any purpose consistent with any refunding, including the funding of an escrow fund or account to be used for the payment or redemption of any outstanding obligations, moneys made available as a consequence of such refunding, including, without limitation, any moneys then on deposit in debt service reserve funds, principal accounts, interest accounts and sinking fund accounts in respect of the outstanding obligations being refunded and, subject to the approval of the Council of State, any moneys appropriated by the General Assembly for the payment of principal of or interest on the outstanding obligations being refunded; and

(8)   to invest any moneys, including any moneys held in trust, in authorized investments. (1935, c. 445, s. 4; 1985 (Reg. Sess., 1986), c. 823, s. 1.)

§ 142-29.5. Authorization of refunding obligations.

By and with the consent of the Council of State, the State Treasurer is authorized to issue and sell, from time to time, refunding obligations for the purpose of refunding outstanding obligations as and to the extent authorized by this Article. The principal amount of any such refunding obligations shall not exceed the principal amount of outstanding obligations to be refunded unless (i) the refunding results in an aggregate debt service savings and (ii) the increase in the principal amount issued does not create cash-in-hand available for new capital improvements.

Refunding obligations issued pursuant to the provisions of this Article shall not be subject to limitations imposed by any other law including, without limitation, the other Articles of this Chapter. (1935, c. 445, s. 5; 1985 (Reg. Sess., 1986), c. 823, s. 1; 1993, c. 542, s. 13.)

§ 142-29.6. Sale of refunding obligations and provisions thereof.

(a)   The bonds shall bear such date or dates, shall be serial or term bonds, shall mature in such amounts and at such times, not exceeding 40 years from their date or dates, and shall bear interest at such rate or rates, which may vary from time to time as hereinafter authorized, and which may be represented, in part, by evidences of additional interest, and the bonds may be made redeemable before maturity, at the option of the State or otherwise as may be provided by the State, at such price or prices and under such terms and conditions, all as may be fixed by the State Treasurer with the consent of the Council of State.

(b)   The bonds shall be signed on behalf of the State by the Governor or shall bear his facsimile signature; shall be signed by the State Treasurer or shall bear his facsimile signature; and shall bear the Great Seal of the State or a facsimile thereof impressed or imprinted thereon; and interest coupons, if any, shall bear a facsimile of the signature of the State Treasurer. If the bonds shall bear the facsimile signatures of the Governor and the State Treasurer, the bonds shall also bear a manual signature which may be that of a bond registrar, trustee, paying agent or designated assistant of the State Treasurer. Should any officer whose signature or facsimile signature appears on any bonds or coupons (if any) cease to be such officer before the delivery of the bonds, such signature or facsimile signature shall nevertheless have the same validity for all purposes as if the officer had remained in office until delivery and any bond or coupon may bear the facsimile signatures of such persons who at the actual time of the execution of such bond or coupon shall be the proper officers to sign any bond or coupon although at the date of such bond or coupon such persons may not have been such officers. The form and denomination of the bonds and any coupons, including the provisions with respect to registration of the bonds, shall be as the State Treasurer may determine in conformity with this Article; provided, however, that nothing in this Article shall prohibit the State Treasurer from proceeding, with respect to the issuance and form of the bonds, under the provisions of the Registered Public Obligations Act as well as this Article.

(c)   Subject to determination by the Council of State as to the manner in which the bonds shall be offered for sale, whether at public or private sale and whether by publishing notices in certain newspapers and financial journals, mailing notices, inviting bids by correspondence, negotiating contracts of purchase or otherwise, the State Treasurer is authorized to sell the bonds, at one time or from time to time, at a price equal to, greater than or less than the face amount of the bonds as the State Treasurer may determine to be in the best interests of the State.

All expenses incurred in the preparation, sale and issuance of the refunding obligations shall be paid by the State Treasurer from the proceeds of any such refunding obligations or any other available moneys.

(d)   (1)   By and with the consent of the Council of State, the State Treasurer is hereby authorized to borrow money at such rate or rates of interest as the State Treasurer may determine to be in the best interests of the State, which may vary from time to time as hereinafter authorized, and to execute and issue bond anticipation notes or notes of the State for the same, but only in the following circumstances and under the following conditions:

a.   For anticipating the sale of any bonds to the issuance of which the Council of State shall have given consent, if the State Treasurer shall deem it advisable to postpone the issuance of such bonds;

b.   For the payment of interest upon or any installment of principal of any of the bonds then outstanding, if there shall not be sufficient funds in the State Treasury with which to pay the interest or installment of principal as they respectively become due; or

c.   For the renewal of any loan evidenced by bond anticipation notes or notes herein authorized.

(2)   Funds derived from the sale of bonds may be used in the payment of any bond anticipation notes issued under this Article. Funds provided by the General Assembly for the payment of interest on or principal of bonds shall be used in paying the interest on or principal of any notes and any renewals thereof, the proceeds of which shall have been used in paying interest on or principal of such bonds.

Nothing in this Article shall be construed as a limitation on the duration of any deposit in trust for the retirement of outstanding obligations which shall not have matured and which shall not be then redeemable or, if then redeemable, shall not have been called for redemption.

(e)   Coupons (if any) and any evidences of additional interest appertaining to bonds and notes shall, after the maturity of such coupons or evidences of additional indebtedness, be receivable in payment of all taxes, debts, dues, licenses, fines and demands of any kind whatever due the State.

(f)   All refunding obligations shall be exempt from all State, county and municipal taxation or assessment, direct or indirect, general or special, whether imposed for the purpose of general revenue or otherwise, except for inheritance and gift taxes, income taxes on the gain from the transfer of the obligations, and franchise taxes. The interest on the refunding obligations is not subject to taxation as income.

(g)   Refunding obligations, coupons (if any) and any evidences of additional indebtedness are hereby made securities in which all public officers, agencies and public bodies of the State and its political subdivisions, all insurance companies, trust companies, investment companies, banks, savings banks, building and loan associations, credit unions, pension or retirement funds, other financial institutions engaged in business in the State, executors, administrators, trustees and other fiduciaries may properly and legally invest funds, including capital in their control or belonging to them. Such refunding obligations, coupons (if any) and any evidences of additional indebtedness are hereby made securities which may properly and legally be deposited with and received by any officer or agency of the State or political subdivision of the State for any purpose for which the deposit of bonds, notes or obligations of the State or any political subdivision is now or may hereafter be authorized by law.

232

(h)   The full faith, credit and taxing power of the State are hereby pledged for the payment of the principal of and the interest on refunding obligations, coupons (if any) and any evidences of additional indebtedness to the same extent as pledged to the outstanding obligations being refunded. To the extent additional security has been pledged to outstanding obligations, such additional security may, at the discretion of the State, be continued and similarly pledged to the appropriate refunding obligations, coupons (if any) and any evidences of additional indebtedness. (1935, c. 445, s. 6; 1985 (Reg. Sess., 1986), c. 823, s. 1; 1995, c. 46, s. 15.)

§ 142-29.7. Additional refunding obligation provisions.

In fixing the details of refunding obligations, the State Treasurer may provide that any of the refunding obligations:

(1)   May be made payable from time to time on demand or tender for purchase by the owner thereof provided a credit facility supports such refunding obligations, unless the State Treasurer specifically determines that a credit facility is not required upon a finding and determination by the State Treasurer that the absence of a credit facility will not materially and adversely affect the financial position of the State and the marketing of the refunding obligations at a reasonable interest cost to the State;

(2)   May be additionally supported by a credit facility;

(3)   May be made subject to redemption prior to maturity with such variations as may be permitted in connection with a par formula;

(4)   May bear interest at a rate or rates that may vary as permitted pursuant to a par formula and for such period or periods of time, all as may be provided in the proceedings providing for the issuance of such refunding obligations; and

(5)   May be made the subject of a remarketing agreement whereby an attempt is made to remarket the refunding obligations to new purchasers prior to their presentment for payment to the provider of the credit facility or to the State.

If the aggregate principal amount repayable by the State under an agreement is in excess of the aggregate principal amount of refunding obligations secured by the related credit facility, whether as a result of the inclusion in the credit facility

233

of a provision for the payment of interest for a limited period of time or the payment of a redemption premium or for any other reason, then the amount of authorized but unissued refunding obligations during the term of such agreement shall not be less than the amount of such excess, unless the payment of such excess is otherwise provided for by agreement of the State executed by the State Treasurer. (1935, c. 445, s. 7; 1985 (Reg. Sess., 1986), c. 823, s. 1.)

Article 4.

Sinking Fund Commission.

§§ 142-30 through 142-43: Repealed by Session Laws 1983, c. 913, s. 30.

Article 5.

Sinking Funds for Highway Bonds.

§§ 142-44 through 142-46: Repealed by Session Laws 1983, c. 913, s. 30.

Article 5A.

Exchange and Cancellation of Bonds Held in Sinking Funds; Investment of Moneys.

§§ 142-47 through 142-49: Repealed by Session Laws 1983, c. 913, s. 30.

Article 7.

General Fund Bond Sinking Fund.

§§ 142-50 through 142-54: Repealed by Session Laws 1983, c. 913, s. 30.

§§ 142-55 through 142-59. Reserved for future codification purposes.

Article 8.

State Energy Conservation Finance Act.

§ 142-60. Short title.

This Article is the State Energy Conservation Finance Act. (2002-161, s. 9.)

§ 142-61. Definitions.

The following definitions apply in this Article:

(1)   Certificates of participation. - Certificates or other instruments delivered by a special corporation as provided in this Article evidencing the assignment of proportionate and undivided interests in the rights to receive payments to be made by the State pursuant to one or more financing contracts.

(2)   Cost. - The term includes:

a.   The cost of construction, modification, rehabilitation, renovation, improvement, acquisition, or installation in connection with an energy conservation measure.

b.   The cost of engineering, architectural, and other consulting services as may be required, including the cost of performing the technical analysis in accordance with G.S. 143-64.17A and inspection and certification in accordance with G.S. 143-64.17K.

c.   Finance charges, reserves for debt service and other types of reserves required pursuant to a financing contract or any other related documentation, and interest prior to and during construction, and, if deemed advisable by the State Treasurer, for a period not exceeding two years after the estimated date of completion of construction.

d.   Administrative expenses and charges.

e.   The cost of bond insurance, investment contracts, credit and liquidity facilities, interest rate swap agreements and other derivative products, financial and legal consultants, and related costs of the incurrence or issuance of the financing contract to the extent and as determined by the State Treasurer.

f.   The cost of reimbursing the State for payments made for any costs described in this subdivision.

g.   Any other costs and expenses necessary or incidental to implementing the purposes of this Article.

(3)   Credit facility. - An agreement that:

a.   Is entered into by the State with a bank, savings and loan association, or other banking institution, an insurance company, reinsurance company, surety company or other insurance institution, a corporation, investment banking firm or other investment institution, or any financial institution or other similar provider of a credit facility, which provider may be located within or without the United States of America; and

b.   Provides for prompt payment of all or any part of the principal or purchase price (whether at maturity, presentment or tender for purchase, redemption, or acceleration), redemption premium, if any, and interest with respect to any financing contract payable on demand or tender by the owner in consideration of the State agreeing to repay the provider of the credit facility in accordance with the terms and provisions of the agreement.

(4)   Energy conservation measure. - Defined in G.S. 143-64.17.

(5)   Energy conservation property. - Buildings, equipment, or other property with respect to which an energy conservation measure is undertaken.

(6)   Financing contract. - An installment financing contract entered into pursuant to the provisions of this Article to finance the cost of an energy conservation measure.

(7)   Person. - An individual, a firm, a partnership, an association, a corporation, a limited liability company, or any other organization or group acting as a unit.

(8)   Special corporation. - A nonprofit corporation created under Chapter 55A of the General Statutes for the purpose of facilitating the incurrence of certificates of participation indebtedness by the State under this Article.

(9)   State governmental unit. - Defined in G.S. 143-64.17.

(10)   State Treasurer. - The incumbent Treasurer, from time to time, of the State. (2002-161, s. 9.)

§ 142-62: Reserved for future codification purposes.

§ 142-63. Authorization of financing contract.

Subject to the terms and conditions set forth in this Article, (i) a State governmental unit that is implementing an energy conservation measure pursuant to G.S. 143-64.17L and financing it pursuant to this Article, (ii) a State governmental unit that has solicited a guaranteed energy conservation measure pursuant to G.S. 143-64.17A or G.S. 143-64.17B, or (iii) the State Treasurer, as designated by the Council of State, is authorized to execute and deliver, for and on behalf of the State of North Carolina, a financing contract to finance the costs of the energy conservation measure. The aggregate outstanding amount payable by the State under financing contracts entered pursuant to this Article shall not exceed five hundred million dollars ($500,000,000) at any one time. (2002-161, s. 9; 2006-190, s. 6; 2009-375, s. 1; 2011-145, s. 9.6D(f); 2013-396, s. 4(b).)

§ 142-64. Procedure for incurrence or issuance of financing contract.

(a)   When a State governmental unit (i) is implementing an energy conservation measure pursuant to G.S. 143-64.17L and financing it pursuant to this Article or (ii) has solicited a guaranteed energy conservation measure, the State governmental unit shall request that the State Treasurer approve the State governmental unit's entering into a financing contract to finance the cost of the energy conservation measure. In connection with the request, the State governmental unit shall provide to the State Treasurer any information the State Treasurer requests in order to evaluate the request. In the event that the State Treasurer determines that financing efficiencies will be realized through the combining of financing contracts, then the State Treasurer is authorized to execute and deliver, for and on behalf of the State of North Carolina, subject to the terms and conditions set forth in this Article, a financing contract for the purpose of financing the cost of the multiple energy conservation measures.

(b)   A financing contract may be entered into pursuant to this Article only after all of the following conditions are met:

(1)   The Office of State Budget and Management has certified that resources are expected to be available to the State to pay the payments to fall due under the financing contract as they become due and payable.

(2)   The Council of State has approved the execution and delivery of the financing contract by resolution that sets forth all of the following:

a.   The not-to-exceed term or final maturity of the financing contract, which shall be no later than 20 years from the date of acceptance of the project.

b.   The not-to-exceed interest rate or rates (or the equivalent thereof), which may be fixed or vary over a period of time, with respect to the financing contract.

c.   The appropriate officers of the State to execute and deliver the financing contract and all other documentation relating to it.

(3)   The State Treasurer has approved the financing contract and all other documentation related to it, including any deed of trust, security agreement, trust agreement or any credit facility.

The resolution of the Council of State shall include any other matters the Council of State considers appropriate.

(c)   In determining whether to approve a financing contract under subdivision (b)(3) of this section, the State Treasurer may consider the factors the State Treasurer considers relevant in order to find and determine all of the following:

(1)   The principal amount to be advanced to the State under the financing contract is adequate and not excessive for the purpose of paying the cost of the energy conservation measure.

(2)   The increase, if any, in State revenues necessary to pay the sums to become due under the financing contract are not excessive.

(3)   The financing contract can be entered into on terms desirable to the State.

(4)   In the case of delivery of certificates of participation, the sale of certificates of participation will not have an adverse effect upon any scheduled or proposed sale of obligations of the State or any State agency.

(d)   The Office of State Budget and Management is authorized to certify that funds are expected to be available to the State to make the payments due under a financing contract entered into under the provisions of this section as the payments become due and payable. In so certifying, the Office of State Budget and Management may take into account expected decreases in appropriations to the State governmental unit that will offset payments expected to be made under the financing contract. (2002-161, s. 9; 2006-190, s. 7; 2011-145, s. 9.6D(g).)

§ 142-65. Security; other requirements.

(a)   In order to secure the performance by the State of its obligations under a financing contract or any other related documentation, the State may grant a lien on, or security interest in, all or any part of the energy conservation property or the land upon which the energy conservation property is or will be located.

(b)   No deficiency judgment may be rendered against the State or any State governmental unit in any action for breach of any obligation contained in a financing contract or any other related documentation, and the taxing power of the State is not and may not be pledged directly or indirectly to secure any moneys due under a financing contract or any other related documentation. In the event that the General Assembly does not appropriate funds sufficient to make payments required under a financing contract or any other related documentation, the net proceeds received from the sale, lease, or other disposition of the property subject to the lien or security interest created pursuant to subsection (a) of this section shall be applied to satisfy these payment obligations in accordance with the deed of trust, security agreement, or other documentation creating the lien or security interest. These net proceeds are hereby appropriated for the purpose of making these payments. Any net proceeds in excess of the amount required to satisfy the obligations of the State under the financing contract or any other related documentation shall be paid to the State Treasurer for deposit to the General Fund of the State.

(c)   Neither a financing contract nor any other related documentation shall contain a nonsubstitution clause that restricts the right of the State to (i) continue to provide a service or conduct an activity or (ii) replace or provide a substitute for any State property that is the subject of an energy conservation measure.

(d)   A financing contract may include provisions requesting the Governor to submit in the Governor's budget proposal, or any amendments or supplements to it, appropriations necessary to make the payments required under the financing contract.

(e)   A financing contract may contain any provisions for protecting and enforcing the rights and remedies of the person advancing moneys or providing funds under the financing contract that are reasonable and not in violation of law, including covenants setting forth the duties of the State in respect of the purposes to which the funds advanced under a financing contract may be applied, and the duties of the State with respect to the property subject to the lien or security interest created pursuant to subsection (a) of this section, including, without limitation, provisions relating to insuring and maintaining any property and the custody, safeguarding, investment, and application of moneys.

(f)   The interest component of the installment payments to be made under a financing contract may be calculated based upon a fixed or variable interest rate or rates as determined by the State Treasurer.

(g)   If the State Treasurer determines that it is in the best interest of the State, the State may enter into, or arrange for the delivery of, a credit facility to secure payment of the payments due under a financing contract or to secure payment of the purchase price of any certificates of participation delivered as provided in this Article. (2002-161, s. 9.)

§ 142-66. Payment provisions.

The payment of amounts payable by the State under a financing contract and any other related documentation during any fiscal biennium or fiscal year shall

240

be limited to funds appropriated for that purpose by the General Assembly in its discretion. No provision of this Article and no financing contract or any other related documentation shall be construed or interpreted as creating a pledge of the faith and credit of the State or any agency, department, or commission of the State within the meaning of any constitutional debt limitation. (2002-161, s. 9.)

§ 142-67. Certificates of participation.

(a)   If the State Treasurer determines that the State would realize debt service savings under one or more financing contracts if certificates of participation are issued with respect to the rights to receive payments under the financing contract, then the State Treasurer is authorized to take actions, with the consent of the Council of State, that will effectuate the delivery of certificates of participation for that purpose.

(b)   Terms; Interest. - Certificates of participation may be sold by the State Treasurer in the manner, either at public or private sale, and for any price or prices that the State Treasurer determines to be in the best interest of the State and to effect the purposes of this Article, except that the terms of the sale must also be approved by the special corporation. Interest payable with respect to certificates of participation shall accrue at the rate or rates determined by the State Treasurer with the approval of the special corporation.

(c)   Trust Agreement. - Certificates of participation may be delivered pursuant to a trust agreement or similar instrument with a corporate trustee approved by the State Treasurer. (2002-161, s. 9.)

§ 142-68. Tax exemption.

Any financing contract entered pursuant to this Article, and any certificates of participation relating to it, shall at all times be free from taxation by the State or any political subdivision or any of their agencies, excepting estate, inheritance, and gift taxes; income taxes on the gain from the transfer of the financing contract or certificates of participation; and franchise taxes. The interest component of the installment payments made by the State under the financing contract, including the interest component of any certificates of participation, is not subject to taxation as income. (2002-161, s. 9.)

§ 142-69. Other agreements.

The State Treasurer may authorize, execute, obtain, or otherwise provide for bond insurance, investment contracts, credit and liquidity facilities, credit enhancement facilities, interest rate swap agreements and other derivative products, and any other related instruments and matters the State Treasurer determines are desirable in connection with entering into financing contracts and issuing certificates of participation pursuant to this Article. The State Treasurer is authorized to employ and designate any financial consultants, underwriters, fiduciaries, and bond attorneys to be associated with any financing contracts or certificates of participation under this Article as the State Treasurer considers appropriate. (2002-161, s. 9.)

§ 142-70. Investment eligibility.

Financing contracts entered into pursuant to this Article, and any certificates of participation relating to them, are securities or obligations in which all of the following may invest, including capital in their control or belonging to them: public officers, agencies, and public bodies of the State and its political subdivisions; insurance companies, trust companies, investment companies, banks, savings banks, savings and loan associations, credit unions, pension or retirement funds, and other financial institutions engaged in business in the State; and executors, administrators, trustees, and other fiduciaries. Financing contracts entered pursuant to this Article, and any certificates of participation relating to them, are securities or obligations that may properly and legally be deposited with and received by any officer or agency of the State or any political subdivision of the State for any purpose for which the deposit of bonds, notes, or obligations of the State or any political subdivision is now or may later be authorized by law. (2002-161, s. 9.)

§ 142-71: Reserved for future codification purposes.

242

§ 142-72: Reserved for future codification purposes.

§ 142-73: Reserved for future codification purposes.

§ 142-74: Reserved for future codification purposes.

§ 142-75: Reserved for future codification purposes.

§ 142-76: Reserved for future codification purposes.

§ 142-77: Reserved for future codification purposes.

§ 142-78: Reserved for future codification purposes.

§ 142-79: Reserved for future codification purposes.

Article 9.

State Capital Facilities Finance Act.

§ 142-80. Short title.

This Article may be cited as the State Capital Facilities Finance Act. (2003-284, s. 46.2; 2003-314, s. 1; 2004-203, s. 79.)

§ 142-81. Findings and purpose.

The General Assembly finds as follows:

(1)   There is a continuing need for capital facilities for the State, many of which will continue to be provided on a "pay-as-you-go" basis by direct appropriations.

(2)   The State will also continue to provide capital facilities through the issuance of general obligation bonds.

(3)   There is a need, however, for the use of alternative financing methods, such as authorized in this Article, to facilitate the providing of capital facilities

243

when circumstances and conditions warrant the providing of capital facilities through financing methods in addition to direct appropriations and the issuance of general obligation bonds.

(4)   The use of these alternative financing methods as authorized in this Article will provide financing flexibility to the State and permit the State to take advantage of changing financial and economic environments. (2003-284, s. 46.2; 2004-203, s. 79.)

§ 142-82. Definitions.

The following definitions apply in this Article:

(1)   Bonded indebtedness. - Limited obligation bonds and bond anticipation notes, including refunding bonds and notes, authorized to be issued under this Article.

(2)   Bonds or notes. - Limited obligation bonds and notes authorized to be issued under this Article.

(3)   Capital facility. - Any one or more of the following:

a.   Any one or more buildings, utilities, structures, or other facilities or property developments, including streets and landscaping, and the acquisition of equipment, machinery, and furnishings in connection with these items.

b.   Additions, extensions, enlargements, renovations, and improvements to existing buildings, utilities, structures, or other facilities or property developments, including streets and landscaping.

c.   Land or an interest in land.

d.   Other infrastructure.

e.   Furniture, fixtures, equipment, vehicles, machinery, and similar items.

(4)   Certificates of participation. - Certificates or other instruments delivered by a special corporation evidencing the assignment of proportionate undivided interests in rights to receive payments pursuant to a financing contract.

(5)   Certificates of participation indebtedness. - Financing contract indebtedness incurred by the State under a plan of finance in which a special corporation obtains funds to pay the cost of a capital facility to be financed through the delivery by the special corporation of certificates of participation.

(6)   Cost. - Any of the following in financing the cost of capital facilities as authorized by this Article:

a.   The cost of constructing, reconstructing, renovating, repairing, enlarging, acquiring, and improving capital facilities, including the acquisition of land, rights-of-way, easements, franchises, equipment, machinery, furnishings, and other interests in real or personal property acquired or used in connection with a capital facility.

b.   The cost of engineering, architectural, and other consulting services.

c.   The cost of providing personnel to ensure effective management of capital facilities.

d.   Finance charges, reserves for debt service, and other types of reserves required pursuant to the terms of any special indebtedness or related documents, interest before and during construction or acquisition of a capital facility and, if considered advisable by the State Treasurer, for a period not exceeding two years after the estimated date of completion of construction or acquisition.

e.   Administrative expenses and charges.

f.   The cost of bond insurance, investment contracts, credit enhancement facilities and liquidity facilities, interest rate swap agreements or other derivative products, financial and legal consultants, and related costs of the incurrence or issuance of special indebtedness.

g.   The cost of reimbursing the State, a State agency, or a special corporation for any payments made for any cost described in this subdivision.

h.   Any other costs and expenses necessary or incidental to the purposes of this Article.

(7)   Credit facility. - An agreement that:

245

a.   Is entered into by the State with a bank, savings and loan association, or other banking institution, an insurance company, reinsurance company, surety company, or other insurance institution, a corporation, investment banking firm, or other investment institution, or any financial institution or other similar provider of a credit facility, which provider may be located within or without the United States of America; and

b.   Provides for prompt payment of all or any part of the principal or purchase price (whether at maturity, presentment or tender for purchase, redemption, or acceleration), redemption premium, if any, and interest with respect to any special indebtedness payable on demand or tender by the owner in consideration of the State's agreeing to repay the provider of the credit facility in accordance with the terms and provisions of the agreement.

(8)   Department of Administration. - The North Carolina Department of Administration, created by Article 36 of Chapter 143 of the General Statutes or, if the Department is abolished or otherwise divested of its functions under this Article, the public body succeeding it in its principal functions or upon which are conferred by law the rights, powers, and duties given by this Article to the Department.

(9)   Financing contract. - A contract entered into pursuant to this Article to finance capital facilities and constituting a lease-purchase contract, installment-purchase contract, or other similar type installment financing contract. The term does not include, however, a contract that meets any one of the following conditions:

a.   It constitutes an operating lease under generally accepted accounting principles.

b.   It provides for the payment under the contract over its full term, including periods that may be added to the original term through the exercise of options to renew or extend, of an aggregate principal amount of not in excess of five thousand dollars ($5,000) or any greater amount that may be established by the Council of State if the Council of State determines (i) the aggregate amount to be paid under these contracts will not have a significant impact on the State budgetary process or the economy of the State and (ii) the change will lessen the administrative burden on the State.

c.   It is executed and provides for the making of all payments under the contract, including payment to be made during any period that may be added to the original term through the exercise of options to renew or extend, in the same fiscal year.

(10)   Financing contract indebtedness. - Indebtedness incurred pursuant to a financing contract, including certificates of participation indebtedness.

(11)   Fiscal period. - A fiscal biennium or a fiscal year of the fiscal biennium.

(12)   Fiscal year. - The fiscal year of the State beginning on July 1 of one calendar year and ending on June 30 of the next calendar year.

(13)   Limited obligation bond. - A limited obligation bond issued pursuant to G.S. 142-88 and payable and secured as provided in G.S. 142-89.

(14)   Par formula. - A provision or formula adopted by the State to provide for the adjustment, from time to time, of the interest rate or rates borne or provided for by any special indebtedness, including any of the following:

a.   A provision providing for an adjustment so that the purchase price of special indebtedness in the open market would be as close to par as possible.

b.   A provision providing for an adjustment based upon a percentage or percentages of a prime rate or base rate, which percentages may vary or be applied for different periods of time.

c.   Any provision that the State Treasurer determines is consistent with this Article and will not materially and adversely affect the financial position of the State and the marketing of special indebtedness at a reasonable interest cost to the State.

(15)   Person. - An individual, a firm, a partnership, an association, a corporation, a limited liability company, or any other organization or group acting as a unit.

(16)   Special corporation. - Either of the following:

a.   A nonprofit corporation created under Chapter 55A of the General Statutes for the purpose of facilitating the incurrence of certificates of participation indebtedness by the State under this Article.

247

b.   A private corporation or other entity issuing certificates of participation pursuant to this Article.

(17)   Special indebtedness. - Financing contract indebtedness and bonded indebtedness issued or incurred pursuant to this Article.

(18)   State. - The State of North Carolina, including any State agency.

(19)   State agency. - Any agency, institution, board, commission, bureau, council, department, division, officer, or employee of the State. The term does not include counties, municipal corporations, political subdivisions, local boards of education, or other local public bodies.

(20)   State Treasurer. - The incumbent Treasurer, from time to time, of the State. (2003-284, s. 46.2; 2003-314, s. 1; 2004-203, s. 79.)

§ 142-83. Authorization of special indebtedness; General Assembly approval.

(a)   General Assembly Approval. - The State may incur or issue special indebtedness subject to the terms and conditions provided in this Article for the purpose of financing the cost of capital facilities that meet one of the following conditions:

(1)   The General Assembly has enacted legislation describing the capital facility and authorizing its financing by the incurrence or issuance of special indebtedness up to a specific maximum amount.

(2)   The General Assembly has enacted legislation authorizing the incurrence or issuance of special indebtedness up to a specific maximum amount for a specific category of capital facilities and the capital facility meets all of the conditions set in that legislation.

(b)   Limitation. - The General Assembly may enact legislation to incur or issue special indebtedness under subsection (a) of this section only if it determines at the time the legislation is enacted that the amount of special indebtedness authorized by the legislation does not exceed the limitation in this subsection. The determination of the General Assembly must be based upon reasonable estimations and once made may be relied upon as conclusive.

248

The sum of the special indebtedness authorized by the legislation and all other special indebtedness authorized by legislation enacted after January 1, 2013, may not exceed twenty-five percent (25%) of the bond indebtedness of the State supported by the General Fund that was authorized pursuant to legislation enacted after January 1, 2013. For purposes of this section, bond indebtedness supported by the General Fund includes both special indebtedness and general obligation bond indebtedness of the State that is supported by the General Fund. (2003-284, s. 46.2; 2003-314, s. 1; 2004-203, s. 79; 2013-78, s. 1.)

§ 142-84. Procedure for incurrence or issuance of special indebtedness.

(a)   Notice and Certificate. - Whenever the State or a State agency determines that special indebtedness is appropriate to finance capital facilities, it shall notify the Department of Administration. If the Department of Administration concurs, it shall provide written notice to the State Treasurer advising the State Treasurer of this determination.

After the filing of the notice and after any preliminary conference, the State Treasurer shall consult with the Office of State Budget and Management as to the revenues expected by that Office to be available to pay all sums to come due on the special indebtedness during its term. If, after consulting with the Office of State Budget and Management, the State Treasurer determines by written certificate that it may be desirable to use special indebtedness to finance the capital facilities, the Department of Administration shall request the Council of State to give its preliminary approval of the use of special indebtedness to finance the capital facilities. The Department of Administration must promptly file copies of the notice and certificate required by this subsection with the Governor and the Council of State.

(b)   Preliminary Approval. - The Council of State, upon receipt of the notice and certificate required by subsection (a) of this section, shall adopt a resolution granting or denying preliminary approval of the financing. A resolution granting preliminary approval may include any other terms, conditions, and restrictions the Council of State considers appropriate and not inconsistent with the provisions of this Article.

(c)   Final Approval. - Before any special indebtedness may be incurred or issued pursuant to this Article, the Council of State must authorize the indebtedness by resolution, either as part of or separate from the resolution required by subsection (b) of this section. The resolution must do all of the following:

(1)   Authorize the providing of a particular capital facility or, in general terms, the types or classifications of capital facilities to be provided.

(2)   Set the aggregate principal amount or maximum principal amount of the special indebtedness authorized.

(3)   Set the maturity or maximum maturity of the special indebtedness authorized.

(4)   Set the rate, rates, or maximum rate of interest, which may be fixed or vary over a period of time, of the special indebtedness authorized.

(5)   Include any other conditions or matters not inconsistent with the provisions of this Article in the discretion of the Council of State, which may include the adoption or approvals as may be authorized in G.S. 142-88 and G.S. 142-89.

(d)   Financing Terms. - No special indebtedness shall be incurred or issued without the prior written approval of the State Treasurer as provided in this subsection, which is in addition to the certificate given by the State Treasurer pursuant to subsection (a) of this section. In determining whether to approve the proposed financing, the State Treasurer may consider any factors the State Treasurer considers relevant in order to find and determine all of the following:

(1)   The amounts to become due under the special indebtedness, including the interest component or rate, are adequate and not excessive for the purpose proposed.

(2)   The increase, if any, in State revenues, including taxes, necessary to pay the sums to become due under the special indebtedness is not excessive.

(3)   The special indebtedness can be incurred or issued on terms desirable to the State.

(e)   Designation of Facilities. - If the Council of State has authorized in general terms the types or classifications of capital facilities to be financed, then the particular capital facilities and the principal amount of special indebtedness to be incurred or issued for each particular capital facility shall be determined by

250

the Department of Administration after considering any factors it considers relevant in order to determine that the particular capital facility to be provided is desirable for the efficient operation of the State and its agencies and is in the best interests of the State.

(f)   Type of Debt and Security. - In the absence of a determination by the Council of State, the State Treasurer, after consultation with the Department of Administration, shall determine the specific security offered and whether the special indebtedness to be issued or incurred shall be financing contract indebtedness, certificates of participation indebtedness, bonded indebtedness, or some combination of these.

(g)   Administration. - The State Treasurer, after consultation with the Department of Administration, shall develop appropriate documents for use under this Article. The State Treasurer shall employ and designate the financial consultants, fiduciaries and other agents, underwriters, and bond attorneys to be associated with the incurrence or issuance of special indebtedness pursuant to this Article.

(h)   Oversight by Joint Legislative Commission. - After all the requirements for approval and oversight provided in this section have been met, and at least five days before the issuance or incurrence of the special indebtedness, the State Treasurer must report to the Joint Legislative Commission on Governmental Operations. This report must include the details of the proposed special indebtedness, including the capital facilities to be financed by the indebtedness, the amount of the proposed indebtedness, the type of indebtedness to be issued or incurred, and any other information required by the Commission. (2003-284, s. 46.2; 2003-314, s. 1; 2004-203, s. 79.)

§ 142-85. Security; other requirements.

(a)   Security. - In order to secure (i) lease or installment payments to be made to the lessor, seller, or other person advancing moneys or providing financing under a financing contract, (ii) payment of the principal of and interest on bonded indebtedness, or (iii) payment obligations of the State to the provider of bond insurance, a credit facility, a liquidity facility, or a derivative agreement, special indebtedness may create any combination of the following:

(1)   A lien on or security interest in one or more, all, or any part of the capital facilities to be financed by the special indebtedness.

(2)   If the special indebtedness is to finance construction of improvements on real property, a lien on or security interest in all or any part of the land on which the improvements are to be located.

(3)   If the special indebtedness is to finance renovations or improvements to existing facilities or the installation of fixtures in existing facilities, a lien on or security interest in one or more, all, or any part of the facilities.

(b)   Value of Security; Multiple Liens. - The estimated value of the property subject to the lien or security interest need not bear any particular relationship to the principal amount of the special indebtedness or other obligation it secures. This Article does not limit the right of the State to grant multiple liens or security interests in a capital facility or other property to the extent not otherwise limited by the terms of any special indebtedness.

(c)   Governor's Budget. - Documentation relating to any special indebtedness may include provisions requesting the Governor to submit in the Governor's budget proposal or any amendments or supplements to the budget proposed appropriations necessary to make the payments required by the special indebtedness.

(d)   Source of Repayment. - The payment of amounts payable by the State under special indebtedness or any related documents during any fiscal period shall be limited to funds appropriated for that purpose by the General Assembly in its discretion.

(e)   No Deficiency Judgment or Pledge. - No deficiency judgment may be rendered against the State in any action for breach of any obligation under special indebtedness or any related documents. The taxing power of the State is not and may not be pledged directly or indirectly to secure any moneys due under special indebtedness or any related documents. In the event that the General Assembly does not appropriate sums sufficient to make payments required under any special indebtedness or any related documents, the net proceeds received from the sale or other disposition of the property subject to the lien or security interest shall be applied to satisfy these payment obligations in accordance with the deed of trust, security agreement, or other documentation relating to the lien or security interest. These net proceeds are appropriated for the purpose of making these payments. Any net proceeds in

252

excess of the amount required to satisfy the obligations of the State under any special indebtedness or any related documents shall be paid to the State Treasurer for deposit to the General Fund.

(f)   Nonsubstitution Clause. - A financing contract, issue of bonded indebtedness, or other related document shall not contain a nonsubstitution clause that restricts the right of the State to (i) continue to provide a service or conduct an activity or (ii) replace or provide a substitute for any capital facility.

(g)   Protection of Lender. - Special indebtedness may contain any provisions for protecting and enforcing the rights and remedies of the person advancing moneys or providing financing under a financing contract, the owners of bonded indebtedness, or others to whom the State is obligated under special indebtedness or any related documents as may be reasonable and proper and not in violation of law. These provisions may include covenants setting forth the duties of the State in respect of any of the following:

(1)   The purposes to which the proceeds of special indebtedness may be applied.

(2)   The disposition and application of the revenues of the State, including taxes.

(3)   Insuring, maintaining, and other duties with respect to the capital facilities financed.

(4)   The disposition of any charges and collection of any revenues and administrative charges.

(5)   The terms and conditions of the issuance of additional special indebtedness.

(6)   The custody, safeguarding, investment, and application of all moneys.

(h)   State Property Law Exception. - Chapter 146 of the General Statutes does not apply to any transfer of the State's interest in property authorized by this Article, whether to a deed of trust trustee or other secured party as security for special indebtedness, or to a purchaser of property in connection with a foreclosure or similar conveyance of property to realize upon the security for special indebtedness following the State's default on its obligations under the special indebtedness. (2003-284, s. 46.2; 2003-314, s. 1; 2004-203, s. 79.)

§ 142-86. Financing contract indebtedness.

(a)   Documentation. - Financing contract indebtedness shall not be incurred until all documentation providing for its incurrence has been approved by the State Treasurer after the State Treasurer has consulted with the Department of Administration.

(b)   Interest Component. - A financing contract may provide for payments under the contract to represent principal and interest components of the cost of the capital facility to be financed, as determined by the State Treasurer.

(c)   Bidding. - Financing contracts may be entered into pursuant to any applicable public or competitive bidding process or any private or negotiated process, to the extent required by applicable law and, if not so required, as may be determined by the Department of Administration after consulting with the State Treasurer.

(d)   Party. - All financing contracts shall be executed on behalf of the State by the State Treasurer or, upon delegation by the State Treasurer after the State Treasurer's having approved the financing contract, by the Department of Administration.

(e)   Credit Facility. - If the State Treasurer determines that it is in the best interest of the State, the State Treasurer may arrange for the delivery of a credit facility to secure payment under any financing contract. The State Treasurer may also provide that payments by the State representing the interest component of the payments to be made under a financing contract may be calculated based upon a fixed or a variable rate of interest.

(f)   Terms and Conditions. - All other conditions set forth elsewhere in this Article with respect to financing contract indebtedness shall also be satisfied prior to incurring any financing contract indebtedness. To the extent applicable as conclusively determined by the State Treasurer, the provisions of G.S. 142-89, 142-90, and 142-91 apply to financing contract indebtedness. (2003-284, s. 46.2; 2003-314, s. 1; 2004-203, s. 79.)

§ 142-87. Additional requirements for certificates of participation indebtedness.

254

(a)   Documentation. - A financing contract shall not be used in connection with the delivery of certificates of participation by a special corporation until all documentation providing for its use has been approved by the State Treasurer after the State Treasurer has consulted with the Department of Administration. All documentation providing for the delivery and sale of certificates of participation must be approved by the State Treasurer.

(b)   Procedure. - The special corporation, if used, shall request the approval of the State Treasurer in writing and shall furnish any information and documentation relating to the delivery and sale of the certificates of participation requested by the State Treasurer. In determining whether to approve the financing in the documentation, the State Treasurer shall consider the factors set forth in G.S. 142-84(d), as well as the effect of the proposed financing upon any scheduled or proposed sale of debt obligations by the State or a unit of local government in the State.

(c)   Terms; Interest. - Certificates of participation may be sold by the State Treasurer in the manner, either at public or private sale, and for any price or prices that the State Treasurer determines to be in the best interest of the State and to effect the purposes of this Article, except that the terms of the sale must also be approved by the special corporation. Interest payable with respect to certificates of participation shall accrue at the rate or rates determined by the State Treasurer with the approval of the special corporation.

(d)   Trust Agreement. - Certificates of participation may be delivered pursuant to a trust agreement or similar instrument with a corporate trustee approved by the State Treasurer, and the provisions of G.S. 142-89(h) apply to the trust agreement or similar instrument to the extent applicable.

(e)   Other Conditions. - All other conditions set forth elsewhere in this Article with respect to certificates of participation indebtedness, including the conditions set forth in G.S. 142-86, must be satisfied before any certificates of participation indebtedness is incurred. (2003-284, s. 46.2; 2003-314, s. 1; 2004-203, s. 79.)

§ 142-88. Bonded indebtedness.

The State Treasurer is authorized, by and with the consent of the Council of State as provided in this Article, to issue and sell at one time or from time to time bonds of the State to be designated "State of North Carolina Limited

Obligation Bonds, Series_____ " or notes of the State as provided in this Article, for the purpose of providing funds, with any other available funds, for the uses authorized in this Article. (2003-284, s. 46.2; 2003-314, s. 1; 2004-203, s. 79.)

§ 142-89. Issuance of limited obligation bonds and notes.

(a)   Terms and Conditions. - Bonds or notes may bear any dates; may be serial or term bonds or notes, or any combination of these; may mature in any amounts and at any times, not exceeding 40 years from their dates; may be payable at any places, either within or without the United States, in any coin or currency of the United States that at the time of payment is legal tender for payment of public and private debts; may bear interest at any rates, which may vary from time to time; and may be made redeemable before maturity, at the option of the State or otherwise as may be provided by the State, at any prices, including a price greater than the face amount of the bonds or notes, and under any terms and conditions, all as may be determined by the State Treasurer, by and with the consent of the Council of State.

(b)   Signatures; Form and Denomination; Registration. - Bonds or notes may be issued in certificated or uncertificated form. If issued in certificated form, bonds or notes shall be signed on behalf of the State by the Governor or bear the Governor's facsimile signature, shall be signed by the State Treasurer or bear the State Treasurer's facsimile signature, and shall bear the great seal of the State or a facsimile of the seal impressed or imprinted on them. If bonds or notes bear the facsimile signatures of the Governor and the State Treasurer, the bonds or notes shall also bear a manual signature which may be that of a bond registrar, trustee, paying agent, or designated assistant of the State Treasurer. If any officer whose signature or facsimile signature appears on bonds or notes issued under this Article ceases to be that officer before the delivery of the bonds or notes, the signature or facsimile signature shall nevertheless have the same validity for all purposes as if the officer had remained in office until delivery of the bonds or notes. Bonds or notes issued under this Article may bear the facsimile signatures of persons who, at the actual time of the execution of the bonds or notes, were the proper officers to sign any bond or note although at the date of the bond or note those persons may not have been officers.

The form and denomination of bonds or notes, including the provisions with respect to registration of the bonds or notes and any system for their

256

registration, shall be as prescribed by the State Treasurer in conformity with this Article.

(c)   Manner of Sale; Expenses. - Subject to the approval by the Council of State as to the manner in which bonds or notes will be offered for sale, whether at public or private sale, whether within or without the United States, and whether by publishing notices in certain newspapers and financial journals, mailing notices, inviting bids by correspondence, negotiating contracts of purchase, or otherwise, the State Treasurer is authorized to sell bonds or notes at one time or from time to time at any rates of interest, which may vary from time to time, and at any prices, including a price less than the face amount of the bonds or notes, as the State Treasurer may determine. All expenses incurred in the preparation, sale, and issuance of bonds or notes shall be paid by the State Treasurer from the proceeds of bonds or notes or other available moneys.

(d)   Application of Proceeds. - The proceeds of any bonds or notes shall be used solely for the purposes for which the bonds or notes were issued and shall be disbursed in the manner and under the restrictions, if any, that the Council of State may provide in the resolution authorizing the issuance of, or in any trust agreement securing, the bonds or notes.

Any additional moneys that may be received by means of a grant or grants from the United States or any agency or department thereof or from any other source to aid in financing the cost of a capital facility may be disbursed, to the extent permitted by the terms of the grant or grants, without regard to any limitations imposed by this Article.

(e)   Notes; Repayment. - By and with the consent of the Council of State, the State Treasurer is authorized to borrow money and to execute and issue notes of the State for the same, but only in any of the following circumstances and under the following conditions:

(1)   For anticipating the sale of bonds, the issuance of which the Council of State has approved, if the State Treasurer considers it advisable to postpone the issuance of the bonds.

(2)   For the payment of interest on or any installment of principal of any bonds then outstanding, if there are not sufficient funds in the State treasury with which to pay the interest or installment of principal as they respectively become due.

(3)   For the renewal of any loan evidenced by notes authorized in this Article.

(4)   For the purposes authorized in this Article.

(5)   For refunding bonds or notes or financing contract indebtedness as authorized in this Article.

Funds derived from the sale of limited obligation bonds or notes may be used in the payment of any bond anticipation notes issued under this Article. Funds provided by the General Assembly for the payment of interest on or principal of bonds shall be used in paying the interest on or principal of any notes and any renewals thereof, the proceeds of which have been used in paying interest on or principal of the bonds.

(f)   Refunding Bonds and Notes. - By and with the consent of the Council of State, the State Treasurer is authorized to issue and sell refunding bonds and notes for the purpose of refunding special indebtedness and to pay the cost of issuance of the refunding bonds or notes. The refunding bonds and notes may be combined with any other issues of State bonds and notes issued pursuant to this Article. Refunding bonds or notes may be issued at any time prior to the final maturity of the debt or obligation to be refunded. The proceeds from the sale of any refunding bonds or notes shall be applied to the immediate payment and retirement of the obligations being refunded or, if not required for the immediate payment of the obligations being refunded, the proceeds shall be deposited in trust to provide for the payment and retirement of the obligations being refunded and to pay any expenses incurred in connection with the refunding. Money in a trust fund may be invested in (i) direct obligations of the United States government, (ii) obligations the principal of and interest on which are guaranteed by the United States government, (iii) to the extent then permitted by law, obligations of any agency or instrumentality of the United States government, or (iv) certificates of deposit issued by a bank or trust company located in the State if the certificates are secured by a pledge of any of the obligations described in (i), (ii), or (iii) above having an aggregate market value, exclusive of accrued interest, equal at least to the principal amount of the certificates so secured. This section does not limit the duration of any deposit in trust for the retirement of obligations being refunded but that have not matured and are not presently redeemable or, if presently redeemable, have not been called for redemption.

(g)   Security. - Payment of the principal of and the interest on bonds and notes shall be secured as provided in G.S. 142-85.

(h)   Trust Agreement. - In the discretion of the State Treasurer, any bonds and notes issued under this Article may be secured by a trust agreement or similar instrument between the State and a corporate trustee or by a resolution of the Council of State providing for the appointment of a corporate trustee. The corporate trustee may be, in either case, any trust company or bank that has the powers of a trust company within or without the State. The trust agreement or similar instrument or resolution, hereinafter referred to as "the trust", may provide for security and pledges and assignments that are permitted under this Article and may provide for the granting of a lien or security interest as authorized by G.S. 142-85. The trust may contain any provisions for protecting and enforcing the rights and remedies of the owners of any bonds or notes issued under the trust that are reasonable and not in violation of law, including covenants setting forth the duties of the State with respect to the purposes for which bond or note proceeds may be applied, the disposition and application of the revenues or assets of the State, the duties of the State with respect to the capital facilities financed, the disposition of any charges and collection of any revenues and administrative charges, the terms and conditions of the issuance of additional bonds and notes, and the custody, safeguarding, investment, and application of all moneys. All bonds and notes issued under this Article pursuant to the same trust shall be equally and ratably secured as provided in the trust, without priority by reasons of number, dates of bonds or notes, execution, or delivery, in accordance with the provisions of this Article and of the trust. The trust may, however, provide that bonds or notes issued pursuant to the trust shall, to the extent and in the manner prescribed in the trust, be subordinated and junior in standing, with respect to the payment of principal and interest and to the security of the payment, to any other bonds or notes issued pursuant to the trust. It is lawful for any bank or trust company that may act as depositary of the proceeds of bonds or notes, revenues, or any other money under this Article to furnish any indemnifying bonds or to pledge any securities that may be required by the State Treasurer. The trust may set out the rights and remedies of the owners of any bonds or notes and of any trustee and may restrict the individual rights of action by the owners. In addition to the foregoing, the trust may contain any other provisions the State Treasurer considers appropriate for the security of the owners of any bonds or notes. Expenses incurred in carrying out the provisions of the trust may be treated as a part of the cost of any capital facility or as an administrative charge and may be paid from the proceeds of the bonds or notes or from any other available funds. (2003-284, s. 46.2; 2003-314, s. 1; 2004-203, s. 79.)

§ 142-90. Variable rate demand bonds and notes and financing contract indebtedness.

(a)   In fixing the details of special indebtedness, the State Treasurer may make the special indebtedness subject to any of the following conditions:

(1)   It is payable from time to time on demand or tender for purchase by the owner thereof if a credit facility supports the special indebtedness, unless the State Treasurer specifically determines that a credit facility is not required upon a determination by the State Treasurer that the absence of a credit facility will not materially and adversely affect the financial position of the State or the marketing of the bonds or notes or financing contract indebtedness at a reasonable interest cost to the State.

(2)   It is additionally supported by a credit facility.

(3)   It is subject to redemption or mandatory tender for purchase prior to maturity.

(4)   It bears interest at a rate or rates that may be fixed or may vary over any period of time, as may be provided in the proceedings providing for the issuance or incurrence of the special indebtedness, including any variations that may be permitted pursuant to a par formula.

(5)   It is the subject of a remarketing agreement under which an attempt is made to remarket special indebtedness to new purchasers before its presentment for payment to the provider of the credit facility or to the State.

(b)   If the aggregate principal amount payable by the State under a credit facility is in excess of the aggregate principal amount of special indebtedness secured by the credit facility, whether as a result of the inclusion in the credit facility of a provision for the payment of interest for a limited period of time or the payment of a redemption premium or for any other reason, then the amount of authorized but unissued bonds or notes and financing contract indebtedness during the term of the credit facility shall not be less than the amount of the excess, unless the payment of the excess is otherwise provided for by agreement of the State executed by the State Treasurer. (2003-284, s. 46.2; 2003-314, s. 1; 2004-203, s. 79.)

§ 142-91. Other agreements.

The State Treasurer may authorize, execute, obtain, or otherwise provide for bond insurance, investment contracts, credit and liquidity facilities, credit enhancement facilities, interest rate swap agreements and other derivative products, and any other related instruments and matters the State Treasurer determines are desirable in connection with the issuance of special indebtedness. The State Treasurer is authorized to employ and designate any financial consultants, underwriters, fiduciaries, and bond attorneys to be associated with any incurrence or issuance of special indebtedness under this Article as the State Treasurer considers appropriate. (2003-284, s. 46.2; 2003-314, s. 1; 2004-203, s. 79.)

§ 142-92. Tax exemption.

Special indebtedness shall at all times be free from taxation by the State or any political subdivision or any of their agencies, excepting estate, inheritance, and gift taxes; income taxes on the gain from the transfer of the indebtedness; and franchise taxes. The interest component of any payments made by the State under special indebtedness, including the interest component of any certificates of participation, is not subject to taxation as to income. (2003-284, s. 46.2; 2003-314, s. 1; 2004-203, s. 79.)

§ 142-93. Investment eligibility.

Special indebtedness are securities or obligations in which all of the following may invest, including capital in their control or belonging to them: public officers, agencies, and public bodies of the State and its political subdivisions; insurance companies, trust companies, investment companies, banks, savings banks, savings and loan associations, credit unions, pension or retirement funds, and other financial institutions engaged in business in the State; and executors, administrators, trustees, and other fiduciaries. Special indebtedness are securities or obligations that may properly and legally be deposited with and received by any officer or agency of the State or political subdivision of the State for any purpose for which the deposit of bonds, notes, or obligations of the State or any political subdivision of the State is now or may later be authorized by law. (2003-284, s. 46.2; 2003-314, s. 1; 2004-203, s. 79.)

§ 142-94. Procurement of capital facilities.

The provisions of Articles 3, 3B, 3C, 3D, and 8 of Chapter 143 of the General Statutes and any other laws or rules of the State that relate to the acquisition and construction of State property apply to the financing of capital facilities through the use of special indebtedness pursuant to this Article. This section does not apply to the construction and lease-purchase, including leases with an option to purchase at the end of the lease term for a nominal sum, of State office buildings pursuant to proposals submitted before the effective date of this Article in response to requests for proposals, to the extent any of those proposals, as they may be supplemented or amended, are approved by the Department of Administration and any of these leases or lease-purchase agreements are approved by the Council of State in accordance with G.S. 143-341(4)d2. With the exception of Article 8 of Chapter 143 of the General Statutes, this section does not apply to any special indebtedness issued pursuant to this Article for the purchase, construction, or operation of capital facilities by Gateway University Research Park, Inc., a joint Millennial Campus in Greensboro. (2003-284, s. 46.2; 2003-314, s. 1; 2004-203, s. 79; 2008-204, s. 3.)

§ 142-95: Repealed by Session Laws 2007-527, s. 39, effective August 31, 2007.

§ 142-96: Reserved for future codification purposes.

§ 142-97: Reserved for future codification purposes.

§ 142-98: Reserved for future codification purposes.

§ 142-99: Reserved for future codification purposes.

Article 10.

Managing Debt Capacity.

§ 142-100. Purpose.

The purpose of this Article is to provide tools for sound debt management by providing an annual debt affordability study to establish guidelines for maintaining prudent debt levels and by establishing a system for prioritizing State capital needs when the needs exceed the State's capacity for new debt. (2004-179, s. 5.1.)

§ 142-101. Debt Affordability Advisory Committee.

(a)   Membership. - The Debt Affordability Advisory Committee is created in the Department of State Treasurer. The Committee shall consist of five ex officio members or their designees and four appointed members, as follows:

(1)   The State Treasurer.

(2)   The Secretary of Revenue.

(3)   The State Budget Officer.

(4)   The State Auditor.

(5)   The State Controller.

(6)   Two members of the public appointed by the President Pro Tempore of the Senate.

(7)   Two members of the public appointed by the Speaker of the House of Representatives.

(b)   Officers and Staff. - The State Treasurer shall serve as the chair of the Committee. The Committee shall meet at the call of the chair. The Department of State Treasurer shall provide space for the Committee to meet. The Department shall also provide the Committee with necessary staff and supplies to enable it to carry out its duties in an effective manner.

(c)   Compensation. - Members of the Committee shall serve without pay but shall receive per diem and allowances provided by G.S. 138-5 and G.S. 138-6.

(d)   Duties. - The Debt Affordability Advisory Committee shall annually advise the Governor and the General Assembly on the estimated debt capacity of the State for the upcoming 10 fiscal years. The Committee shall oversee the undertaking of an annual debt affordability study and the establishment of guidelines for evaluating the State's debt burden. The guidelines should include target and ceiling ratios of net tax-supported debt to personal income and debt service to revenues, target and floor percentages for the 10-year payout ratio, and target and floor percentages for the unreserved General Fund balance. The Committee's recommendations shall include recommendations on debt capacities for debt supported by the General Fund, the Highway Fund, and the Highway Trust Fund. The Committee shall also recommend any other debt management policies it considers desirable and consistent with sound management of the State's debt.

(e)   Reports. - The Committee shall report its findings and recommendations to the Governor, the President Pro Tempore of the Senate, the Speaker of the House of Representatives, and the Fiscal Research Division by February 1 of each year. (2004-179, s. 5.1; 2007-551, s. 1.)

§ 142-102: Reserved for future codification purposes.

§ 142-103: Reserved for future codification purposes.

§ 142-104: Reserved for future codification purposes.

§ 142-105: Reserved for future codification purposes.

§ 142-106: Reserved for future codification purposes.

Vision Books Order Form

Fax Orders:	1-980-299-5965
Phone Orders:	1-704-898-0770
E-mail Orders:	www.visionbooks.org
Mail Orders:	Vision Books, LLC P.O. Box 42406 Charlotte, NC 28215

Shipp To:
Name_____
Address_____
City_____State_____Zip_____
Phone_____Fax_____
Email_____@_____

Bill To: We can bill a third party on your behalf.
Name_____
Address_____
City_____State_____Zip_____
Phone____(_____)_____Fax_____
Email_____@_____

Pamphlet Number ($15.00 Each)	Qty	Total Cost
_____	_____	_____
_____	_____	_____
_____	_____	_____
_____	_____	_____
_____	_____	_____
_____	_____	_____
_____	_____	_____
Full Volume Set 1-92	92 Pamphlets	1,380.00

Free Shipping & Handling on Full Volume Orders
Add $1.00 Shipping & Handling per pamphlet $_____

Total Cost $_____

Thank you for your support. Management!

DID YOU ENJOY THIS BOOK?

Vision Books, LLC would like to hear from you! If you or someone you know has been fasely imprisoned, we would like to hear your story. If the 'North Carolina Criminal Law and Procedure' has had an effect in your life or if you have suggestions, we would like to hear from you. Send your letters to:

Vision Books, LLC
Attn: Staff Writers
P.O. Box 42406
Charlotte, NC 28215
Email: staff@visionbooks.org

Order Additional Copies:

Fax Orders: 1-980-299-5965

Phone Orders: 1-704-898-0770

E-mail Orders: www.visionbooks.org

Mail Orders: Vision Books, LLC
                     P.O. Box 42406
                     Charlotte, NC 28215

www.ingramcontent.com/pod-product-compliance
Lightning Source LLC
Chambersburg PA
CBHW051634170526
45167CB00001B/193